Localist Movements in a Gl

RENEWALS 458-4574
DATE DUE

GAYLORD			PRINTED IN U.S.A

Urban and Industrial Environments

Series editor: Robert Gottlieb, Henry R. Luce Professor of Urban and Environmental Policy, Occidental College

For a list of the series, see pages 321–323.

Localist Movements in a Global Economy

Sustainability, Justice, and Urban Development
in the United States

David J. Hess

The MIT Press
Cambridge, Massachusetts
London, England

© 2009 Massachusetts Institute of Technology

For information on quantity discounts, email special_sales@mitpress.mit.edu.

Set in Sabon by SNP Best-set Typesetter Ltd., Hong Kong. Printed and bound in the United States of America.

Library of Congress Cataloging-in-Publication Data

Hess, David J.
Localist movements in a global economy : sustainability, justice, and urban development in the United States / David J. Hess.
p. cm.—(Urban and industrial environments)
Includes bibliographical references and index.
ISBN 978-0-262-01264-5 (hardcover : alk. paper)—ISBN 978-0-262-51232-9 (pbk. : alk. paper)
1. Sustainable urban development—United States. 2. Globalization. 3. Central-local government relations. I. Title.
HC110.E5H47 2009
338.973'07091732—dc22

2008035958

10 9 8 7 6 5 4 3 2 1

Contents

Acknowledgments

This book is based partly on research funded by the National Science Foundation under the title "Sustainable Technology, the Politics of Design, and Localism" (SES-00425039). Any opinions, findings, conclusions, or recommendations expressed in this book are my own and do not necessarily reflect the views of the National Science Foundation or others who are acknowledged. Under the grant, I had the opportunity to team-teach a course with Langdon Winner on sustainability and local democracy, and I worked with him to supervise a team of four graduate research assistants (Richard Arias-Hernández, Colin Beech, Rachel Dowty, and Govind Gopakumar). The graduate students developed some of the case studies that are discussed in chapters 4 and 5, and the grant also provided me with the resources needed during a sabbatical semester to conduct site visits and other case studies that are discussed in chapters 4–6. The thirty case studies that provide the background for this book are now posted on my website (www.davidjhess.org). Langdon graciously read some of the chapters and commented on them. I also greatly appreciate the willingness of the many people who consented to be interviewed for the case studies. I wish to thank especially Jim Boon, Leanne Krueger-Braneky, Betsy Johnson, and Ray Schutte.

I appreciate comments from the graduate students who read a draft of the book: Jennifer Barton, Doug Clark, Jessica Kyle, Anna Lamprou, Jennifer Maniere, and Ross Mitchell. Attorney Harry Miller provided some important insights into the differences among types of nonprofit organizations and the fiduciary limitations of privately held corporations. Comments on various aspects of the work from colloquia at the University of Illinois and Virginia Tech were also helpful. My long-term colleague Patric Giesler has influenced my attention to the internal diversity and variation of a social phenomenon. MIT Press editor Clay Morgan and series editor Robert Gottlieb oversaw a very helpful peer-review process that led to significant improvements. Melanie DuPuis also read the entire manuscript. Although she may not agree with all of my analyses, her comments were invaluable.

I also wish to thank the people who helped build Capital District Local First, Inc. During the time I spent attending meetings of that nonprofit organization and various national conferences of its national umbrella organization, the Business Alliance for Local Living Economies, I learned a great deal about localism. My hope is that this book will be valuable not only for academic researchers but also for people involved in the localist movement who want a broader perspective on both challenges and potentials that localism offers for enhancing environmental sustainability and social justice.

There may be some overlap of content with the following previously published essays: "Enhancing Justice and Sustainability at the Local Level: Affordable Policies for Local Government" (*Local Environment*, 2007); "Localism and the Environment" (*Sociology Compass*, 2008), and "What Is a Clean Bus?" (*Sustainability: Science, Policy, and Practice*, 2007). A contractual agreement provides permission for republication of any overlapping material. I began my discussion of localism in chapter 6 of the companion volume, *Alternative Pathways in Science and Industry* (MIT Press, 2007).

Localist Movements in a Global Economy

Introduction

It is 7 o'clock on a Thursday evening, and people are headed to a meeting of the "local first" business association of Springfield. The members have come together under the banner of supporting the locally owned independent businesses in their community. They are a politically diverse group, and they try to leave their partisan politics at the door. For example, Abby works for a microfinance organization that assists Springfield's minority-owned small businesses. Ben works for a large retail food cooperative and is heavily involved in sustainable local agriculture. Cathy works for a reuse center that provides job training for at-risk youth, but she also sees her work as helping to solve the problem of solid waste. Daniel, an independent software developer who is involved in a campaign against Wal-Mart, was arrested in the Seattle demonstrations against the World Trade Organization. Edna, who runs an independent bookstore, is facing debilitating competition from the chain stores, and is coming to the meeting partly because "buy local" campaigns have become a cornerstone of independent bookstores' survival. Frank, a political conservative who runs a hardware store, has seen sales dwindle since a "big-box" store came to his neighborhood and has come to the conclusion that life was much better in the era of small, neighborhood retail shops.

The names and identities of the people involved in Springfield's "local first" organization are fictitious, but the diversity of motives for joining an "independent business association" (that is, a nonprofit organization, usually restricted to a metropolitan region, that brings together small businesses and other organizations that are locally owned and not part of a franchise, a corporate chain, or a national nonprofit organization) is characteristic of what I have experienced in three years of involvement in localist politics in the United States. By 2008 there were about 100 independent business associations across the United States that were affiliated with either the American Independent Business Alliance (AMIBA) or the Business Alliance for Local Living Economies (BALLE). The annual meetings of BALLE provided one gathering point for the movement. At those meetings, owners of small businesses, officials from local governments, and representatives of nonprofit organizations could hear talks by localist leaders and attend dozens of smaller "break-out" sessions. The topics included community capital, employee ownership, fair trade, "green" buildings, inner-city entrepreneurship, local food, and renewable energy.

Advocates of independent businesses and nonprofit organizations argue that locally owned and locally controlled organizations are the backbone of the economy and provide leadership in local civil society and politics. They sometimes also claim that such organizations provide good job opportunities and that they are more responsive than large corporations to concerns about a region's quality of life and environment. More generally, advocates of what is often called "localism" see invigorating locally owned independent businesses as the basis for building and maintaining not only a region's economic well-being but also its environmental, political, and social well-being. In this book, I will examine those and related premises with the aim of developing a better understanding of a variety of social change efforts directed at revitalizing local ownership and local democracy.

Localism, Globalization, and Localization

The idea of localism engenders many controversies, of which perhaps the most basic is the definition of the term "localism" itself. Many researchers have recognized that the historical changes generally referred to as "globalization" have brought about a paradoxical reemergence of the local; indeed, it is widely assumed that globalization and localization are two sides of the same coin. As a result, to understand localism and localization, it is necessary to begin with a basic understanding of globalization.[1]

From an economic perspective, globalization is a historical change characterized by the increasing complexity and density of global supply chains, the internationalization of finance, and the concentration of wealth in large multinational corporations and the elites who benefit from them. Far from a natural evolution driven by economic laws such as increasing returns to scale, the economic changes have been guided by national policies and international treaties that support trade liberalization, reduce welfare-state obligations, restructure markets, and facilitate industrial consolidation. The changes have generated enormous wealth, but inequalities in the distribution of wealth have increased in many countries, including the United States.

From a political perspective, globalization involves the weakening of the capacity of a nation-state to direct and organize its economy. Although small post-colonial governments have long experienced such limitations, even powerful national governments such as that of the United States have found their economic sovereignty limited by the growing web of international treaties, international governmental organizations, multinational corporations, trade relationships, and transnational civil-society organizations. Furthermore, state and city governments have developed their own relationships to the global economy that, to some degree, bypass national politics and policies. Government, at all levels, has undergone changes as functions once deemed to be the proper purview of governments have been passed on to the nonprofit and private sectors and as representative decision making by elected and appointed officials has been displaced by governance among stakeholders. As a result, "democracy deficits" have become more prominent, not only at the international level (where the global population lacks the franchise), but also at the national and local levels. Such changes have tended to block political opportunities for redress of local claims through conventional political channels. Because political opportunities can be blocked, the conditions are set for the emergence of anti-globalization and localist movements.

Along with the economic and political transformations have come tremendous social changes. Previously important forms of identity, such as working-class and national identities, have been reconfigured. The growth of the Internet and the availability of air travel to the masses have enabled the proliferation and maintenance of identities linked to transnational and translocal communities, such as identities based on ethnicity, religion, lifestyle, hobbies, or occupational interest. Local, place-based identities have also been reconfigured as people have come to see their home towns through the lens of comparison with other places and times. They may find the environmental side effects of local industry and the visible deterioration of neighborhoods unacceptable, especially if they have seen alternative models as they are being developed throughout the world.

From an ecological perspective, globalization has increased the awareness of the limits on the carrying capacity of the planet. Attention to greenhouse-gas emissions increased after 2000, but climate change is only one part of a complex web of interlocking environmental and infrastructural crises that include persistent pollutants in the biosphere (including in human bodies); ongoing destruction of natural habitats by resource-extraction ventures and human populations; increasing demands for and shortages of water; technological and investment gaps for renewable energy; and broken, decaying, and nonexistent infrastructures in many of the world's cities and rural areas. The poor often bear the greatest burden of such changes, so environmental and social justice problems are also deeply intertwined. Global in scope and local in effect, the changing relationship between humans and the environment, and our understanding of that relationship, are also elements of what "globalization" has come to mean.

One way of thinking about "the local" in an era of globalization is to view it as a disappearing phenomenon as the world becomes more transnational, cosmopolitan, de-territorialized, and culturally homogeneous. However, most theorists of globalization have dismissed that perspective as simplistic. Rather than the mere absorption of the local into the global, they say, we are witnessing a remaking of the relationship between the local and the global. The term "glocal," which has been used to refer to the production of standardized goods in global commodity chains that simultaneously reproduce and alter local cultures through product differentiation, represents one attempt to capture the complexities of new local-global relationships. Likewise, the concept of "global cities" draws attention to the emergence of specialized, place-based nodes in a globalized economy. In a world characterized by rapidly changing local-global relationships, there are various forms of localization that accompany changes associated with globalization. I find it useful to distinguish localism as a movement from four other forms of localization: the technopole or regional industrial cluster, Internet-based hyperlocalism, environmentally oriented relocalization, and political devolution.[2]

With respect to the first type of localization, the growth of global political institutions, multinational corporations, transnational nongovernmental organizations, and regional trading blocks has coincided with a growing awareness of the importance of subnational regions and their direct connections to global systems. Saskia Sassen, Manuel Castells, Peter Hall, and other social scientists have explored the growth of "global cities" and "technopoles," where high-tech industrial clusters achieve a better position in the global economy as a result of place-based synergies that occur with the co-location of businesses. When a business locates in a region that has other businesses in the same industry, it is possible to take advantage of informal innovation networks, a talented labor force, industry-appropriate financial and legal services, and networks of linkages with regional governments and universities. All around the world, national and regional governments struggle to build metropolitan industrial clusters with the hope of becoming the next Silicon Valley. The advantages of co-location are now well known and carefully cultivated. The cluster model of economic development seeks to strengthen the complex networks of relationships of the high-tech firms of a regional economy in order to foster a dynamic network of innovative businesses in a particular industry.[3]

The model of the urban industrial cluster is not the only example of localization that has emerged in an era of globalization. In the media, retail, and information-technology industries there is also increasing discussion of "hyperlocalism"—that is, the use of localized knowledge and local social networks as a new source of corporate profits. One form of hyperlocalism takes local knowledge, such as knowledge about restaurant service and food quality, and converts it into reviews and commentaries that provide guidance to potential consumers. Informal, word-of-mouth, local knowledge is converted into nonlocal, Internet-based discussions; in turn, the readers' attention can be sold to local and nonlocal advertisers. Another form of hyperlocalism involves retail chains' use of the computerization of inventories to develop localized databases that customers can search. Although the first phase of online superstores did not entail inventories for local branches of a chain, the next wave of databases increasingly enabled customers to find out quickly which products are available at a local branch. What was once informal and local knowledge, or at least an action that involved a phone call and a conversation with a sales representative about which store actually has what items in stock, has become codified, Internet-based knowledge that is used to attract local consumers in order to enhance the profits of corporate retailers. Increasingly, retail chains are taking the next step in hyperlocal marketing by tailoring merchandise to local neighborhoods. A third example of hyperlocalism involves large media companies. Urban newspapers, in the wake of circulation declines (attributable to the migration of readers to the Internet), have turned to supporting local social networks and online communities of local interest groups. By becoming more deeply integrated into the local society, urban newspapers are able to develop novel content that complements the readily available national and international content of the nonlocal media. The local content and social networks drive website visits and create the potential for new streams of advertising revenue. The three examples of hyperlocalism all utilize local knowledge and Internet-mediated connections with place-based communities as ways of generating new revenue, which in turn is converted into profits, usually for nonlocal shareholders.[4]

A third form of localization is directly related to environmental movements. The "back to the land" movement of the 1970s had the goal of returning to a simpler, agrarian lifestyle in order to live in greater harmony with nature and to experiment with appropriate technologies such as organic agriculture and renewable energy. Ecovillages and other experimental living arrangements also involved local communities that aimed to achieve some degree of self-sufficiency through more communal lifestyles. In the early 2000s, the Post-Carbon Institute launched the Relocalization Network, which helped more than 150 chapters around the world to develop plans and projects for life in an "energy-constrained future." Considerably more pragmatic and less utopian than some of its historical predecessors, the Relocalization Network represents another iteration of environmentalism and localization. Here the focus is less on building new types of community than on shifting existing cities and towns toward local self-reliance in food and energy. Although similar to localism, the Relocalization Network is much more driven by environmental concerns and less concerned with local ownership. As a result, for the purposes of this book it is classified as an example of localization but not of localism.[5]

A fourth example of localization involves the changing relationship among levels of governments. In the United States since 1980, there has been a general trend toward the devolution of responsibilities from the federal government to state and local governments. Although federal funding has sometimes followed devolution, in many cases the funding has not been adequate for the new responsibilities of state and local governments, and consequently the changes have in some cases created gaps in service delivery. Furthermore, devolution has often been accompanied by privatization, or the shifting of the implementation of programs from the public sector to the nonprofit and for-profit sectors, often via public-private partnerships. As the anthropologist Dorothy Holland and her colleagues have shown, the "outsourcing of government" has created opportunities for local governments and civil-society organizations, but it has also created new patterns of exclusion. Furthermore, the devolution and privatization of government have tended to shift both local governments and civil-society organizations from a role of advocacy to one of service delivery. In the United Kingdom, similar policy changes associated with the Labour Party were called "the New Localism"; to avoid confusion, I will call this type of localization "devolution."[6]

I will use the term "localism" to refer to a fifth pattern of renewed emphasis on the local in a globalized world. "Localism" is understood here as the movement in support of government policies and economic practices oriented toward enhancing local democracy and local ownership of the economy in a historical context of corporate-led globalization. Although cluster-based synergies emerge in networks of locally owned independent businesses, they differ from the export-oriented, high-tech clusters that economic development offices favor in their quest for the next technopole. The high-tech clusters may involve some local ownership, but in general the financing of such enterprises involves venture capital. The goal of a high-tech start-up is an initial public offering of stock or sale to a large company, either of which leads to geographically dispersed ownership. Likewise, the Internet can be used to network associations of locally owned and independent businesses, and even to network independent business associations across countries, but the goal of localism is not to channel local knowledge and consumption into the profits of multinational corporations, which is the general logic behind hyperlocalism. Regarding the third type of localization, localism has an environmentally oriented strand, but it is not fundamentally concerned with environmental issues in the way that the Relocalization Network is. There are environmental dividends associated with localist politics, but localist politics focus on local democracy and economic sovereignty. Finally, although in some cases the localist goals of small-business development mesh with those of microenterprise development and other market-oriented anti-poverty initiatives, localism focuses less on the politics of devolution and privatization and more on restoring economic and political democracy to communities that have increasingly found their worlds dominated by multinational capital.

Localism as a Movement

Is it appropriate to think of localism as a movement? There are some good reasons why the concept of a movement may be helpful in understanding localism, as opposed to thinking of it as merely a new strategy for owners of small businesses to act as an interest group. Although a diverse group of citizens and small-business owners may come together in a "local first" meeting under the shared banner of supporting locally owned independent businesses and family farms, they do not come together only under that banner. They also meet because they are concerned with global problems (addiction to oil, ongoing warfare, decay of old neighborhoods, rising crime and poverty), and with a general sense of degradation of the economy, of politics, of neighborhoods, and of the quality of life in a place they call home. In other words, there is a second, political and social dimension to localism that in many ways encompasses the narrow economic calculus of local businesses that are banding together to resist the negative side effects of corporate consolidation. There is a sense of civic purpose, of not spending an evening bowling alone but instead spending time building something together with other people who share a similar concern for their community. The sense of opposition to the dominant direction of the world politics and economics is one reason why one might think of localism as a movement.[7]

Another reason for thinking of localism as a movement is that the word "movement" appears in the language of localist organizations. At localist conferences and meetings, I have often heard people refer to their activities as a movement. A more objective indication of the self-identification of localism as a movement is that at the time of writing there were more than 30,000 webpages that used the phrase "buy local movement." In the minds of many people who support the basic principle of restoring local and independent ownership to the economy, localism is a movement.

Arguably, localism is also a movement in the more technical social-scientific sense, because it involves a social-change agenda based on a long-term, multi-organizational challenge to powerful social institutions, specifically an economy and a polity dominated by large multinational corporations. However, very little of the action of localist organizations involves street protests and other extra-institutional actions. We social scientists often use the criterion of extra-institutional action as an essential feature in our definitions of social movements. In cases where the repertoires of action occur mostly within existing institutions but there is still a multi-organizational, multi-campaign effort with a social-change agenda that challenges elite authority, I prefer to use the term "reform movement" instead of "social movement." Furthermore, because much localist action takes place through the marketplace rather than in civil society or in the political arena, it might be better to think of localism in more general terms as an "alternative pathway" for social change in the global economy. Although I will use the term "localist movement" occasionally in this book, the term "alternative pathway" helps to free the imagination to recognize other types of reform action that are characteristic of localism, such as use of the market and consumption as vehicles of social change.[8]

As with most broad movements, the category of localism embraces a variety of inter-related movements, activist networks, and advocacy groups. The most common expressions of localism as a movement occur in "buy local" campaigns and in other forms of political action that are driven primarily by locally owned independent retail businesses and by locally oriented agrifood networks (a category that I will define to include community gardening). I will explore aspects of those dimensions of localism in chapters 4 and 5, but I have also tried to open up thinking about localism by exploring what localism can and does mean in other industries where efforts to enhance or preserve local ownership occur. Examples include advocacy in favor of community choice and local public ownership of electricity production, better and greener public transportation systems, and community-oriented and community-controlled media. Although each of the topics is vast, I have been guided by a general interest in exploring the extent to which localism is in a tradeoff relationship or a synergetic relationship with goals of social and environmental responsibility. As a result, rather than attempt a comprehensive coverage of all forms of localism, I have focused this investigation of localism on examples that make it possible to analyze the degree to which localist politics are consistent with or in tension with goals of sustainability and justice.

By interpreting localism as a movement, I will also argue that its political goals are broadly consistent with those of the anti-corporate, anti-globalization movement. As I will show, there is evidence to support the argument in the writings of localist leaders and in some of the practices of localist organizations. I do not deny that there are also significant differences between the localist and anti-globalization movements. Localism does not involve dramatic street protests against global financial organizations, as the anti-globalization movement does. With a largely middle-class social composition (in the sense of a primary class location in the small-business sector and the local nonprofit sector), localism may involve alliances with teamsters, students, and "turtles," but it is not a labor-youth-environmental movement. Although it is important to recognize the differences with the anti-globalization movement, one should also recognize the points of convergence. Support of independent local ownership is defined in opposition to the increasing control of local economies everywhere by large publicly traded corporations. Localist leaders also criticize the huge government subsidies, tax breaks, and incentives that go to large corporations, while small businesses are left to fend for themselves. In short, the loss of democracy to corporatocracy is a common theme for the localist and anti-globalization movements.[9]

Types and Ranges of Localism

The geographical scope of "local" is another controversial topic that warrants some initial discussion. At the upper end of the scale, the term can be used as an equivalent for "domestic" or "national" in the context of global trade. It can also refer to a country within the European Union, or to a North American state or province. For example, many American states support labels, such as "made in Vermont," that draw attention to the state-level provenance of products. At a smaller scale, "local" has sometimes been used to refer to a neighborhood or a small city within a metropolitan region. In this book, "local" will designate a geographic scale that is generally larger than a small city or a neighborhood and smaller than most American states. To be specific, "local" will refer to the scale outlined by the economic-development researchers Edward Blakely and Ted Bradshaw:

Regional and local are used interchangeably to refer to a geographical area composed of a group of local government authorities that generally share a common economic base and are close enough together to allow residents to commute between them for employment, recreation, or retail shopping. (2002: xvi)

Although "local" in this sense could be used to refer to a rural geographical area, my focus in this book will be on metropolitan or urban regions. I choose this level and this urban focus because in the United States it is in such regions that localism as a movement has taken off.

Another definitional problem involves the economic dimension of localism. In its most "pure" or ideal form, localism involves a confluence of four features: locally sourced resources or inputs into food and manufactured goods, production of goods by locally owned businesses, sales through locally owned organizations, and consumption by a population that shares a geographical locale with the producers and retailers. An organization that exemplifies all four features is a farm that utilizes mostly local inputs (by saving seeds and by using waste from one animal or plant as food for another), is owned locally, sells to consumers in a nearby city (either directly or through locally owned organizations such as food cooperatives), and restricts most of its sales to local customers. Another example is a credit union that serves a geographically restricted region and invests primarily in loans to members and to locally owned independent businesses. A third example is a community radio station that is funded by local donations and serves a local listening area with locally developed programming that focuses on local news and features. These three examples might be thought of as representing "pure" localism, but it is obvious that even in such cases not everything is local; the farm's tools and machines, the credit union's computers and software, and the radio station's broadcasting equipment are all likely to have come from other regions of the country or the world.[10]

A more common, hybrid form of localism is found among owners of small service businesses and Main Street retailers who have banded together under the threat of competition from chains and franchises. Because most of their wares are purchased from nonlocal producers and made with nonlocal inputs, the localist component involves only two of the four aspects of localism: local ownership and sales to local markets. Another example of a hybrid type of localism is a local government agency that provides goods and services to a region, such as a publicly owned utility or a public transit system. The products used, such as buses and fuel (diesel or natural gas), are generally not manufactured or extracted in the region, but the other two aspects of localism—ownership and sale to local customers—are present. Today, much of what passes as localism more closely approximates the hybrid type of small retailers and public agencies than the pure type. However, the pure type is useful to keep in mind as a yardstick against which other types of localism might be measured.

It is also necessary to have in mind a third concept in addition to the pure and hybrid forms of localism: some locally owned independent businesses that cater mostly to the local economy purchase some supplies and services from other locally owned businesses outside the region. Here, there is a direct relationship between independent producers in one region and independent retailers in another region, and we need a third category to describe such local-to-local supply chains. I use the terms "global localism" and "alternative global economy" to describe the interesting transnational networks of alternative commodity chains that operate outside the mainstream global economy of large food, manufacturing, and retail corporations.[11]

Although there is tremendous variation in the geographical scope and the organizational forms associated with localism, there are important boundaries that figure in localist politics. For example, the line between a locally owned independent business and a publicly traded global business is by no means easy to draw. For some publicly traded corporations, a group of stockholders may control a significant portion of the company and live in the region where the company is headquartered. This type of organization is in some sense locally owned, but it is not "independent" in the sense of being closely held by a few owners who live in the region where they work. The distinction becomes important because publicly traded corporations, or start-up companies that have significant equity from "angel" investors or from venture-capital firms, tend to be vulnerable to acquisition by larger corporations. The story of the ice cream producer Ben and Jerry's—once locally owned and independent—is well known in the localist movement. In an effort to maintain its mission of social responsibility, the company's initial public offering was limited to residents of Vermont, but gradually the shareholders sold their stocks to nonlocal buyers. Eventually Ben and Jerry's became a target for acquisition and was purchased by Unilever, a huge international firm that produces a wide variety of domestic household and food brands. Although the parent company maintained Ben and Jerry's "peace politics" as part of its strategy of occupying a niche market position with a well-known brand, the original owners lost control of the company, and about 20 percent of the workforce was laid off. Once a locally owned independent business with roots in a region and obligations to the local workforce and communities, Ben and Jerry's became a local brand in a global business.[12]

Another distinction is that between localism in the modern, globalized economy and locally oriented production and distribution in the premodern, subsistence economy. The first human societies had locally based economies (generally with limited inter-societal trading), and even in the great empires much agricultural production was for local subsistence. In the United States, the frontier communities of the seventeenth and eighteenth centuries engaged in locally oriented subsistence farming, and even the export-oriented cotton and tobacco plantations were supported by an infrastructure of locally produced food, clothing, and other goods. With the development of transportation and communication infrastructures during the nineteenth and twentieth centuries (canals, railroads, steamships, telephones, highways, airplanes, the Internet), the localized subsistence economy increasingly gave way to a continental and then a global economy. However, the ideal of a return to the subsistence lifestyle reemerged in other localization movements, such as the "back to the land" movement, and there are some points of overlap between participants in those movements and participants in the localist movement. Although such points of overlap exist, in twenty-first century America localism is primarily an urban movement. The primary social address of localism is not the hippie farmer who wants to return to a simpler way of life but the local retailer, credit union, restaurant, city government department, radio station, or nonprofit organization.

Localism, Sustainability, and Justice

In this book I will provide an overview of localism in the United States and a perspective on some of the scholarly debates that have emerged. In doing so, I will focus on the question of the extent to which localism can contribute solutions to the world's environmental and social problems. The first of my two central arguments will be that any understanding of localism in the United States, not to mention in other countries, should take into account considerable variation, and not only across geographical locales but also across industries. As a result, one should be cautious about generalizations based on a narrow slice of localist politics and reform efforts. Second, the redevelopment of locally owned independent businesses can contribute to solving environmental and equality problems, but such contributions are uneven, and I am skeptical that localism alone can provide complete solutions. As the agrifood scholars E. Melanie DuPuis and David Goodman have suggested, it would be a recipe for ineffectiveness to focus only on the local level of politics and to ignore the need to address policy problems at the state, federal, and global levels. DuPuis and Goodman advocate "reflexive politics of localism"—that is, an approach that would make localism "an effective social movement of resistance against globalism" (2005: 364). In this book, I develop their suggestion. I explore both the potentials and the challenges of localism across a variety of industries, and I suggest ways in which such reflexive politics have already emerged and can be developed further. There are already examples of localism that show concern with environmental and social justice goals and that are connected with reform efforts at multiple scales. Those examples suggest the potential to develop a global localism that is anchored in the project of building an alternative global economy that potentially could be more effective in addressing global problems of sustainability and justice than a global economy dominated by large multinational corporations.[13]

As a background for understanding my argument, I should clarify what I mean by "sustainability" and "justice." I use a definition of "sustainability" that is more or less in line with that of the ecological economist Herman Daly, who drew attention to the ultimate question of global ecosystem collapse. In my rendition of his definition, human life is sustainable if our use of global ecosystem resources is less than the ability of the ecosystem to replenish consumed resources (or to supply substitutions), and if environmental "sinks" (pollution and waste) do not exceed the capacity of the global ecosystem to process them. To address sustainability, we should think about the fundamental question of the carrying capacity of the planet and the growth logic of human societies. Because the growth logic of human societies is driven in part by a financial system that rewards short-term growth in revenue and profitability, the long-run solution to the underlying problem of sustainability will require developing alternative ways of organizing the global economy. The localist model of privately held companies with a mission of community stewardship and an ability to choose environmental and social values over growth provides one pathway for restructuring the global economy in an era of environmental limits.[14]

The ecologically oriented definition of sustainability does not draw attention to issues of justice. As most students of environmental issues recognize, environmental burdens are not borne equally across the world. The poor, especially those who live in coastal regions or in areas subject to droughts in the less developed countries, are most likely to undergo hardship in response to climate change. Among the poor it is often women, children, and the elderly who shoulder the heaviest burdens of poverty. The poor also tend to suffer more from environmental pollution, such as the hazards of chemical plants and the effects of mineral-extraction projects. Furthermore, when people are so poor and so resource constrained that they must choose between resource conservation and staying alive, they are not able to integrate sustainability considerations into their livelihoods. As a result, the problem of sustainability is closely linked to the problem of justice. By "justice" I mean mainly the effects of a globalized economy on wage and income inequality and on the quality of life in diverse regions of the world. This focus does not imply that other perspectives on justice are unimportant, but my focus will be on distributive or social justice, understood here to involve how society's goods and bads are distributed across class, geographical, ethnic, gender, and other social divisions. However, I will also make reference to the concept of procedural justice, using that term loosely to refer to issues of fairness in democratic process and transparency in decision making across the political system.

Matters of sustainability and justice can be understood as social problems, but sustainability and justice are also social values in the sense that they refer to general notions about the way the world should, ideally, be organized. When referring to the way values are instantiated in organizations, I will use the term "goals," and often I will use "social and environmental responsibility goals" as a substitute for "sustainability and justice." Often such goals are considerably narrower than the concepts of sustainability and justice as defined here, but I will view them as aligned with the overarching values of achieving a more sustainable and just world. There is a range of benefits that localism could, in theory, provide for the project of building a more just and sustainable world, and we might think of them in terms of environmental and social benefits or dividends. However, the relationships among localism, sustainability, and justice are not always as straightforward as might first appear.

Method and Organization

In the pages that follow, I seek to understand, explicate, and occasionally criticize the arguments, strategies, and projects of those who gather under the banner of localism today. It should be clear at the outset that I am optimistic about the possibilities of localism, but I also see it as a complex social phenomenon that has some strands that are more able than others to contribute solutions to global problems of sustainability and justice. In order to understand localism, I have become immersed in localist politics, not only by attending localist events as a dispassionate observer but also by becoming actively involved in the long and hard work of building an independent business association in the area where I live. I have accepted that challenge partly because, after decades of studying knowledge and social movements, I have increasingly wanted to bridge the gap between the academy and activism, and I am drawn to the prospect of building an alternative global economy that one strand of localism offers. I have chosen not to write about my personal experience in upstate New York because I considered it community service rather than fieldwork, and ethically it is best to treat such work as providing background insight, which for me has been considerable. I prefer instead to use formal, semi-structured interviews as a source of data, as I have done in some of the chapters below. As a result, this book draws on a variety of sources of empirical evidence gathered between 2005 and 2008: books, articles, and other documents written by localist advocates, critics, and scholars; interviews; visits to about thirty locally owned independent organizations that were selected for their potential to address problems of sustainability and of justice in a variety of industries; attendance at annual conferences of BALLE and regional conferences where localist themes were prominent; and participation in localist networks and in an independent business association.

Independent business associations have been growing rapidly across North America, and similar efforts can be found in other parts of the world, especially Europe. Although a comparative perspective on localism would be helpful, it is beyond the scope of the present book, which is limited to localism in the United States. To some extent the narrowing of focus is based on the empirical research that I have completed to date, and to some extent the focus on the United States can be justified as important because it examines how the world's cradle of neoliberal globalization has also produced a counter-movement that challenges the assumptions of the "Washington consensus."[15]

To date there has been very little social-scientific reflection on localism, and consequently there is a need for a book that steps back and probes the conditions, challenges, and potential of the movement. Here I adopt an interdisciplinary strategy that combines theoretical reflection, empirical research, and policy analysis. In the first three chapters, I draw on a wide range of theories about sustainability, the global corporate economy, and economic development. In the next four chapters, which constitute the empirical portion of the book, I develop an analysis of localism based on organizational case studies and other empirical evidence. In the final chapters, I assess both the challenges to and the potentials of localism, and I examine a variety of proposals that might enhance the prospect of developing an alternative global economy.

In chapter 1, I explore localism as a political ideology or philosophy. Specifically, I examine the mainstream debate between neoliberal and liberal approaches to the global problems of environmental sustainability and social justice. I then consider radical alternatives in the socialist and communalist tradition. Localism has points in common with all four political positions but cannot be reduced to one or the other. Furthermore, localism draws attention less to the relationship between the government and the economy, which is the basis of debate between and within radical and mainstream political positions, than to the question of the relationship between the large publicly traded corporation and society as a whole. Likewise, localism also draws more attention to the problem of the rights of place-based communities to self-determination than to economic justice in the distributive sense of the reduction of poverty and protection of the working class. In common with some of the critics of mainstream politics, localism suggests that an economy based on the large publicly traded corporation may be maladapted to solving today's social and environmental problems. However, the alternatives developed by advocates of increased local ownership are different from those articulated by socialists and communalists.

In chapter 2, I consider localism as a system of knowledge and as a critique of the research field of economic development studies. Specifically, the history of export-oriented economic development strategies in American cities has generated increasing awareness of the limitations of the strategies, and the growth of import substitution provides a complementary economic development strategy. In this chapter I examine the legacy of import substitution as a strategy for economic development in less developed countries, the reasons for the shift to export-oriented policies, and the reasons why trade liberalization policies have provoked increasing skepticism in both the more and less wealthy countries. In addition, I examine the arguments that have been raised against localism as a regional development strategy, and I review "localist research," an emerging field that evaluates the economic and social impact of local ownership.

In chapter 3, I develop a theoretical reflection on localism by examining arguments that have been raised against the localist vision of an alternative global economy that could bring about a more just and sustainable world order. Criticisms that localism is neither more just nor more sustainable than an economy based on corporate globalization are useful because they help sharpen our understanding of both the challenges and the potential of localism. I suggest that the criticisms cannot be the basis of a facile rejection of localism. Instead, one must examine localism as a highly variable reform movement, some elements of which address issues of sustainability and of justice better than others. The argument becomes the basis for the explorations in the next four chapters, in which I consider localism in five industries: retail, food, energy, transportation, and the media.

In chapter 4, I examine the type of localism that is organized as a movement in support of locally owned businesses. I compare the history of the anti-chain-store movement of the 1920s and the 1930s with the growth of grassroots "buy local" campaigns since 1995. I note a possible tension within the "buy local" form of localism between defense of locally owned independent businesses and broader goals of social and environmental responsibility. I also trace out the implications of the tension in both an analysis of organizational mission statements of independent business associations and a more detailed inquiry into cases of selected issues that have emerged in some of the associations. Further, I analyze some of the patterns found in my case studies of reuse centers as one example of a form of retail localism where sustainability goals and justice goals can be found together.

In chapter 5, I review the background literature in agrifood studies, which is generally critical of the reformist aspirations of localism. Because agrifood scholars have produced the most developed academic literature on localism, they provide some valuable insights into the challenges of sustainability and justice that localism as a pathway for change faces. The literature focuses on local agricultural networks that connect urban and suburban consumers with regional farms via food cooperatives, farmers' markets, locally oriented restaurants, and community-supported agriculture. Agrifood scholars note a disjuncture that can occur between local ownership and sustainable agricultural practices, a lack of concern with farmworkers' rights, and some general convergences between this form of localism and neoliberalism. Again, I argue that one should be careful about generalizing from one form of localism to the movement as a whole or even to the food industry as a whole. I analyze case-study material on urban community gardening and urban nonprofit farms to show that government-oriented protest politics of variable scale and substantial concern with issues of sustainability and justice can be found in this field of localist politics.

In chapter 6, I examine localism in the context of municipal, regional, or state government ownership. I study three cases of local ownership in the electric power industry: public power, community choice, and conservation utilities. In each case I examine the potential and challenges with respect to producing higher levels of energy conservation and/or renewable energy, the effects of the organizations on low-income energy access and savings, and the potential for renewable energy and energy conservation to be configured as an import-substitution approach to economic development. In the second section of the chapter, I examine the greening of public transportation as a complex network of relationships among transit technology innovations, government regulations, environmental justice groups, and the economics and practices of fleet management. I examine the environmental and social dimensions of the definitional conflicts regarding urban transit and the potential for the greening of public transportation to be linked to the generation of local businesses and economic development based on import substitution.

In chapter 7, I explore the history of media-reform movements in the United States and the emergence of alternative and community media as one strategy for opposing corporate control of the media. At both the national and the local level, independent media that support the goals of local ownership and social and environmental responsibility have faced severe financial struggles. I examine the problem of consolidation of for-profit alternative media, appropriation by and opposition from National Public Radio, and the potentials and pitfalls of nonprofit ownership as a strategy of survival. A historical analysis of print and broadcast media grounds the next section, in which I examine claims about the grassroots and democratic potential of Internet-based media. With that background in mind, I go on to examine the emergence of negative coverage of localism in the American media and investigate the hypothesis that negative coverage of localism is beginning to emerge more from large media corporations.

In chapter 8, I cover various proposals for policy change that would strengthen opportunities for creating stronger locally oriented economies. I examine new financial products and new ways of thinking about investment that would open up capital flows into locally owned independent businesses and nonprofit organizations. I then examine policy changes needed at the local and national levels of government, and suggest how reforms in support of localism could be connected with other reform efforts oriented toward the social and environmental responsibility of multinational corporations. The policy issues outlined in this chapter form the basis for my assessment of localism in the concluding chapter.

In this book I map out some of the underlying ideas and assumptions of the localist movement in the United States and some of the differences across industries. I weigh the environmental and social challenges of localism and ponder their potential consistency with, or conflicts with, parallel projects for economic reform. As an alternative pathway in urban development, localism raises fundamental questions about economic development strategies that are based on attracting large corporate manufacturers, big-box stores, and high-tech start-up companies. On that ground alone it provides a valuable way of rethinking issues related to the economic development, inequality, and urban and industrial environments. Localism is by no means a panacea for the problem of rechanneling economic development in more sustainable and just directions, but some forms of localism can serve as ingredients in projects to build more democratic, just, and sustainable politics for the twenty-first century, or at least for mitigating what some believe to be an inevitable future of environmental and social collapse. Understanding the potential of localism to contribute to social and environmental responsibility goals requires a perspective on the movement that explores its variations, its challenges, and its limitations. Much of that potential rests on building connections with other reform movements that seek to build an alternative global economy.

1
Global Problems and Localist Solutions

Can the global economy solve global problems, especially the paired sustainability and justice crises? In answering the question, political and civic leaders carve out a variety of positions based on opposing political ideologies that constitute a field of debates over future policies. The mainstream debates involve various mixes of liberalism (which views relatively high levels of government intervention in the economy as necessary and desirable) and neoliberalism (which advocates less regulation, lower levels of government spending, and reliance on markets to solve social and environmental problems). In the United States, there was a transition from the dominance of liberalism during the era of Presidents Franklin Roosevelt through Jimmy Carter to neoliberalism during and after the administration of President Ronald Reagan. Against the mainstream, a radical tradition in American politics articulated a parallel set of differences between a state-centered, socialist approach to policy and a decentralized, communalist approach. In this chapter, I will map out the mainstream and radical debates as a background for understanding localism. I will argue not only that understanding the field of mainstream and radical political ideologies is essential for grasping localism as political thought, but also that localism cannot be reduced to the existing positions in the field. Rather than constituting a rehash of political traditions, localism borrows from previous political ideologies but is also in some ways a unique response to the historical situation of corporate-led globalization.

Liberalism and Neoliberalism

In the United States and other industrialized democracies, the dominant approach to economic and social policy from 1932 to 1980 was welfare-state liberalism, sometimes also known as social democracy. Tolerant of relatively high levels of government intervention in the economy, political leaders established policies that corrected market failures such as pollution and steered the economy to full employment. The policies often drew on Keynesian economics, which was based on the idea that the economy could achieve equilibrium at undesirable levels of output and employment, and hence government intervention was needed to bring the economy to a socially desirable equilibrium. As a political ideology, liberalism invoked a broad concept of "freedom," such as was articulated in the "four freedoms" speech of President Franklin Roosevelt. The four freedoms included freedom from want and positioned social welfare as an acceptable task of government.

During and after the 1980s an alternative perspective came to dominate policy in the United States, Britain, and increasingly other countries. As the geographer and social theorist David Harvey has argued, neoliberalism also emphasized the role of government as the protector of freedom, but the types of freedom emphasized were those of contracting individuals and large firms. In direct contrast with the Roosevelt's interpretation of freedom, the focus on marketplace freedoms emphasized the rights of firms to engage in free trade, to hire workers without interference from unions, and to conduct business without burdensome government regulations and taxes. Under neoliberal policies the poor would be helped not by welfare and labor policies but instead by increased investment in high-technology jobs that would result in higher productivity and wages.[1]

Two of the principle policies associated with neoliberalism, trade liberalization and deregulation, can be viewed as exemplars of marketplace freedom. The reduction and elimination of trade barriers allowed corporations in wealthy countries to move production to countries where wages were low and profits were higher. Likewise, policies that dismantled environmental, labor, and other regulations allowed businesses to be free to pursue the most efficient opportunities anywhere in the world.

The neoliberal perspective suggested that by freeing the marketplace from government interference, the global economy would become more economically efficient. Small farms and stores, not to mention expensive factories in unionized areas of wealthy countries, would be forced to innovate or go out of business. The demise of local ownership that accompanied such changes was understood to be the result of improved policies that allowed marketplace efficiencies to take their natural course, untrammeled by government regulation.

Neoliberals readily admit that economic liberalization causes some dislocations, but they view such collateral damage as necessary for the longer term gains of increased productivity and efficiency. The developmental scenarios for neoliberalism were roughly as follows: Factories in wealthy countries would close down, and the more entrepreneurial workers would find new and even better-paying jobs in the innovation economy. They would earn higher wages as a result of the higher productivity of labor in industries such as nanotechnology, biotechnology, financial services, entertainment, and information and communication technologies. Meanwhile, the older manufacturing jobs would migrate to the low-income countries, where the rural poor would find new opportunities and higher wages as they joined the urban industrial working class. Inequality between nations would decline, and the world as a whole would become more equitable.

As liberals have been quick to point out, the record for neoliberal policies on social inequality has not corresponded to the rosy predictions. Although it is true that since 1990 there has been a decline in between-nation inequality, the improvement in global inequality is attributable largely to the growth of the newly industrializing Asian economies, and conditions have worsened in some parts of the world, especially sub-Saharan Africa. Furthermore, inequality within many countries has increased, a phenomenon that has been subjected to diverse explanations. In the United States, firms shifted their manufacturing operations to areas of the world with lower wages, first to the American South and West, then increasingly to Mexico and overseas. Hourly workers in unionized jobs lost their bargaining power and often their jobs, and their transition to lower-paying service jobs has been one factor that has caused increasing inequality. In the less wealthy countries of the world, the structural adjustment programs of the 1980s and the 1990s forced economic changes that resulted in the rapid growth of urban slums. A liberal might admit that the neoliberal promise of a "tide that lifts all boats" was fulfilled from the limited perspective of between-nation inequality, but the tide ended up lifting the yachts more than the rafts.[2]

The changes associated with neoliberal policies also had direct implications for the environment. The transition to an economy independent of oil that had been envisioned by some members of the administrations of President Jimmy Carter and California Governor Jerry Brown during the 1970s never happened, and instead government investments in renewable energy research were frozen or reduced. Three decades later the United States found itself embroiled in an unpopular war that, like previous wars of the twentieth century, was largely based on geopolitical rivalry over oil. As the country continued on a foreign-policy course oriented toward control of global oil supplies, it lost valuable time that could have been spent in a transition away from fossil fuels. Opportunities to "green" manufacturing, to restore habitats, and to reduce pollution were also lost.[3]

Mainstream political debate in the United States on the continuing problems of inequality and environmental degradation has been largely limited to advocacy of continued neoliberalization versus a return to liberal approaches that would sanction higher levels of government intervention in the economy. Regarding environmental problems, a neoliberal purist would argue that rising prices for fossil fuels and new market opportunities for clean technologies should be the sole determinant of the transition from an economy dependent on fossil fuels. At the other extreme, an ideal typical liberal would propose huge government investment in renewable energy with mandates and targets. For neoliberals, if the world is running out of oil, then the price of oil should continue to rise, and new investments will follow. Marginal sources of oil (shale, deep ocean drilling, and coal liquidification) or substitutes such as biofuels will become profitable, and investment will flow into the new sources. Neoliberals are confident that the greening of the economy will occur in response to marketplace signals. In reply, liberals argue that the price signals will not come quickly or strongly enough and that the signals will continue to be dampened by the failure of the market to capture the true value of the use of the environment as a source of new resources and a sink for waste deposits. As a result, much more government intervention is needed. Occasionally a broad political consensus is reached in favor of some type of government intervention, but then the debate between neoliberal and liberal perspectives continues between more market-oriented policies, for example a cap-and-trade approach to carbon reduction, versus more interventionist policies, such as a carbon tax.

Regarding poverty, an ideal typical neoliberal would emphasize economic development programs that reduce taxes for businesses that locate in targeted, low-income areas. Neoliberals believe that a return to government-supported poverty, labor, and welfare programs would plunge the economy into stagnation by strangling innovation and the marketplace. They argue that if liberals can be prevented from strangling the economy, then the twenty-first century will see rising incomes, enormous wealth, and spreading democracy. In contrast, an ideal typical liberal would emphasize the need for government retraining programs, assistance for the poor, education in general, and assistance to small businesses. Some proposals call for a floor below which no person would be allowed to sink. Liberals argue that neoliberal policies will plunge the twenty-first century into increasing poverty, social instability, and ultimately political instability.

Table 1.1 provides a schematic outline of mainstream political debate for environmental and social inequality issues. Regarding environmental problems, from an ideal typical neoliberal perspective the main problem is to identify government regulations that restrict the greening of the corporate sector based on profitability considerations. Government policy should identify impediments to investment, such as restrictions on distributed generation, and remove them. From the liberal perspective the main problem is to identify opportunities for government investment in new technologies and industries that need assistance in order to reach economies of scale that make them competitive, and to correct for externalities such as pollution and resource withdrawal that may not be properly priced by markets. Regarding poverty, neoliberals emphasize identifying regulations and other impediments to entrepreneurialism and

Table 1.1
Neoliberal and liberal approaches to environmental and social problems.

	Neoliberalism	Liberalism
Environmental problems	Eco-efficiency: reduce government impediments to eco-innovation by ending many regulations and taxes	Green interventionism: increase government regulations to address risk, crises, and externalities
Social problems	Developmentalism: solve poverty by encouraging economic development and entrepreneurialism	Welfare statism: solve poverty with government programs to provide assistance and training

economic development in low-income neighborhoods, whereas liberals emphasize the need to establish a floor for poverty and to fund government-sponsored programs for education, training, and economic development. On the whole, since 1980 the neoliberal end of the spectrum has tended to triumph, but many policy outcomes reveal elements of both strands of political thought.

As I have suggested, the positions outlined in table 1.1 are meant to be exemplary or ideal types; in practice the mainstream debate involves a wide range of contested positions, compromises, and mixed policies and proposals. Two examples of proposals made within the field of mainstream political debates to address environmental problems can give an example of how neoliberal and liberal strands of thinking tend to coexist. In their 1999 book *Natural Capitalism: Creating the Next Industrial Revolution*, Paul Hawken, Amory Lovins, and L. Hunter Lovins attempted to convince business readers that what was good for the environment was also good for a corporation's bottom line. In support of their win-win scenario that questioned the "profits-versus-environment" assumption, Hawken et al. discussed many technological innovations that could simultaneously enhance profits and improve the environmental performance of companies. Their emphasis on profitability as a driver of greening was exemplary of green neoliberalism, and their book was an excellent example of thinking that has become known as eco-efficiency. Although those strands of thinking might lead the reader to classify the book as an exemplar of a neoliberal approach to corporate greening, the arguments put forward also revealed a liberal strand. Building on tax policies that have been implemented in some of the northern European countries, the authors suggested that a thorough tax shift was needed to motivate producers and consumers alike to make the dramatic changes in practices that would be necessary to solve the world's environmental crisis. For example, they called for the elimination of taxes on both business and personal income and their replacement with tolls on activities that generate emissions and waste, such as transportation, electricity, heating, industrial pollutants, and the use of natural resources. Such a high level of government intervention in the economy was more suggestive of liberalism, and indeed the authors were careful to distinguish their approach from the laissez-faire policies of pure neoliberalism. However, the authors generally retreated from the challenge of examining the broader relationship between the environmental crisis and global poverty. Although the subsequent work of Hawken would be more clearly classified as social liberalism, this particular book suggested policies based on a greater awareness of eco-efficiency and market-based solutions and some tax restructuring, but with relatively little attention to distributional issues.[4]

Another mainstream proposal, one developed at roughly the same time as *Natural Capitalism* but with a more globalist and liberal orientation, was the World Energy Modernization Plan. The plan was developed in a meeting of an international group of energy company presidents, economists, and policy experts who believed that the Kyoto Protocol process was inadequate. Addressed more to the world's political leaders than to its business leaders, the World Energy Modernization Plan suggested how to think about the environmental crisis from a more comprehensive perspective than one based on technological innovation and market-oriented tax reforms. As in the case of Hawken et al., one can find strands of liberal and neoliberal thinking in the proposal. A strand of neoliberal thinking was evident in the support for a market-based emissions trading scheme, but in the liberal tradition the plan called for a shift in energy subsidies in industrialized countries from carbon-based industries to renewable ones, and it also called for government intervention to reduce the consumption of fossil fuels by 5 percent per year. Furthermore, the plan also showed more concern than Hawken et al.

with global inequality by including a proposal for a renewable energy transfer fund, supported by small tax on international currency transactions (known as a "Tobin tax"), that would bring the new technologies to less wealthy countries at a rate of about $300 billion per year. The internationalist and redistributive elements of the plan were in many ways continuous with the liberal or social democratic sentiment of the United Nations reports such as *Our Common Future*, which encouraged the world's business and government leaders to develop a vision that involved government intervention in the economy to solve both environmental and inequality problems.[5]

As the two examples suggest, concrete policy proposals to solve global environmental and/or social problems may tilt toward liberal or neoliberal political perspectives, but they often have strands of both types of political ideology. The categories of liberal and neoliberal are useful to identify and track strands of political thought, a project that may help one to discern the values that guide policy proposals. As the two examples show, the greening of the economy can tilt toward either neoliberal or liberal solutions, and it can be either more or less separated from concern with distributional issues raised by globalization. The political debate focuses on the details of such mixed proposals and what role the government will play in steering a transition toward a greener economy.

Underneath the endless positions, counter-positions, compromises, and standoffs that characterize the political field of contestation between neoliberalism and liberalism is a body of unquestioned assumptions, or what the sociologist Pierre Bourdieu described as a "doxa" of beliefs, that neither neoliberals nor liberals question. The fundamental elements of the doxa involve reducing trade barriers, opening financial markets, harmonizing regulatory policies across world regions, and using monetary policy to keep inflation under control. The elements of the doxa are linked together by a common belief in a global economy that has as its fundamental unit the large publicly traded corporation. Other types of organizations may exist in the interstices of the global economy—"mom and pop" retail stores, micro-enterprises, cooperatives, nonprofits, and the occasional publicly owned enterprise—but they are marginal, not central to the economy. Rather, the corporate economy is the centerpiece

of a global order that ensures economic growth and technological innovation, which in turn are assumed to be central to producing the greatest
good for the greatest number.[6]

If the advocates of mixed neoliberal and liberal policies are correct,
then a combination of profit-led corporate innovation and government-
sponsored regulations and incentives will soon usher in a new generation
of clean technologies, including carbon sequestration, biofuels from
switchgrass, hybrid-electric flex-fuel and electric vehicles, ubiquitous
solar and wind energy, hydrogen fuel cells, lightweight nanomaterials,
bioplastics, and smart green buildings. If the redistributional and inter-
nationalist proposals of social liberalism are integrated into the greening
of the economy, then the mixes of neoliberal and liberal environmental
policies could also be configured to reduce global poverty. Furthermore,
as the economies of the developed countries undergo greening, they will
achieve energy independence, and they will no longer need to support
militaries and neocolonial control of resource-rich countries. As military
dominance recedes, terrorism could also recede, and democracy and
peace might flourish. By 2050 the world's population will have peaked,
and the positive effects of a newly green, democratic, corporate global
order could be visible everywhere. At that point economic growth would
coincide with greater per capita income, and poverty would begin to
recede even in the worst areas of the world. The debate is all about which
types of taxes, regulatory policies, government subsidies, and technology
transfer are needed, and what kinds of policy reforms are best, to get
from here to there. But how realistic are the hopeful scenarios of mainstream political debates?

Some Challenges for Mainstream Optimism

The mainstream political debates are based on the hope that the global
economy can simultaneously undergo greening and continued economic
growth without destroying the environment or plunging the world's poor
into epidemics and starvation. The hope is based on the assumption that
technological innovation can be rapid enough to compensate for the
environmental impact that accompanies increased economic growth,
and that governments can provide adequate policy solutions before the

catastrophic environmental effects of ongoing economic growth are widely felt.

Critics of mainstream economics and policy have long raised skeptical questions about the capacity of the capitalist system to solve the world's problems of social inequality. In the nineteenth century Karl Marx viewed the conflict between the profit-seeking activities of elites and the quality of life of the working class as generating increasing misery and eventually revolutionary potential in the advanced industrial societies. Since that time Marx's prognosis has been partially borne out in a century of worker-peasant revolutions in less developed countries, including Russia and China, but in the advanced industrial societies the class conflict was kept under control by the development of the welfare state and collective bargaining. To some degree the wealthy, democratic countries were also able to export class conflict to less developed countries by establishing terms of trade that allowed for higher wages for the working class of their own countries. From the Marxist perspective, the fundamental conflict between the desire of owners of capital for profitability and the desire of workers for fair working conditions and wages did not disappear. Rather, the history of the twentieth century involved developing institutions to manage the conflict, ranging from labor negotiations in wealthy, democratic countries to violent repression and military dictatorships in colonial and post-colonial countries. Awareness of the fundamental conflict between labor and capital has been the basis of skepticism that mainstream policies will ever solve the pervasive and growing problems of social inequality.[7]

During the 1970s a related critique drew attention to another fundamental problem of capitalism: the conflict between the quest for ongoing profitability and the quality of the natural environment. The concern raised was that the ongoing quest for increased profits, which drives economic growth in general, will eventually hit a wall of ecological limits, because economic growth entails increasing use of natural resources and deposits of waste and pollution. In order to surmount the fundamental conflict between economic growth and environmental limits, growth must coincide with the dematerialization of the economy. In other words, economic growth must take place in a way that reduces the ecological impact of the global economy. For example, if a source of

cheap, plentiful, clean energy were to become available, it might be possible to have 9 billion people all living at a high standard of living
without causing the global ecosystem to crash. Such was once the promise
of nuclear energy, and it is now replaced by visions of a wind-solar-
hydrogen economy with virtual workplaces enabled by information technology and dense cities redesigned along smart growth principles. In
theory the large industrial corporation could be tapped to serve technological innovation in energy conservation, renewable energy, green chem-
istry, building design, and urban design. This vision of the ecological
modernization of the economy as a solution to the conflict between
growth and environmental limits would require, at the minimum, government intervention in the economy in a manner similar to the construction of the welfare state as a means of mitigating the conflict between
capital and labor. In other words, in addition to building a welfare state,
the world's national governments would also have to build an environmental state.[8]

Since the 1970s the world's national governments have begun constructing environmental agencies and programs, but the mainstream
scenarios of corporate greening and environmental regulation face several
shortcomings as solutions to growth within ecological limits. One limitation involves the sincerity and pace of the greening of industry. On a
first impression, the ostensible greening of large corporations appears to
be a hopeful sign of a transition toward the scenario of dematerialization
and sustainable production. Certainly the business press shows increasing interest in corporate greening. However, when one looks a little more
carefully at the actions of even the greenest of corporations, the record
is often more complicated. For example, the sociologist Leslie Sklair has
found that corporate greening is often highly opportunistic and not
deeply embedded in corporate strategy. Even the business press has
recognized the difficulties that corporate environmental officers face
when attempting to gain support for green innovations that do not have
an equivalent return on investment to other investment options. From
Sklair's analysis and the ongoing coverage of greenwashing in both the
business press and the environmentalist media a picture of the modern
corporation as a Janus-faced enterprise emerges. One side looks like a
case study of corporate greening, whereas the other side reveals a record

of ongoing environmental destruction and support of anti-environmental policies. The split in corporate strategy on the issue of greening is not due to dishonesty or mere greed; rather, it is a product of structural conditions that require corporate leaders to maximize shareholder value, even when the goal runs into conflict with plans for corporate greening.[9]

Another weakness that critics identify in mainstream nostrums is the failure of corporate greening to lead to a decline in absolute environmental impact. To date corporate greening has coincided with continued growth in absolute levels of resource consumption and environmental degradation at a global level. For example, automobile companies have continued to develop fabulous green concept vehicles and a new generation of hybrid and flex-fuel vehicles, but they also compete to put increasing numbers of cars and trucks on the roads rather than envision a transition to intensive use of public transportation. Likewise, the big-box retailers are greening their stores and their product lines along the best eco-efficiency principles, but they continue to construct global commodity chains that require increasing amounts of fossil-fuel energy for transportation. The electrical utilities are building some wind farms and offering some energy-conservation measures, but their revenues remain tied to increased electricity consumption, much of which, in the United States, is based on coal and natural gas. Some oil companies are diversifying to reposition themselves as energy companies, but their profits remain linked to increased petroleum consumption, and they continue to compete with each other to explore and exploit new oil fields all over the world. Furthermore, there are many other environmental issues for which change seems much less likely to be forthcoming, such as the environmental risks associated with nanotechnology and persistent chemical pollutants, the ongoing destruction of habitats as a result of mineral extraction and agriculture, the continued use of coal as an energy source, and the depletion of aquifers.[10]

A third obstacle to the credibility of the rosy scenarios of mainstream political debate is the continued existence of "brown corporations," that is, anti-green companies that continue to support the longstanding battle against environmental reform. After a wave of environmental legislation during the 1960s and the 1970s that addressed some of the most egregious environmental challenges in the United States, brown corporations in industries most affected by environmental regulations regrouped and developed increasingly stiff opposition to environmental regulations under the banner of neoliberalism. By the 1990s the companies had developed a wide range of techniques used to convince voters to oppose environmental regulation. For example, in attempts to manage the influence of science on environmental policy for global warming, brown corporations funded climate change skeptics, who served as a small minority of contrarian scientists but leveraged a disproportionately large amount of media coverage throughout the 1990s and well into the first decade of the twenty-first century. Brown corporations also influenced political leadership to stifle environmentally oriented science. For example, one corporation's memo in 2001 to the administration of President George W. Bush called for the removal of Robert Watson as chair of the Intergovernmental Panel on Climate Change, and within a year the administration had achieved the goal of receiving Watson's resignation.[11]

A fourth deficiency in mainstream scenarios is that even where innovation in favor of green technology is successful, the innovations may generate a new wave of environmental problems that will in turn take years to solve. From a technological perspective, many of the promised new technologies are possible but undeveloped and unproven. For example, carbon sequestration for coal-burning plants has unknown risks, especially when the carbon is stored as a gas. As the lethal carbon eruption in the Lake Nyos region in Cameroon indicated, concentrated eruptions of carbon dioxide are both odorless and fatal. Regarding the promise of biofuels as a bridge technology to a hydrogen-based or electricity-based transportation system, coal is used to run ethanol distilleries; petroleum is used as a basis for fertilizer and to run farm equipment and tanker trucks; more pesticides must be applied, resulting in increased land and water pollution; conversion of forested or fallow land to cropland will result in increased greenhouse-gas emissions; the net energy return on energy invested is, at least for corn and under some assumptions, negative; the emissions of ethanol may be less healthy than those of gasoline; and food prices are rising in response to higher demand for corn and other feedstocks. Fuel-cell and hydrogen technologies remain very expensive and replete with technical problems, especially if one assumes that the source of hydrogen will be renewable energy. Wind and solar are promising alternatives, but they remain tiny percentages of energy production, and a transition to them is slowed by many technical and economic problems. Furthermore, the negative side effects of new green innovations would likely be borne most heavily by the poor: people located near carbon-sequestration sites or nuclear waste sites, small farmers who lose access to land and water as their resources are absorbed into biofuel production, factory workers in nanotechnology plants, and those whose family budgets are heavily affected by rising food prices.[12]

As the new side effects of environmentally oriented technological innovations become evident, it takes another 20 years of scientific research and grassroots mobilization to point out the problems, work out solutions, and develop the political will to convert the solutions into policy. In each case we are likely to make a new history that repeats that of carbon emissions, where interested corporations resist attempts to remediate known environmental problems. A new segment of the private sector that is benefiting substantially from pollution and other negative environmental externalities is likely to slow down attempts to ameliorate the situation until well after a crisis has become widely visible. Although it is true that some large publicly traded corporations can, in some cases, be enrolled in efforts to solve environmental problems—indeed, we are unlikely to solve environmental problems if they are not—the enrollment often occurs after a huge amount of damage has been done, a significant mobilization of civil society and scientific research has been brought to bear on the problem, and the industry gives up on its first-line strategy to suppress or slow reform efforts.

A fifth shortcoming is the tendency for the very definition of "greening" to undergo dilution. Under the gun of profitability considerations, companies are tempted to water down sustainable design (that is, design that utilizes zero-waste cycles of production and consumption with a goal of dematerializing the economy so that ecological collapse is avoided) to green tech (design that addresses problems such as chemical pollution and greenhouse gases, but not necessarily at sufficient scale) to clean tech (design that mitigates some of the worse effects of existing technologies).

Far from a mere question of semantics, the changes involve a shift in perspective from solution to reduction of harm, often in the form of technologies that create new problems of their own. It is too easy to lose track of the fundamental driver of the environmental crises: a global economy that is continuing to grow in absolute levels of environmental sinks and withdrawals. Instead, the focus shifts to innovation that reduces impacts but ignores the difficult politics of the environmental impact of continued growth.

From the perspective of critics of mainstream neoliberal and liberal politics, the five deficiencies just outlined—the Janus-faced attributes of many of the self-proclaimed green corporations, the coexistence of corporate greening and continued expansion of environmental sinks and withdrawals, the rearguard actions of brown corporations, the potential negative environmental effects of green technology, and the tendency to water down sustainable design to clean tech—make it very unlikely that the rosy scenarios of mainstream political prognostication will be realized in the coming decades. The solutions have been around for a while, such as those proposed by Hawken et al. or the advocates of the World Energy Modernization Plan. There is little doubt that the greener segments of the corporate world will support some environmental reforms, such as carbon-based emissions trading, partly because the reforms have become necessary in the United States in order to harmonize state-level initiatives. However, a deep and lasting ecological transition of the economy is likely to be held up by the brown corporations that benefit most from environmental degradation or by groups within so-called green corporations whose profitability growth is threatened by new regulatory proposals. The policy-making process will continue to involve conflicts between relatively green and brown segments of industry and society, and to the extent that solutions emerge from the political process, the solutions are likely to be piecemeal and watered down. Because the solutions are likely to be diluted in comparison with what needs to be done to bring about the high degree of dematerialization of the economy that would allow economic growth to occur within environmental limits, critics of mainstream political scenarios envision a much less rosy future: an ongoing environmental crisis and an uneven, decades-long historical transition to societal collapse.[13]

To be clear, the critique of mainstream debate and policies is less about the technical capacity of the political and economic system to solve problems and more about its political capacity to realize its technical potential in a comprehensive and timely way. There is little doubt that under liberal and neoliberal policies the economy will undergo a greening process, and we may even see declines in energy intensity or other metrics of relative sustainability, but the problem is that environmental reforms will not keep pace with the need to limit the absolute growth of global ecosystem sinks and withdrawals to a sustainable level. Furthermore, the reforms will also tend to define one aspect of environmental destruction, such as climate change, as *the* global crisis. As policies emerge to address carbon emissions, there will be great rounds of self-congratulations for a job well done. But if one looks a little more carefully, overall growth in emissions will continue, new generations of toxic chemicals will be released on the environment, and habitats will continue to degrade. Furthermore, in the political compromises that emerge, environmental solutions are likely to be severed from social problems such as poverty. Indeed, the potential of the large corporation to generate an effective response to global problems of poverty and inequality appears to be even weaker than that of governments. Companies that are under siege for questionable labor practices—such as sweatshops, minimal benefits, lock-ins, and race and gender discrimination—have in some cases put forward major public-relations campaigns about their eco-efficiency measures as way to burnish images that have been tarnished by labor controversies.[14]

Rather than approach environmental and social problems as an interwoven whole, the greening of the corporate world can end up driving a wedge between them. From the perspective of critics of the mainstream political debates, it is likely that under a regime of neoliberalism, and even one of timid liberalism, a situation of "one step forward, one step backward" will continue to characterize environmental policy in the United States and many other countries for much of the twenty-first century. Large publicly traded industrial corporations will continue to undergo greening, and regulatory policy will continue to address environmental issues, but the changes are likely to be too little, too late to solve the full range of interconnected environmental and social problems, not to mention the side effects generated from the new technological fixes.

With scenarios of collapse rather than amelioration looming, why do the world's economic and political elites not embrace a precautionary politics and rush to enact a wide range of social and environmental reforms? To answer the question, one needs to remember that collapse will mean many things to many people. In a world of increasing natural disasters and climate-generated risk, the wealthy have much less to lose than do the poor, and indeed they have much to gain. Elites have the financial resources to diversify their wealth, insure their investments against risk, and get out of harm's way when the disasters strike. The more conservative segments of the elites, those who support the neoliberal dream of dismantling the public sector, have also begun to find new economic opportunities in a world of privatized disaster relief. A halting policy process of taking one step backward on solving environmental problems, followed by one step forward, provides the wealthy with all sorts of economic opportunities to benefit from both the greening of the economy and the unraveling of the ecology, at least in the short term, which is the only time horizon for the publicly traded corporations in which they are invested. If the critics of mainstream political debate are correct, then the mainstream political field, with its mixes of aggressive neoliberalism and timid liberalism, will provide an ongoing mixture of half-hearted responses that lead to uneven collapse, environmental degradation, and human immiseration throughout the world.[15]

Radical Alternatives

Whereas the mainstream political debate draws attention to the problem of more or less government steering of the economy, and what kinds of steering are necessary, the radical perspective—and one might remember that the word "radical" comes from "radix," Latin for "root"—suggests that the problem goes much deeper. There is a fundamental contradiction between an economy based on the large publicly traded industrial corporation, with its narrow focus on earnings growth and stock prices, and the general societal goal of adapting the global economy to ecological limits and distributing wealth in a manner that accords with widely held understandings of basic fairness. The fundamental economic organization of modern society, the industrial corporation, was developed during an era when the society-environment relationship was considerably different. Five hundred years ago, when the first modern corporations were chartered, the contours of the world's continents were largely unmapped, and the agricultural societies of both colonizing and colonized societies had much smaller ecological footprints than their industrial successors do today. In an era of colonial expansion, the corporation was a valuable tool for European political elites who wished to motivate their subjects to extend the rule of national governments across the world. Likewise, in the nineteenth century a central challenge for the US government was to extend sovereignty over a large continent, much of which was populated by native peoples who wreaked much lower levels of ecological destruction on the environment. During that period public offerings of stock became necessary to raise the capital required for railroads, and a more modernized species of capitalist organization emerged: the publicly traded corporation.[16]

The publicly traded corporation as an engine of economic growth served the interests of colonizing nation-states well. In a world with relatively distant ecological limits, as was the case throughout the nineteenth century for the United States, the growth orientation of the large corporation was beneficial for both workers and elites. However, the era of ecological limits has now set in, and we are faced with the question of how well adapted the publicly traded corporation is to a world in which economic growth needs to occur within global ecological limits. Radical sociologists and heterodox economists have suggested that in order to put our modern societies on a path toward life within sustainable limits, economic policy would have to end economic growth or at least shift to a low growth scenario that would enable a "steady state" of ecosystem sinks and withdrawals. Although they recognize that technological developments will enable some economic growth without additional environmental destruction, they argue that to date the pace of technological innovation has not been not been rapid enough to make up for the environmental effects of economic growth. The greening of industry creates the illusion of motion toward a goal, but because absolute levels of environmental withdrawals and sinks increase as a result of economic growth, there is no forward motion on the fundamental issue of creating a global economy that operates within sustainable limits.[17]

Radical critics of the twinned global crises of sustainability and poverty offer a perceptive diagnosis and prognosis of the patient, but their prescriptions tend to be less satisfying. When pushed, many radical critics embrace the need for changes in taxes, regulations, treaties, and other government policies that place them in the camp of aggressive liberalism in the political field. However, there is also a tradition of radical solutions that charts out an alternative set of policy directions to that of the liberal-neoliberal debate. The solutions, which I will discuss here under the loose rubrics of socialism and communalism, are outlined, again as ideal types, in table 1.2.

Socialism, the most widely known of the radical policy proposals, has historically been viewed as a means of redistributing wealth in society from elites to working-class and poor people. If large corporations were nationalized, profits that would have gone to wealthy shareholders would instead accrue to the government owner, which could then redistribute the wealth either directly to the workers via higher wages or indirectly through welfare programs. Although socialism is widely understood through the lens of distributive justice, it can also be configured as a radical solution to the environmental problems outlined in the previous section. The nationalization of industry under a socialist government

Table 1.2
Socialist and communalist approaches to environmental and social problems.

	Socialism	Communalism
Environmental problems	Restriction of growth in environmental damage by government ownership of corporations with a dematerialization mandate	Restriction of growth in environmental damage by local, communal organization of society and use of sustainable technologies
Social problems	Government ownership of large corporations to appropriate profits for redistribution to the poor and working class	Local sharing of wealth through collective decision making and ownership

provides one possible resolution of the conflict between the publicly traded corporation's endless thirst for profitability and growth and society's need for changes in production that reduce the growth in the effect of the economy on the environment. If a government were to nationalize the most environmentally damaging industries or even just the brownest corporations, it could potentially transform industrial priorities to meet environmental goals. The leaders of the nationalized companies would not need to worry about short-term profits and their fiduciary responsibility to shareholders, because their shareholders would be government owners with a different approach to the balance between economic growth and social and environmental responsibility. If the government were to demand sustainable technology and dematerialization of production ahead of growth in profits and revenue, industry could be brought in line with the goal of a radical restructuring of the economy, and an environmental state would become something more than the mirage that it has become after decades of neoliberal policy making.

An example of a socialist approach to environmental issues in the United States is the proposal of Barry Commoner (a biologist who ran for president in 1980 as the candidate of the Citizens Party) for limited nationalization of industry. Commoner has sometimes been portrayed as advocating the "deindustrialization" or "demodernization" of industry, but the terms can be misleading if interpreted to imply that he wanted to close down advanced industry and return to an agrarian past. Instead, Commoner advocated a mixture of green liberalism—that is, a strong government role in the steering of the economy—and limited socialism in the form of the nationalization of the energy, transportation, and health industries. He hoped that a combination of liberal and socialist approaches to industrial policy would bring about a rapid greening of industry. He argued that twentieth-century industrial technology was faulty from an ecological perspective, and he suggested instead that industry had to be rebuilt along "ecologically sound lines." In order to accomplish the radical restructuring of the technological basis of crucial industries, he argued, government ownership was necessary.[18]

Commoner, like many other twentieth-century radical critics of capitalism, recognized the imperfections of socialist policies. Specifically, the environmental record of government ownership in communist countries appeared to be no better than in the capitalist West. One could extend the point and argue that with some exceptions the former communist governments, like other countries that nationalized some industries, did not make environmental goals prominent in the mission of the state-owned corporations. However, as Commoner noted, "socialist economics does not appear to require that growth should continue indefinitely" (1971: 281). If cases could be found where national governments had mandated that government-owned corporations pursue environmental goals, it might be possible to demonstrate that a socialist approach could contribute to a rapid greening of industrial technologies. But even if it would be possible to make that argument in a convincing way, another problem haunts the history of government-owned corporations: a record of lack of innovation and inefficiency. The lack of efficiency is enough for some to claim that the history of the twentieth century proves that socialism is a failure. Socialist solutions continue to be explored in some of the newly industrializing countries and in the former communist countries, where foreign corporations have extracted national resources at low prices, and government ownership has been used to recapture profits for national governments. Those cases would provide the empirical basis for making an ongoing assessment of the social and environmental benefits of publicly owned corporations. There are also instances of relatively uncontroversial forms of government ownership of industry in the United States. For example, local government ownership of public transit and electrical services has been both successful and popular in various urban areas. This small-scale, American variant of socialism, which one might call "localist socialism," remains a vibrant part of the local economy and political culture in many towns and cities. As I will explore in chapter 6, there is evidence that public ownership of electricity generation and transmission has been accompanied by environmental leadership.[19]

A broader problem than inefficiency is that the nationalization of industry presupposes that the new owner of the corporation, the national government, is capable of wanting a more radical transition to a more socially just and less environmentally damaging economy than private shareholders. However, national governments are often as deeply invested in the growth economy as the publicly traded corporation, because a growing national economy is necessary to maintain political hegemony and to maintain a standard of living for a growing population. For example, the population of the United States is projected to rise to about 400 million by 2050 and nearly 600 million by 2100. The continued growth in population will place exceptional demands on global resources, especially as other countries with large populations, such as China and India, continue to increase per capita resource consumption. When one large economy, such as China, is growing much more rapidly than another, such as the United States, then it will not be long before the smaller economy catches up with the larger one. China has already surpassed Germany as the world's third-largest economy, and it is projected to surpass Japan by 2020 and the United States by 2050. As the smaller economy continues to grow, it will compete not only economically for precious global commodities such as oil and natural gas but also politically, because it has a greater surplus available to convert into military resources, foreign aid, and general geopolitical influence. In such circumstances, a national policy of slow or no growth could dramatically alter the international balance of power. Without rapid growth, the United States could become the "Argentina" of the twenty-first century. Indeed, financial projections by Goldman Sachs suggest that by 2050 the economies of the "BRIC" countries (Brazil, Russia, India, and China) will be larger than those of France, Germany, Italy, Japan, the United Kingdom, and the United States combined. If purchasing-power parity is used as the metric, then the Chinese economy will surpass that of the United States by as early as 2015.[20]

Owing to geopolitical competition, a powerful nation-state that undertakes a transition to a low-growth economy, and does so while its own population is growing and its competitors' economies are growing more rapidly, could be committing political suicide. A rapidly growing private sector can help ensure that a country will have the resources to support an extensive military, maintain its geopolitical position on the world stage, and therefore maintain access to commodities, especially oil and natural gas under conditions of post-peak shortages. Even if the country were to socialize only the largest corporations in the energy and transportation industries, it would still need to have a growing economy in order to compete militarily. As a result, the government would probably put pressure on the publicly owned corporations to grow, and the end result might not be different from an economy based on publicly traded corporations. Although socialism may provide a better solution to problems of justice, especially in developing countries that wish to recapture profits from extractive industries, the nationalization of industries is of questionable value as a solution to the fundamental contradiction between economic growth and environmental limits. As long as there is an international system based on competition among nation-states, with war as the ultimate measure of power, the ameliorative capacity for socialism will be limited.

The argument about the environmental weaknesses of socialism should not be interpreted to imply that there might be some benefits of the nationalization of resource-intensive industries over a liberal order with no public ownership. For example, government ownership of brown corporations would reduce the flows of capital toward anti-environmental think tanks and political candidates. Consequently, the nationalization of some companies may increase the political system's autonomy and its capacity to develop effective policies to reduce the energy intensity of the economy. Socialism might also be more effective for countries that are not militarily dominant and are less concerned with geopolitical hegemony. However, in the United States, which requires ongoing growth to retain its position as global hegemon, socialism would be unlikely to enable the radical shift of the economy toward lower growth with dematerialization. Socialism would work as a solution to the sustainability problem only if the United States were to solve its dependence on foreign fossil fuels, which would then allow it to relax the need to maintain geopolitical dominance, which in turn would allow it to focus on dematerialization more than on economic growth. The question, which will be left unanswered here, is whether the transition to an economy based on self-sufficient and renewable energy sources can take place rapidly under mainstream policy regimes, or whether the nationalization of the fossil-fuel industries would be necessary to achieve the rapid transition without undue political obstruction.

Another branch of radical political thought, communalism, also purports to provide a better solution than policies developed within the frameworks of mainstream political thought. In the United States the communalist tradition can be traced back to religious communities of the colonial era and to the utopian experiments of the nineteenth century. The debate between the socialist and communalist strategies for social change was already well formulated by the middle of the nineteenth century, when Friedrich Engels criticized utopian socialism as an unrealistic response to the social ills of industrialism. By the late nineteenth century, socialists and anarchists were debating their differing approaches to radical solutions. In the twentieth century, the countercultural communes of the 1960s and the "back to the land" movement of the 1970s provided further experiments in the tradition.[21]

In a commune, wealth is typically owned collectively and distributed through a collective decision-making process. Although there is usually some limited private ownership, tools, vehicles, computers, land, buildings, food, energy, and other things are collectively owned. As a result, the gap in wealth and income between the richest and the poorest members of the community is very small. Even more than socialism, communalism provides a solution to the problem of inequality. Of course, the per capita wealth of a commune may be much lower than that of the society as a whole, and consequently there is a range of collectivist experiments that permit varying mixes of individual and collective ownership. Modifications of the ideal typical commune, such as the ecovillage and cohousing, allow even greater degrees of family ownership and wealth accumulation. In effect they trade inequality for flexibility and attractiveness.

Many of the communes of the 1960s and the 1970s were deeply concerned with sustainability, at least at the local level. The anarchist intellectual Murray Bookchin brought communalist politics into dialogue with environmental concerns and advocated the formation of liberatory, decentralized communities that he variously described as anarchist, social ecological, communalist, and libertarian socialist. Bookchin advocated decentralization less as communal living than as a return to direct democracy in the form of federations of neighborhood assemblies that would own and direct fundamental economic units. Collective, local ownership of the means of production would replace both private-sector capitalism and federal-government socialism as the fundamental basis of the US economy. Municipalization of the economy based on local, direct democracy would coincide with a technological shift toward sustainable agriculture, renewable energy, and other green technologies. Bookchin's position on technology was complicated. Although in some ways he might be classified as advocating de-industrialization, he saw computerization and other forms of modern technology as offering the potential for a more decentralized society with greater leisure.[22]

Eco-anarchist thought influenced some of the communal experiments of the 1960s and the 1970s, but the colorful history of attempts to communalize American society during that period is largely one of failure. Utopian communities often faced transition crises as members adjusted their ideals of shared ownership and collective decision making to the realities of interpersonal conflict. Communes and related community experiments that lasted more than 10 years faced problems of reproduction and recruitment. Many children of the hippie communes migrated back to the world their parents had left behind, and some of the older and more successful American communes faced a problem of caring for an aging population. Although urban ecovillages and environmentally oriented cohousing have been more successful, those variants of communalism have not proven to have mass appeal.[23]

Nationalization, municipalization, or communalization could, in theory, solve the fundamental contradictions of capitalism by fostering a deep restructuring of the economy so that additions and withdrawals to the environment would be managed under a democratic political process and brought within ecologically sustainable limits. Likewise, the solutions could enhance social equality through the redistribution of corporate profits from elites to the working class and the poor. However, if the United States were to embark on an extensive program of reform such as outlined by Commoner or Bookchin, the shifts of wealth would likely entail intense resistance from elites, who benefit from the status quo of economic growth and military domination. As revolutionary socialists suggested in the nineteenth century, a violent confrontation would be a likely outcome of such radical restructurings. Although in theory a radical policy program that blends ecosocialism and ecocommunalism could bring about a significant social and technological transformation of the economy, it does not appear to have especially good prospects in our time. Both socialist and communalist approaches to organizing society were outside mainstream political debate during the 1960s and the 1970s, and they became even more marginal in the decades that followed. The prospects for policy approaches that draw on radical political thought of either the socialist or the communalist variety are quite low in the United States of the early twenty-first century.

Although the radical alternatives are politically quite marginal in the United States, they are important for the purpose of understanding localism as political thought and action. It may even be tempting to situate localist thought historically as a continuation of socialist or communalist politics, but there is almost no evidence that radicals such as Barry Commoner and Murray Bookchin have influenced the present-day US localist movement. Nevertheless, there are some connecting strands. The primary example is E. F. Schumacher, the author of *Small Is Beautiful*. Schumacher had an enthusiastic audience in the United States, especially on college campuses, between 1973 (the year his book was published) and 1977 (when he died). *Small Is Beautiful* can still be found for sale at the annual BALLE meetings, and the E. F. Schumacher Society (headquartered in Great Barrington, Massachusetts) has built on his legacy by developing local currencies and other localist initiatives in the United States.

Schumacher was a socialist who spent most of his career working as an economist for the National Coal Board, an organization that controlled the United Kingdom's nationalized coal industry. From that vantage point he was able to see the limitations of government ownership of industry and the unflattering similarities between large publicly owned companies and large publicly traded corporations. His thinking also drew on his experiences as a director on the board of an employee-owned company, as an economic advisor for the country of Burma, as an organic gardener, and as a student of the Gandhian, village-centered strategy of rural development. Those experiences came together in his advocacy of a transition to economies based on renewable resources, people-centered and employee-owned business organizations, and technologies of development appropriate to the needs of a country's poor and working-class people. In terms of the typology of political positions developed above, his work synthesized elements of socialist and communalist thinking, especially the cooperativist strand of socialist thought that emphasized employee ownership and the Gandhian version of village-centered communalism. In an intellectual move that was in many ways a precursor of twenty-first-century localist politics, Schumacher also (to a degree) stepped out of the classic "state-versus-economy" debate by analyzing the type of economic organization that would be the best to solve environmental and social problems. He concluded that neither the large publicly traded corporation nor the large government-owned corporation was necessarily the best solution for building a more socially just and environmentally sustainable society. Instead, he sought answers in new forms of economic organization and ownership.[24]

Schumacher's legacy of appropriate technology and small firms owned by employees, much like the thought and the policy prescriptions of Commoner and Bookchin, seems almost quaint after decades of neoliberal policies and corporate globalization. For the less wealthy economies, the legacy of the appropriate-technology movement can be found today in organizations such as Engineers Without Borders, but Schumacher's focus on appropriate technology and national economic self-sufficiency has been marginalized by waves of structural adjustment programs and direct foreign investment. For the developed Western countries, Schumacher's goals of reforming the large publicly owned enterprise and awakening the potential of employee ownership have also been swept aside, in this case by waves of privatization and industrial consolidation. Here, there is some influence of Schumacher's thought on the present-day localist movement. For example, there is considerable interest in employee ownership as an exit strategy for aging entrepreneurs who do not wish to take their company public or sell their business to Multinational, Inc. Cooperatives and credit unions, which have democratic organizational structures, have also been active in the localist organizations with which I am familiar.

Although it is important to recognize the influence of E. F. Schumacher, there are significant differences between his vision of an alternative economy and that of present-day localists. For today's localist movement in the United States, the emphasis on appropriate technology has been replaced by a more general concern with sustainability and community, and likewise the organizational focus is much more on small businesses than on employee-owned firms. If one wishes to push the comparison, it may be best to think of present-day localism as "Small Is Beautiful 2.0," this time with an economic base in a pre-existing economic class and with greater concern for independent ownership than for appropriate technology. Even that qualified comparison should not be pushed too far, because the class basis of present-day localism is considerably different from that of "small is beautiful" economics, which remained rooted in a vision of building appropriate organizations and technologies for the world's working-class and poor people.

Localism as a Political Ideology

Although one can identify pro-localist individuals who are influenced by Schumacher and other political thinkers in the socialist or communalist tradition, it would be a mistake to position localism merely as a continuation of radical political thought. Instead, one can identify affinities between localism and all four strands of political ideology. To the radical side, the support of locally owned public enterprises and employee-owned enterprises resonates with socialism. But there are also wings of the localist movement that draw on the radical heritage of decentralization and communalism; for example, on the agricultural side of localism, there is an emphasis on developing local food networks. In this sense one might classify localism as a continuation of radical political traditions and debates. However, strands of mainstream political thought also are evident in the localist movement. For example, localism is consistent with the neoliberal trend in favor of the devolution of national government responsibilities to the states and to communities. A focus on local governance has flourished in the neoliberal climate of government-driven devolution and privatization. Furthermore, by asking consumers to support locally owned independent businesses, "buy local" campaigns, and other localist mobilizations, advocates of localism work through the market under the consumerist logic of voting by spending. But against this neoliberal strand one can also find strands of thought and policy advocacy that would be better characterized as liberal. For example, localist campaigns can also involve local government regulatory interventions and calls for policy support from the federal government, both of which are consistent with the tradition of twentieth-century political liberalism.[25]

The continuities of localism with socialist, communalist, neoliberal, and liberal politics should all be recognized, and likewise any attempts to reduce localism to one or the other strands of political ideologies would best be greeted with questions about oversimplification. It is too easy for analysts who have sympathies with positions within the existing political field of mainstream and radical politics to misinterpret localism as small-scale socialism or liberalism, an iteration of the communalist politics of the late 1960s and the early 1970s, or an expression of neoliberalism via marketplace reformism. Rather, if one starts with recognition of the diversity of the localist movement, it becomes possible to recognize that the new types of coalitions are being built at the grassroots and to explore both the continuities with and differences from political legacies. Localism can appeal to socialists who want to see more local government ownership, to communalists and decentralists who wish to see the growth of independent local economies, to neoliberals who support the small-business sector as a solution to social and environmental problems, and to liberals who seek greater regulation of local land use and federal legislation that ends corporate handouts. The bluest of Democrats may find themselves agreeing with the reddest of Republicans, at least on the strategy of local economic control as a means for improving the environmental, health, and quality of life of their shared, place-based communities. Furthermore, the selection of which strands come to the fore is likely to vary depending on broader political opportunities.[26]

To some degree, localism reveals the doxa, or the "peace in the feud," that occurs between advocates of mainstream policies and the radical alternatives. The debates largely assume that the central political issue is the degree of participation of the national government in the economy: from very little at the extreme of anarcho-communalists to significantly reduced among neoliberals to moderate and aggressive among liberals to government ownership among socialists. The terms of the radical and mainstream political debate can be used to inform an analysis of the articulations of localist politics with existing political ideologies, but they can also become a template that fails to reveal the departures from those ideologies. Just as the radical critique steps outside the mainstream debate between neoliberalism and liberalism, so the localist perspective cannot be understood as limited by the terms of the debate between mainstream and radical politics. To avoid the misinterpretation and to understand localism on its own terms, it is necessary to develop a more succinct vocabulary for its politics.

I suggest that the crucial differences between localist political thought and both radical and mainstream ideologies are the emphasis on the role of small-businesses and nonprofit organizations, the call for independent and local ownership, and the goal of extending that project to locations throughout the world in the form of a global economy based on locally owned independent enterprises. Local autonomy translates largely into a concern with ownership, that is, the question of who owns the means of production. However, in contrast with both radical and mainstream traditions, localism does not entail framing the ownership issue in terms of more or less public ownership, as occurs in debates over privatization and nationalization. The mainstream political debates focus on more or less government intervention in the economy, and the radical debate pushes either for federal ownership in the socialist tradition or for municipal and communal ownership in the communalist tradition. Localism departs somewhat from the existing political debates by shifting attention from the government-economy relationship to the relationship between multinational corporations and society. At the heart of concept of local independent ownership is a political project of building an alternative economy that is distinct from the world of the large publicly traded corporation. This position has resonances with radical critiques of capitalism, either from a socialist or an anarchist perspective. However, the focus on small-business development through market development and government programs also has resonances with neoliberalism and liberalism. The strong attention drawn to the shortcomings of a global economy dominated by enormous corporations with little concern for nation-states or for place-based communities, and often with little concern for the environment and hourly workers, represents a kind of politics that seems especially geared toward addressing the problems that have emerged in an era of globalization.

In addition to drawing attention to the large publicly traded corporation as the central unit in need of reform, localism also adopts a "one-off" position from existing political traditions by configuring the problem of justice in a different way. The "peace in the feud" between mainstream and radical debates on justice concerned the problem of social inequality, especially the fates of working-class and poor people. The debate has always been about how to solve the problem of helping those at the bottom of the social ladder, both at home and abroad. The solutions range from neoliberals' emphasis on enterprise development zones and workfare to welfare-state liberalism to redistribution of profits through communal or government ownership. Although the positions are quite different from each other, the overall debate shares an emphasis on justice in the distributive sense of solving social inequality and poverty.

Localist politics broaden the discussion of justice by injecting what might be considered a procedural perspective into the debate. For localist politics the more central justice issue is the loss of economic and political sovereignty of place-based communities to global capital, which implements new regimes of governance through control of federal government policies, continental trade agreements, and global trade and financial organizations. By sovereignty I mean nothing more complicated than the traditional understanding of a government's ability to regulate and otherwise control the economics and politics of its territory and population. In a world dominated by multinational corporations, it has become increasingly difficult for local communities, and even large nation-states, to achieve autonomy from the priorities set by global capital. Localism draws attention to an underlying problem that is a precondition for a community or larger political unit to be able to address issues of distributive justice. If the democratic governance of the economy is broken as a result of corporate control of local, state, national, and international governments and governing bodies, then it will be difficult for governments to address significant social and environmental problems. Conversely, a community with high economic sovereignty could be in a better position to address issues of poverty within its boundaries than one that is governed by outside forces. However, the two issues are analytically distinct, and the difference is crucial if one is to understand what localism is about as a form of political thought and action.[27]

A helpful context for understanding the localist concern with sovereignty is found in the work of the anthropologists James Ferguson and

Aihwa Ong, who draw attention to the shifts in sovereignty that have occurred in an era of neoliberal globalization. They note that although governments retain formal sovereignty over a territory, in some cases multinational corporations or non-governmental organizations have achieved de facto control. Their examples are drawn from fieldwork in Asia and Africa, but there are parallels with some cities in the United States. Increasingly cities have ceded territorial control over some areas to enclaves of mostly global capital, such as occurs in office parks, shopping malls, and clusters of big-box stores, and other parts of American cities have become largely abandoned to the nonprofit sector. Although neither the corporate enclaves nor the abandoned neighborhoods in American cities are identical to similar shifts of sovereignty in Africa, Asia, and Latin America, the parallels are notable. The comparative work of anthropologists on the transformations of sovereignty associated with globalization provides a good context for understanding the sense of loss of local sovereignty and the desire to reinstate it that is found in the localist movement.[28]

When used as a way of understanding localism in the United States, the concept of sovereignty should be used more loosely than its meaning in international law, where one speaks of a government's military sovereignty over a territory. However, the struggles of indigenous peoples, colonized countries, and post-colonial nations for rights of self-determination provide helpful parallels for understanding the desire for renewed sovereignty that is characteristic of the localist movement in the United States. As in the case of colonized peoples, place-based communities begin with a sense of loss of autonomy, with local knowledge of the degradation of their quality of life and awareness of the gradual shift of economic control to the headquarters of distant corporations. Notwithstanding the parallels, there are also two main differences between concerns with enhanced sovereignty in post-colonial countries and the concept of sovereignty that is crucial to localism in the United States: localist sovereignty is focused more on the question of ownership of economic enterprises, and it is configured within a federated political system. As a result, the idea of local sovereignty is closely connected with a concept of vigorous democracy, the valorization of small businesses, and the insulation of the political system from domination by economic elites. Those concerns are, I suggest, more characteristic of the liberal and radical political traditions than neoliberal thought.

However, because distributive justice is not necessarily congruent with sovereignty, localism departs from the tradition liberal and radical debates on justice. It is possible for localist politics to slide into class-based exclusion and come into conflict with the goal of distributive justice, but the localist concern with sovereignty can also be aligned with struggles to rebuild low-income neighborhoods via the development of small businesses, the growth of the local nonprofit sector, and the invigoration of local governments. In this book I will draw attention to some of the convergences between localism and distributive justice to underscore the argument that localism need not take a path of middle-class retreatism. Nevertheless, the argument that the fundamental concerns of localism focus on the loss of local political and economic sovereignty will be helpful in sorting through the somewhat confusing politics that, in terms of the mainstream and radical field of political positions and traditional left-right polarities, may appear to be all over the political map.

To summarize: Localism emphasizes the problems of the corporatization of the economy and the loss of local sovereignty, and it draws attention to the project of building an economy based on economic units other than large corporations, rather than finding solutions that adjust the role of the government in the economy and that address the pervasive growth of within-nation inequality. (See table 1.3.) The problems that preoccupy the ongoing political field of mainstream and radical positions do not disappear, but instead the terms of the debate about the economy, sustainability, and justice are widened. Just as the radical alternatives to mainstream politics opened up a broader set of political issues for consideration and contestation, so localism opens up the debate of mainstream and radical politics and policies to a broader field of issues.

Middle-Class Radicalism

If one is looking for a historical point of reference for understanding the twenty-first-century localist movement in the United States, in my view the best starting point is what the historian Robert D. Johnston has

Table 1.3
Localist approaches to environmental and social problems.

	Mainstream and radical politics	Localism
Environmental problems	Reforming the government-economy relationship, via either more or less regulation (mainstream) or new forms of ownership (radical, communalist)	Building an alternative global economy to one based on the large industrial corporation
Social problems	Distributive justice either via the state (liberal, socialist) or nonstate institutions (neoliberal, communalist)	Sovereignty in the sense of the right of self-determination of communities

described as the "middle-class radicalism" of the Progressive Era. His book rejected common interpretations of the middle class as politically conservative, interpretations that I would argue are colored by the debates about post-New Deal liberalism. Instead, Johnston argued that during the early twentieth century the middle class of small-business owners can be found in political alliance with the working class in opposition to the politics and policies of the corporate elites.[29]

Progressive political thought also played a significant role in the politically diverse coalitions of the anti-chain-store movement of the 1920s and the 1930s, a direct predecessor of present-day localism and a movement that will be discussed in more detail in chapter 4. The legal scholar Richard Schragger notes that the anti-chain-store movement of the 1920s and the 1930s was "rooted in the anti-monopoly ideology of the Progressive Era" (2005: 1014). As the New Deal coalition emerged, small-town America became a source of opposition to Franklin Roosevelt's centralist liberalism, and "the [anti-chain-store] movement fell on the reactionary side of these new political-cultural lines" (ibid.: 1083). To understand the localism of the early twenty-first century as political thought and action,

I suggest, it is necessary to return to the localism of the early twentieth century, when support for local ownership of the economy was deeply connected to a variety of reform movements. One example from that era is the defense of localism by Supreme Court Justice Louis Brandeis, who had supported Senator Robert LaFollette's presidential bid and had been a founding member of the National Progressive Republican League. Brandeis articulated a doctrine of economic localism that was later displaced by the emerging liberalism of the New Deal. Schragger writes:

> The decentralist strand of the Progressive movement that Brandeis represented fused a localist ideology with political and economic reform—a program that turned out to be more radical in many ways than the New Deal itself. As the commitment to decentralization turned into opposition to the New Deal, however, the reformist valence dissipated, and the remnants of Brandeis's progressive constitution were increasingly associated with resistance to reform. After the New Deal revolution, localist arguments became the province of states' righters. A rhetoric of defensive federalism replaced the Brandeisian rhetoric of reformist localism. (ibid.: 1083–1084)

Anti-corporate but not anti-capitalist, the politics of LaFollette and Brandeis, and more generally the politics of the lower-middle-class movements of the early twentieth century, are better points of comparison for understanding twenty-first-century localism than the mainstream and radical political traditions discussed so far. Nevertheless, present-day advocates of localism share the concern that liberals and radicals have with environmental sustainability and social justice, although the concern is far from universal. In other words, issues that were linked to liberal and radical politics since the 1930s are becoming reconnected with the small-business sector (or, to use the traditional term, the petite bourgeoisie). To the extent that the new linkages, which I will trace out empirically, continue to grow and strengthen, a potential exists for a political reconfiguration that has not been seen since the shifts from the Progressive Era to New Deal liberalism. If one agrees that the liberal tradition from Franklin Roosevelt to present-day liberal Democrats has been unable to stop the advance of corporate domination of the political system, and that the radical alternatives have lacked political traction, then one may be willing to consider that the reconfiguration of the politics of the small-business sector represents a political development of potential historical consequence.

To underscore the point that an important goal of the localist movement is envisioning alternative economies in a world of corporate globalization, consider as an example the political and economic positions articulated by Judy Wicks, a co-founder of BALLE and a leader of the localist movement, at the Twenty-Fourth Annual E. F. Schumacher Lectures:

In order to protect all that I care deeply about, I needed to step out of my own company, out of the White Dog Café, and start to work together with other businesses to build an alternative to corporate globalization. . . . Rather than a global economy controlled by large multinational corporations, our movement envisions a global economy with a decentralized network of local economies made up of what we call living enterprises: small, independent, locally owned businesses of human scale. These living enterprises create community wealth and vitality while working in harmony with natural systems. (2004: 5)

As a vision articulated by a movement leader, Wicks's views are not necessarily shared by all independent business owners or even by all business owners who are affiliated with BALLE, but Wicks does present a way of thinking that explores the potential for this sector of the economy to provide solutions that have not been forthcoming from big business. She opens up a pathway that links the small-business sector to the politics of local, living economies based on principles of increased local ownership, functioning democracies, environmental sustainability, and social justice.

Wicks's vision includes both the ideal typical localist concern with the sovereignty of place-based communities and the invigoration of small businesses (a goal of political reform that echoes the Progressive Era politics of the early twentieth century) and the more conventionally liberal political project of making business more socially and environmentally responsible. In other words, it is suggestive of a configuration of politics that, if Schragger is correct, has been largely absent in the American political landscape since the centralist liberalism of the New Deal displaced Progressivism. For example, Wicks notes that she pays her workers a living wage, that she has campaigned for universal health care, and that her business was the first in the state to have its electricity completely supplied by wind power. In making those decisions, she explicitly rejected the management mantra of "grow or die" and instead created a foundation using the profits from her business. She describes her daughter's experiences in Seattle in 1999 as a protestor against the World Trade Organization, a suggestion of the possible linkages between localism and the politics of anti-globalization movements. "Politicians and government administrators," she writes, "who are frequently former CEOs and lobbyists, often owe their jobs to the corporations that fund political campaigns. The merger of corporate interests with government is defined as fascism." (2004: 27)[30]

Wicks is not alone in linking a defense of locally owned independent enterprises with a critique of a globalized economy based on large publicly traded corporations. For example, Stacy Mitchell, chair of the board of the other major umbrella organization of local independent businesses, AMIBA (American Independent Business Alliance), writes in her book *The Big-Box Swindle*:

The megachains contribute far less to our local economies than they take away. For all of the new jobs that the chains have created, they have destroyed many thousands more—at small businesses and American factories especially, but also, as we will see, at enterprises as diverse as family farms and local newspapers. (2006: 35)

Likewise, David Korten, who sat on the board of BALLE and also served on the advisory board of AMIBA, writes in *The Post-Corporate World*: "What we know as the global capitalist economy is dominated by a few financial speculators and a handful of globe-spanning megacorporations able to use their financial clout and media outreach to manipulate prices, determine what products will be available to consumers, absorb or drive competitors from the market, and reshape the values of popular culture to create demand for what corporations choose to offer." (1999: 40) And Michael Shuman, a board member of BALLE, wrote in the chapter "Wreckonomics" of his book *The Small-Mart Revolution*:

In the TINA ["there is no alternative"] mindset . . . the unemployed are simply excess capacity to be shipped to another community. We're told to keep our bags packed so we can migrate at a moment's notice to another job hundreds or thousands of miles away. Forget about your friends and neighbors. Tell your kids to let go of their silly attachments to teachers and friends. Put away all those memories around your house. Community is just another obstacle to progress. (2006: 38)

Localist leaders' concerns about the negative side effects of a globalized, corporate-dominated economy and their hope for the potential of building a more humane, community-oriented private sector are not just the musings of the leadership of national organizations such as BALLE and AMIBA. I have heard such views expressed widely in meetings and conferences dedicated to local living economies and related topics. Likewise, in dozens of conversations with concerned independent business owners in my own region I have encountered a widespread sense that the region was a more friendly, community-oriented place before the era of big-box retail stores and franchise restaurants. This form of small-business radicalism is not anti-capitalist in the tradition of socialist and communalist politics, nor is it identical to Progressive Era anti-corporatism. Rather, present-day localism reopens a conversation about how markets can be made responsive to social and environmental goals, including the goal of maintaining and strengthening democracy at all levels of government.

Localism, I suggest, identifies a new political opportunity and a new possible configuration of political alliances. The control of global capital over the media, think tanks, and political parties has ushered in an era of neoliberalism and timid liberalism, just as it has removed aggressive liberalism, not to mention socialist or communalist politics, from the acceptable spectrum of political debate. But as political opportunities have closed in some ways, localists have discovered, they have opened in other ways. The very success of neoliberal globalization has generated increasing concern over local quality of life. The concern rests on a local knowledge that cannot easily be distorted through the rhetoric of neoliberal think-tank studies, media pundits of corporate news channels, and corrupted politicians. For example, the question of economic growth and environmental degradation, which at a national level is often abstracted in the form of economic statistics, translates at the local level into debates over green spaces and economic development projects that affect a regional environment and quality of life. Here the question of the limits to growth becomes visceral in political debates over issues such as the preservation of green spaces versus the development of new roads, shopping centers, manufacturing facilities, and housing. Although local governments can be captured by local growth coalitions, there is also substantial potential for provoking a public debate on planning and growth within the local political arena, where citizens who ordinarily might not care about growth and environmental quality may become more involved.

Of course, the opening of a political opportunity is accompanied by some political risk. The growth of localist politics could siphon energy away from the liberal and socialist projects of achieving government policy reform at a national and international level, thereby contributing to the closure of political opportunities at those levels. In other words, localism can play into the neoliberal politics of devolution and privatization. However, it is also possible that participation in localist politics may open the door to a new appreciation of the importance of government policy reform as a strategy for dismantling the corporatocracy. The risk that localism siphons political energy away from government-oriented mobilizations at national and international levels versus the possibility that it mobilizes relatively nonpolitical people to become politically active can be examined empirically and should not be prejudged in a dismissive analysis. What I can say from attending localist meetings and conferences is that there is a confluence between the narrow goal of protecting locally owned businesses and place-based communities from corporate predation and the broader goal of building a more just and equitable global economy. If the first strategy of localism is to develop an alternative global economy that is based on locally owned, independent, values-based businesses rather than global corporations, the strategy can be, and sometimes is, connected with social and environmental responsibility activism oriented toward global corporations. Judy Wicks writes: "I see now that there are two fronts in the movement for responsible business. One front is trying to reform large corporations; the other front is working to create an alternative to corporative globalization that will build economic power in our communities through local business ownership." (2004: 27) Here, there is a potential to reformulate politics in a way that does not cede to the political right the deep concern that citizens across the political field have with place-based communities, local democracy, and local economies.

For some people, affiliation with localist organizations translates into broader political action: to stop a local big-box development project, to engage in shareholder activism and other corporate reform projects, to support political candidates who favor a range of socially and environmentally oriented regulatory interventions in the economy, to attend an anti-globalization protest rally. The call to "buy local" may be the hook that brings in the local independent business owner, but once owners have joined an independent business association they may discover that they are not just small businesses but stewards of their communities with a variety of social, economic, environmental, and political benefits to offer the customers and citizens of a region. In this sense, it would be simplistic to dismiss localism as a reactionary movement of the petite bourgeoisie or of green, middle-class suburbanites who are just trying to save their own skins when confronted with the flood tides of the global economy and ecological collapse. That would be too resolutely economistic, too encompassed by the logic of self-interested class politics, and too tinted by the lenses of New Deal liberalism. Although it is important to keep such criticisms in mind to identify challenges and pitfalls, localists are also concerned with building alternative economic institutions that are dedicated to policies that could transition the world's economy away from a collapse scenario, corporate greed, and a planet of slums. In the words of Seventh Generation CEO Jeffrey Hollender, the localist movement draws attention to "what matters most"; it encourages businesses not to let economic profitability trump social and environmental goals. In the words of an invitation to small-business owners issued by another founder of BALLE, Laury Hammel: "Over the next thirty years . . . entrepreneurs like you can help transform the world of commerce so that human values lead business growth, not only the drive for higher profits. We invite you to join thousands of others in this mission to grow local value and build a just and sustainable world." (Hammel and Denhart 2007: 160–161)[31]

Such are the promises of localism that constitute the basis of its appeal and its potential to reframe positions in the political field. Are the promises credible? What kinds of research support the claims of localism? How do localist businesses and advocacy organizations handle the challenges of conducting business and developing public policies in a more socially and environmentally responsible way? What are the more specific criticisms of localism, and how well founded are they? Which industries work best and worst for localism? What policy changes would make localism more likely to succeed? By avoiding the temptation to situate localism in a template of an existing political ideology, we are prepared to pose a different set of questions with new insights.

Conclusion

Fifty or a hundred years from now, people may look back and say that neoliberals and liberals were right: that the world was able to solve its pressing environmental and social crises without changing the fundamental economic organization of society. When a crisis becomes visible and evident enough, it is possible that an adequate governmental and intergovernmental response will occur. However, I remain skeptical that the political leaders of the twenty-first century will solve its deep problems without first addressing the growing and untrammeled power of corporate globalization and the influence of the economic behemoths on governmental decision making. The growth logic of the large publicly traded corporation is poorly adapted to today's global ecology. Furthermore, the current tendency is for the corporate sector to drive a wedge between environmental and equality issues, so that some limited greening of the private sector occurs while hundreds of millions of people are plunged into worse poverty.

Because corporate power has so much influence over national policy making and the media in the United States, there has been little debate at the national level on the root causes of the environmental and social crises. Politicians who raise such "populist" questions are skewered by the pundits of corporate media and shunned by most wealthy potential donors. With mainstream political debate focused on issues such as renewable portfolio standards and carbon trading, there is little or no space for a deeper discussion of the likelihood that an economic system based on short-term earnings growth is, in the long run, not adapted to life within global ecological limits. The idea that substantial economic reform is a precondition for avoiding a gradual descent into deepening global sustainability and justice crises is outside the limits of the field of mainstream debate.

Those who are concerned with such issues face four not especially palatable strategies:

• They may work within frameworks of neoliberal reasoning as corporate insiders to try to convince managers and owners that eco-efficiency reforms and better labor standards will improve brand image, not to mention profits and stock prices, and therefore should be implemented voluntarily.

• They may take a place within the government and court system as reformers to fight a rearguard battle against ongoing attempts to undo regulations and to gain occasional incremental changes when political opportunities open.

• They may directly confront as activists the worst failures of government regulation by organizing social movements and campaigns in favor of deeper political reforms than those advocated by insiders and reformers.

• They may withdraw into intentional communities where it is possible to enact a better world on a small scale and to test what kinds of arrangements succeed and fail.

In view of the stalemate that has arisen in attempts to transform corporations from amoral engines of growth into social and environmental stewards, it is not surprising that some people have turned to localist strategies of change. Rather than see localist strategies as supplanting the others, it is probably better to view them as constituting an additional pathway to change—one that, like the others, has unique limitations and potentials.

Although localists articulate a message of the need for corporate reform and for support of locally owned independent organizations, the message should not be oversimplified. Not all publicly traded corporations uniformly contribute to injustice and environmental degradation; the emergence of publicly traded corporations in the solar and conservation industries provides one hopeful sign of how financial markets can support dematerialization, especially when government policies and incentives are in place to encourage such developments. Likewise, many small businesses, nonprofit organizations, and public enterprises are far from beacons of social and environmental responsibility. But localism raises an important structural question: closely held private companies; small nonprofit organizations; and local public agencies are not required to set aside social and environmental responsibility goals when stock prices decline and when analysts' reports turn sour. In the place of anonymous stockholders are individual proprietors, employee-owners, small partnerships, volunteer boards, and elected or appointed government officials who are in a position to think about their organizations in terms of the triple bottom line of economic viability, social responsibility, and environmental sustainability. Such organizations have the potential to form the basis of a different type of economy, one which operates more along the lines of civil society organizations than large corporations. An economy governed by such organizations may be in a better position to adapt to the pressing social and environmental problems of the twenty-first century, because such organizations are rooted in their communities and responsive to their needs. Such is the promise and potential of localism.[32]

2

Economic Development and Localist Knowledge

The city in which I live—Schenectady, New York—was once the vibrant headquarters of General Electric and other manufacturers. Old-timers describe the downtown streets during the 1940s and the 1950s as full of pedestrians. The streetcar lines all led to the central city, which was the location of the big department stores and, only a few blocks away, the huge manufacturing factories. By the 1990s, the city that "lights and hauls the world" was all but dead. ALCO, which had manufactured locomotives for most of the twentieth century and tanks during World War II, was long gone. General Electric retained a turbine-manufacturing operation at the site of its historical home, but its world headquarters had been relocated to Connecticut, and the number of employees who worked in the Schenectady plant had declined to a sliver of the past. The shoppers had all defected to malls and big-box stores outside the city limits, and there were many empty storefronts. In 1998, in response to the downturn, some community leaders launched the Schenectady Metroplex Development Authority with the hope of revitalizing the city; a decade later, the downtown area shows a few signs of life, but it remains deserted on nights and weekends.

The story of Schenectady's decline is far from unique. Once thriving industrial centers, many American cities became haunted by the remnants of former factories and vacant retail buildings. The transformation from industrial powerhouses of the world to rustbelt ghost towns was a slow death from many different blows. In the 1950s and the 1960s, the construction of highway systems and suburbs enabled the middle class to move out of central cities and streetcar suburbs to the less congested outer areas of the metropolitan region. Another factor in the decline of central cities was the decision by corporate leaders to shift manufacturing to areas of the country and the world with lower labor costs. Since the 1980s, as government policies have increasingly facilitated the globalization of production, it has been easier for factories to pull up stakes and move elsewhere. It is in this economic development landscape that localism as a movement in the United States articulates an alternative, both as a body of alternative urban development policies and as an epistemic challenge to mainstream thinking in the economic development field. Whereas the previous chapter explored localism as a system of political thought, this chapter will explore localism as a form of theoretical and applied economic knowledge.[1]

High-Tech Clusters and Economic Development Policies

The de-industrialization of American cities contributed to the growth of economic development offices and of a new research field that examined how government policies could improve local economies. Histories of economic development studies in the United States generally recognize three phases of thinking and policy. In the first phase, state and local governments offered incentives to motivate nonlocal firms, usually manufacturers, to set up shop in their region. Pioneered in the southern states to attract firms from northern states in search of places where they could hire workers for lower wages, the policies soon became national. As more and more cities and states adopted the same policies, the economic incentive packages became self-defeating. Competition among regions led to increasingly costly give-aways, and longstanding local firms were also tempted to leave their home regions in search of new advantages. Furthermore, when the economic incentive packages ran out, some firms packed up and left the region. As a result of the deficiencies of the "smokestack chasing" model of economic development, a second wave of policies focused on retaining firms already present and on the incubation of new firms. The third wave built on the second by focusing on clusters of firms and building a regional advantage in specific industries. In other words, the goal shifted from landing "big fish" to building an ecology that would grow schools of fish.[2]

To be successful, a "technopole"—that is, a metropolitan area with a manufacturing cluster, usually high-tech—requires many ingredients, among them state and local governments that support new business development, dense informal networks that allow firm-to-firm learning, the availability of venture capital, and a strong research and development cluster in the local colleges and universities. A literature on the "triple helix"—that is, the interwoven links among government support, university research, and industrial innovation—suggests that a technopole requires substantial infrastructure and sustained investment. When successful, an industrial cluster becomes a magnet for similar businesses, which seek the advantages of co-location because of enhanced access to a skilled workforce, a "quality" service sector, and local information-sharing and venture-capital networks. In other words, when a cluster is successful, it is no longer necessary for economic development professionals to chase smokestacks; the smokestacks come to them. Nor is it necessary to worry about firms that pull up stakes and leave after economic incentives run out; new firms are always being born from the dynamic interactions of the cluster. For this reason, as I noted in the introductory chapter, globalization has produced a paradoxical reemphasis on place, albeit in the form of the "global city" with its focused industrial clusters.[3]

In regard to the goal of building a more sustainable economy, the technopole model of economic development has some limitations. In most cases the high-tech industrial cluster has little connection with the pressing need to shift to "green" technology. Instead, manufacturing facilities in nanotechnology, biotechnology, and information technology generate new environmental health risks for nearby residents. However, it is possible for cities to bridge the goals of developing a high-tech industrial cluster and contributing to a more sustainable world, both by focusing on clean manufacturing techniques and by developing high-tech clusters of green technologies. Examples of green technopoles include the Danish wind turbine industry and the cluster of solar energy manufacturing and research in Freiburg, Germany. In the United States green technology clusters can only be found in incipient stages, but they are emerging in the San Francisco Bay area and in some northeastern cities.[4]

Regarding concerns with distributive justice, the model of economic development based on the high-tech manufacturing cluster has the advantage of providing good jobs, but it tends to benefit skilled and well-educated workers over their unskilled or less skilled counterparts. The less skilled workers can find support positions in service of the high-tech industry, but such service jobs are less likely to be unionized and to offer long-term employment stability than the jobs once available in Fordist manufacturing operations. The sociologist Saskia Sassen concludes that global cities tend to undergo increasing economic polarization as the gaps between high-skill and low-skill jobs increase. Nevertheless, an advocate of the technopole model of economic development could argue that the dislocations are, in principle, capable of correction. By combining a high-tech industrial development policy with job training programs and economic opportunities for low-income workers, it would be possible to configure a technopole that would go a long way toward remediating regional inequalities.[5]

Another possible weakness of the technopole is that not all cities and industries are equally likely to build successful clusters. Small cities that lack a large research university, venture-capital firms, and other intellectual and financial resources are not in a good position to develop internationally competitive industrial clusters. Small state governments also lack the resources to put together a cluster of research universities, government subsidies, and industrial infrastructure. Likewise, cities can flounder on a more piecemeal approach of attracting industrial corporations one by one with promises of tax and land-use concessions. In such cases the original headlines that promise jobs and wealth from the industrial newcomer may turn out to disappoint the long-time inhabitants of the region. The high-wage jobs may not to be as plentiful or lucrative as first promised, and the new factory may expose the community to new forms of pollution and waste. When the tax incentives run out or the calls for environmental amelioration mount, the savior of a regional economy can threaten to leave or to "outsource" jobs.[6]

For many cities the project of developing into a technopole carries high risks. The economic development office may fail as the result of a lack of resources and infrastructure, or it may find itself constantly trying to recruit new companies to replace companies that are leaving. Even a partial success that creates a small manufacturing cluster may not be adequately diversified, and it may collapse when global economic conditions change. In view of the risks inherent in developing a successful economic base of export-oriented manufacturing, localism can provide a hedge on economic development risk through diversification. Because localist strategies may work best in industries other than those associated with the technopole, there is no reason for localist and high-tech development to be construed as mutually exclusive. The technopole is best suited to the world of high-tech manufacturing and information technology, where the pressures of industrial innovation require rapid growth, infusions of venture capital, and a quick transition from start-up company to an initial public stock offering or acquisition by a large corporation. In other industries—such as banking, retail, construction, services, food and agriculture, and energy—rapid growth and large initial investment are often not always as pressing. In those industries, localist strategies may work well for locally owned small businesses that need not pursue the "banana curve" of rapid economic growth fueled by venture capital and terminated by a liquidity event. Furthermore, efforts to develop locally owned and locally oriented businesses may addresses issues of urban poverty and job creation that are not handled well by the trickle-down economics of service jobs associated with high-tech firms.[7]

Localist economic development policies can be framed as providing a more balanced approach to economic development that pays greater attention to the local quality of life, to local environmental health, and to the provision of good jobs for people who do not necessarily have high-tech training and the background to prosper as entrepreneurs of technological innovation. Including not only locally owned independent businesses but also nonprofit organizations, cooperatives, and local government enterprises, localist organizations have another advantage from an economic development perspective: they tend to sink their roots deeply into the regional economy, and they are unlikely to pull up stakes and move away. Unfortunately, in many American cities the quest to attract high-tech manufacturers or to build the next complex of retail superstores gains the ear of urban economic and political leaders, and corresponding efforts to develop locally owned and locally oriented businesses are placed on the back burner if they get any attention at all. It is often headline news when a region lures a big manufacturer, and the press statements usually contain rosy estimates of the number of high-paying jobs that the firm will generate, but advocates of locally owned business find it hard to get economic development officials and other local political leaders to broaden their thinking to consider how that sector of the economy can also be developed.

One of the reasons why localism has not yet become fully integrated into the science and practice of the economic development profession is that there is a widespread assumption that the economic vitality of a region is based on firms that bring money from outside the region into the economy. Certainly, any regional economy requires "export" earnings in order to pay for goods and services acquired outside the region. Those earnings include the sale of manufactured goods and services to consumers outside the region, but they can also include tourism and higher education, which bring external funds into the region. Localism as an economic development strategy complements the outward or export orientation of economic development thought by opening up a parallel set of opportunities for "import," that is, ways to save money that is flowing out of the region by channeling it back into the regional economy. The alternative, inward-looking approach to economic development has a long history involving development policies used for decades in less developed countries. In order to understand localism as an intellectual challenge to, or an alternative pathway of thought in, the science and practice of economic development, it is necessary to understand first some of the history of debates between export-oriented growth strategies and import substitution.

Import Substitution and Economic Development Theory

In many of the less wealthy countries of Asia, Latin America, and Africa, import substitution dominated both the theory and the practice of economic development from 1930 through 1970, and in some cases later. The Great Depression and World War II led to a decline in some export-oriented industries in the developing countries, and political leaders experimented with policies to enhance domestic industries that "substituted" imports in manufactured goods from abroad with those made domestically. In some cases, protective trade barriers for domestic industries were combined with government ownership of the manufacturing and mining industries. As the political scientist Eduardo Silva notes in a comparative analysis of the policies in four South American countries, the term "import substitution" refers to a range of economic policies that changed in response to international economic conditions.[8]

In most cases the new manufacturing industries produced low-tech consumer goods such as appliances, but in some of the larger countries the policies also encouraged the production of capital goods and high-tech products such as airplanes. The import-substitution approach to development relied on policies such as import tariffs, industrial subsidies, and the manipulation of exchange rates. Often populist political leaders also chose to use price controls to hold food prices in check, and they supported negotiations between industrial elites and labor unions. By balancing the development of domestic industries with popular support for the industrial policies, the political leaders hoped to build up a new source of export earnings that would enable them to escape from dependence on agricultural and mineral exports as the primary source of foreign exchange. The higher productivity of the manufacturing companies would then be reflected in higher wages for workers, and the standard of living would rise. Meanwhile, the country would have a more diversified economy that would be better able to withstand rapid changes in commodity prices and the eventual depletion of reserves of mineral resources.[9]

The import-substitution approach to economic development, in combination with welfare-state policies and nationalized industries, had a period of substantial success. In the "Southern Cone" of South America, standards of living rose during the 1940s and the 1950s to levels close to those of developed countries. Economists and sociologists there propagated social science models of development that promised to break the chains of dependency. During the peak decades of the import-substitution era, there were measurable improvements of economic growth, manufacturing, life expectancy, infant mortality, working-class jobs, literacy, infrastructure, and even exports. A crucial metric was the size of the informal sector of the economy, or the amount of people earning a living outside the economy of formal business, nonprofit, and government organizations. Between 1940 and 1980 the informal sector of the economy in Latin America declined slightly or remained constant, depending on measurement assumptions, even though the population was growing. After 1980, when structural adjustment programs were widely implemented, the informal sector grew significantly. In general, import-substitution policies were successful on many metrics, and in retrospect they were more successful in some countries than the neoliberal policies that replaced them.[10]

However, import substitution was by no means a perfect economic policy. The record of economic growth fell short of the original rosy predictions. Investments in industrial development and spending on social welfare created inflationary pressures in countries such as Chile. Because the new industries required capital goods for their factories, imports continued to grow, and the countries failed to industrialize rapidly enough to escape dependency on commodity exports for foreign exchange. As a result, trade deficits and pressures on the currency increased. Another problem was that the governments often placed price controls on food in order to keep the costs of living low for urban workers engaged in manufacturing, but the price controls generated market inefficiencies and squeezed the agricultural industry. The challenges to the network of import-substitution policies were evident as early as the 1950s in some countries, but they became especially visible during the global recession that followed the oil price hikes of 1973. The energy crisis of the 1970s had a doubly negative effect on less wealthy countries: demand for exports to developed countries declined, and the price of petroleum imports rose. Overall productivity also grew at low rates in a variety of developing countries, often at a fraction of a percent, well below rates in developed countries and export-oriented developing countries such as Taiwan.[11]

In addition to the problems generated by inflationary spending, global economic cycles, and internal dislocations, the record of what became known as the Asian tigers was another import factor behind the reconsideration of import-substitution policies. In the late 1950s Taiwan ended its import-substitution policies, instituted an exchange rate policy that did not overvalue the currency, and otherwise helped to develop export-oriented industries. During the 1960s both Taiwan and South

Korea showed tremendous economic success based on the alternative approach of export-led growth or export-oriented development. Their success set the stage for a shift in thinking, and by the late 1970s China, India, and a few other countries were shifting toward an outward-oriented strategy. Statistics such as the growth of gross domestic product suggested that the policies were successful in those countries as well.[12]

For the variety of reasons just enumerated, by the 1970s import-substitution policies were being questioned in many quarters, but much of the debate of that period focused on how to improve or tweak the policies rather than jettison them. After the overthrow of Salvador Allende on September 11, 1973, it became politically possible to destroy popular protections of domestic industry and labor. Chile became the laboratory for an alternative approach to economic development based on the neoliberal approach of the economist Milton Friedman, who had trained Latin American students at the University of Chicago with the support of the US government and the Ford Foundation. The neoliberal approach had not won many adherents among political leaders and leading economists in the Southern Cone countries, but once the dictator-ships of Chile and other Southern Cone countries had silenced political opposition, the door was open for neoliberalism.[13]

Where military dictatorships did not dismantle import substitution and publicly owned corporations, pressure from international financial orga-nizations did. The high oil prices and the global recession of the 1970s caused many countries to go into debt, often by borrowing "petrodollars" recycled from oil-rich countries through American banks. When the indebted countries defaulted on their loans, the International Monetary Fund resolved the crises on the condition that the countries agree to struc-tural adjustment packages. By the 1990s the era of import substitution and public ownership had been replaced by the "Washington consensus," a global financial regime marked by an end to trade protections for domestic industries, privatization of state enterprises, cutbacks in government welfare programs, and the continued transformation of agriculture toward export-oriented cash crops. Although import-substitution policies were discredited in global financial circles, the policies never disappeared com-pletely. Instead, evidence of import substitution can still be found in crucial industries such as information technology in Asia, and there is an ongoing discussion about the benefits of combining import substitution and export-oriented development.[14]

The export-oriented approach to development coincided with the general shift in politics toward trade liberalization. Advocates argued that the tariffs and subsidies of import-substitution policies encourage the protected, local industries to produce substandard and overpriced goods. Their arguments were supported by the many examples of black markets based on the import of higher-quality foreign goods at price premia to shoddy locally manufactured products. The alternative of open markets would eradicate black markets and inefficient industries protected by the fences of import-substitution policies. Trade liberalization would force domestic industries to go out of business or innovate to become competitive in global markets. Although advocates of trade liberalization admitted that workers in inefficient industries would lose their jobs, they argued that the workers would eventually find new jobs in more competitive industries, sometimes with the assistance of government retraining programs. Furthermore, the higher levels of productivity in the new jobs would be reflected in higher wages. In other words, free trade would lead to both lower prices and higher wages, and everyone would win.

By the early 2000s some social scientists were becoming skeptical of the general benefits of trade liberalization and of related neoliberal economic policies (including dismantling of labor and environmental standards, decreased government assistance for the poor, and, in general, reduction of government intervention in the economy). The successes of Taiwan and Korea were not easily replicated in countries where social, economic, and political conditions were significantly different. Moreover, in many countries the industrial workers who were thrown out of work from the closing of import-substituting industries never found the promised new jobs from the countervailing boost in new export-oriented industries. Instead, urban slums proliferated alongside dramatic growth in unemployment, crime, inequality, poverty, and informal economic activity. Although in theory neoliberal policies would eventually lead to new industrial growth and employment, the result for most of the people at the bottom of the world's pyramid has been increased misery and poverty. During the days of import substitution, life was in many ways better, especially in Africa and Latin America, than it was during and after the 1980s.[15]

In a book titled *Planet of Slums*, the urban studies researcher Mike Davis offers a sobering survey of economic development in the less wealthy countries. In those countries globalization has entailed living with the results of structural adjustment programs of the International Monetary Fund and other global financial organizations, which demanded an opening of markets to world trade and a reduction in government spending. To earn foreign exchange, agriculture became more export-oriented, and natural resources were opened to development by multi-national corporations. Rural populations flooded into cities because of the loss of traditional livelihoods and the rise of rural violence that forced them off their land, but when they arrived in the cities, they found few if any jobs waiting for them. Because the national governments were also cutting public bureaucracies and reducing trade protections for domestic industries, former employees in government positions and domestic industries were thrown out of work and forced into the informal urban economy, where they competed for a livelihood with the rural migrants. As a result, many of the world's largest cities have become vast expanses of shantytowns in which basic housing, sanitation, roads, and other infrastructure are unavailable or severely restricted. As the shantytowns and slums proliferated, members of the small middle and upper classes increasingly walled themselves in behind protective barriers of security guards and gated communities. In the place of formal economic organizations such as government agencies, large corporations, and small businesses, slumlords, gangs, and fundamentalist religious organizations became the only significant organizations of the informal economy in the vast slums of the developing world. The import-substituting industries, welfare-state bureaucracies, and domestically oriented small farmers may have been economically inefficient from the point of view of the world's economic elites, but to the former urban workers and newly arrived rural migrants there has been little advantage in the new efficiencies of trade liberalization.[16]

The economic disruptions that have occurred in many cities of the developing countries since 1980 are parallel to the changes (described at the outset of this chapter) in Schenectady and other de-industrialized cities in the United States. Large corporations closed expensive factories and outsourced well-paid, unionized jobs to countries where labor unions were weaker, wages were lower, and environmental standards were nonexistent or poorly enforced. Just as some developing countries (especially in East and Southeast Asia) benefited from the offshoring of manufacturing, in the United States some cities made a successful transition to the knowledge economy, but only some cities made the transition. In the United States, growth in the high-tech and service sectors, together with interregional mobility, made enough new jobs available to prevent the pattern of widespread growth of the informal economy that occurred in the less developed countries, even though overall income inequality increased. Labor and environmental organizations came to see free trade agreements, especially notorious provisions such as chapter 11 of the North American Free Trade Agreement, as bringing about a race to the bottom in labor and environmental standards. The exploitation of workers and of the natural environment in less developed countries made possible lower wages and production costs in the United States. Skepticism of globalization has also grown in the United States, even to the point of becoming an issue in presidential election politics.[17]

The effect of trade-liberalization policies on workers in poor and wealthy countries alike has contributed to the growth of the anti-globalization movement and widespread skepticism over the benefits of the Washington consensus. One type of economic localism, a nationalist form in favor of protectionist trade policies, can be found in some of the labor and left organizations of the movement. For example, in 2000 the former head of the International Economics Unit of Greenpeace, Colin Hines, published a book titled *Localization: A Global Manifesto* in which he argued in favor of "managed trade" that would restore tariffs and import quotas in some industries. He also suggested that national governments or groups of small countries implement a "site here to sell here" policy, which would require global corporations to locate their production in the country where they sell products. If tariffs and subsidies were combined with such policies, large corporations would have a higher stake in maintaining production within national borders, where they potentially would be more amenable to government regulatory policies that protect workers, communities, and the environment. Hines did not address the problem raised by critics of import substitution, namely that protected industries under import-substitution polices can be inefficient. Instead, he sidestepped the issue by pointing to a tradeoff between low industrial efficiency and high regulatory standards, and he suggested that when there is such a choice the latter option should be favored.[18]

Although it may not be surprising that protectionist sentiment is alive and well among the labor-oriented segments of the traditional left and socialist parties throughout the world, it may be more surprising that similar arguments in favor of protectionism can also be found in other quarters. For example, a group of corporate executives and policy experts developed the Horizon Project to advise Democratic Party leaders on a variety of issues, including trade. One intellectual influence is *Global Trade and Conflicting National Interests*, a book by Ralph Gomory (a former vice president of IBM) and William Baumol (a former president of the American Economics Association and a professor at New York University). The book argues that, although trade between countries that are very unequal in technology is beneficial to both, when countries become more technologically equivalent they enter into a "zone of conflict." As the technology gap between American workers and workers in China and other less developed countries has declined, more and more high-wage jobs have disappeared, and the downward pressure on wages in the United States has increased. Meanwhile, trade deficits have mounted as Americans import more and more goods from abroad. To solve the problem, Leo Hindery, chair of the Horizon Project, has suggested an end to illegal and unfair trade practices that harm American workers, a cap on the trade deficit, a national security impact statement for the offshoring of jobs, and a change in tax policy to encourage large manufacturing and technology companies to invest in domestic workers' skills and productivity.[19]

In the context of debates over trade liberalization, the term "local" tends to mean the national economy rather than a metropolitan economy, and it would not be entirely accurate to say that the new policy proposals represent a return of import substitution. Still, there are some obvious similarities. By capping trade or restoring tariffs and import quotas in some industries, and by requiring a "site here to sell here" policy or tax changes that encourage job creation at home, the critics are suggesting policies that represent a fundamental challenge to the orthodoxy of the Washington consensus. The criticisms of neoliberal free-trade policies have yet to be translated into policy reforms at the national level in the United States, but calls for new forms of protectionism are likely to increase as the wealth of Asian economies grows. More important for the understanding of localism, the debates on import substitution and free trade at the international level provide an intellectual background for novel ways of thinking about economic development at a metropolitan level. Although import substitution was discredited for many years in international development circles, the concept has explicitly returned in the debates on urban development.

Import Substitution and American Cities

In 1969—that is, roughly when economists and policymakers were registering reservations about the success of import-substitution policies in international development circles—the iconoclastic urban theorist Jane Jacobs published *The Economy of Cities*. Less well known than her earlier book *The Death and Life of American Cities*, which many see as predating the concern with new urbanist and smart growth approaches to urban planning and design, Jacobs's later books provided a defense of the importance of import substitution as a factor that drives urban growth. Jacobs argued that in cities such as Chicago during the nineteenth century the rise of import-replacing industries was crucial to economic growth spurts. Goods that the city once had to "import" from other American cities or from abroad were increasingly manufactured in the city for local consumption. Furthermore, the "import-replacing" industries often innovated on existing products, and eventually the new locally oriented industries also turned to sales outside the metropolitan area, thus producing a new wave of export-oriented growth.[20]

Jacobs's argument suggested that metropolitan economic development policies could benefit from the strategy of encouraging import-replacing businesses. However, the insight did not receive much attention in economic development circles. Rural self-sufficiency was a prominent theme of some of the "back to the land" efforts of the 1960s counterculture and of the appropriate-technology movement in developing countries, but city planners and economic development offices did not rush to transfer the idea to American cities. An exception was the work of David Morris of the Institute for Local Self-Reliance, who in a 1975 book used the phrase "localism" to describe neighborhood-oriented community development strategies. By 1980, the institute was developing studies of economic leakage (that is, of how money flowed out of a region through purchases of nonlocal goods and services). In many ways, the Institute for Local Self-Reliance during the 1970s and the early 1980s laid the groundwork for the localist movement of the early twenty-first century. One direct connection is Stacy Mitchell, a senior researcher with the Institute for Local Self-Reliance who became the chair of the board of AMIBA.[21]

By the 1980s import substitution was beginning to emerge as a local economic development strategy in the United States. In 1982 the mayor of St. Paul, Minnesota, unveiled the Homegrown Project, which drew on the work of the Institute for Local Self-Reliance in support of import-substitution policies. The project included a "buy local" program and support for small-business development. The green emphasis of the Homegrown Project stirred up some opposition from economic development professionals, and ultimately the plan failed after the mayor left office in 1989. Another experiment with import substitution was a technological innovation known as the Oregon Marketplace, a database that linked local businesses to potential suppliers within the state. The database saved firms up to 50 percent on some purchases and generated $250,000–$500,000 per year of import-substitution revenue for the state economy. Similar programs were set up in Illinois, Nebraska, Minnesota, and Washington. For example, in Chicago the leaders of some of the largest corporations established a database of goods and services that they were willing to purchase from local suppliers, and the program also offered a purchasing fair.[22]

Although the experiments with the import-substitution strategy did not receive widespread attention in the professional literature, a small cluster of articles challenged the assumptions of economic development based mostly or entirely on export-oriented manufacturing. In 1993, the economist Joseph Persky and colleagues developed a theoretical defense of the approach and outlined how it would work for the city of Chicago.

A few years later, the economist Thomas Michael Power developed the environmental implications of import substitution in a book titled *Lost Landscapes and Failed Economies*. Power argued that by shifting from extractive industries to tourism and retirement, a region could preserve its local natural values while also bringing in new sources of revenue. The economist Ann Markusen criticized the export orientation of economic base theory (the theory based on manufacturing as the center of the regional economy) and drew attention to the potential of arts centers and the consumption base for economic development policies. The geographers Ted Rutland and Sean O'Hagan reviewed the small but empirically grounded cluster of research that challenges economic development strategies based wholly on export earnings and showed that most growth in employment in Canadian cities occurred in the local sector of the economy.[23]

In 1998, as the critique of economic base theory and economic development strategies based on high-tech, globally oriented manufacturing firms was being articulated in the economic development literature, the economist and attorney Michael Shuman developed and popularized theories of import substitution for local economic development in a book titled *Going Local*. Because he was connected with BALLE, Shuman brought the theory of import substitution into the language and thinking of independent business associations across the continent. He coined the term "LOIS" for "locally owned import-substituting" businesses, which he opposed to the world of TINA, the "there is no alternative" politics of advocates of corporate-led globalization. Furthermore, he worked with local governments, such as the economically depressed county of St. Lawrence in upstate New York, to develop economic leakage analyses and plans for economic development based on import substitution. He argued that the strategy could also work for larger cities and that it could be especially valuable as a source of employment for workers whose jobs have been outsourced and who are unable to find high-wage or meaningful work elsewhere. His work connected the theory of import substitution to the development of locally owned independent businesses as part of economic development policies.[24]

To some degree a parallel change also took place for rural development strategies. The "back to the land" and organic agriculture movements of the 1960s and the 1970s represented an initial phase in the development of alternative agrifood networks. Although organic food eventually became a niche market and a part of the global food system, local food systems also continued to develop. The agrifood researchers Anne Bellows and Michael Hamm noted the relevance of the concept of import substitution in understanding local food systems as a rural development strategy, and likewise the agrifood researcher Terry Marsden and colleagues discussed the potential for agricultural and food localism to provide an alternative economic development strategy. Marsden's work on the importance of "short food supply chains" is relevant to the broader localist critique of those who advocate high-tech manufacturing as the only or the primary regional economic development strategy. Marsden and his colleagues contrasted "economies of scope"—or dense, locally-based networks of organizations—with two alternative rural development strategies: the export-oriented, agro-industrial logic and the post-productivist approach that utilizes farmland for tourism and recreation. In doing so, Marsden et al. suggested an alternative to the "use values" orientation of Power by arguing for a return to an economy based on production. However, like Power they shared a concern with a local economy based on socially and environmentally responsible enterprises. Although it is quite relevant, to date the thinking of agrifood researchers such as Marsden has had little if any influence on the localist movement of independent business associations in the United States.[25]

The Inefficiency Controversy

As I have suggested, the economic base of the localist movement, at least in the United States during the early twenty-first century, is mostly the small-business sector rather than large high-tech industrial organizations. Especially prominent have been the independent retailers that are facing competitive pressures from chains; small banks and credit unions that invest their resources locally; and small, family farms that have chosen to sell directly to consumers, restaurants, and food cooperatives in cities. Those businesses have united behind the slogans "buy local," "bank local," "think local," "eat local," and so on, which encourage consumers to think about the effects of their purchases on the quality of life in their community. They reframe consumption as a civic and political act, and they encourage consumers to think about shopping in terms other than bargains, prices, and fashion. As "buy local" campaigns have achieved greater visibility, criticisms have begun to mount, and they are often very similar to the criticisms raised in international development economics with the theory and practice of import substitution.

Critics of "buy local" campaigns argue that because small businesses are economically inefficient and charge higher prices, they do not deserve patronage. The critics sometimes draw on neoclassical economics to argue that grassroots campaigns that encourage consumers and governments to buy locally end up helping inefficient firms to stay in business rather than to close their doors. Likewise, local governments create inefficiencies when they use zoning regulations and other policy instruments to restrict land use in ways that make it difficult for franchises and superstores to operate. For critics, the effects of voluntary shifts in consumption, procurement policies, and zoning regulations that restrict big-box stores are much the same as import tariffs, subsidies, and other trade barriers that occurred at a national level under protectionist and import-substitution policies. Although the Commerce Clause of the United States Constitution prohibits state and local governments from enacting tariffs on nonlocal goods, the other pro-local policies operate as nontariff barriers to trade. In view of the parallel with national trade barriers, more or less the same argument of economic inefficiency can be applied to import substitution at a regional or metropolitan level. For example, once a big-box home-supply store has arrived in town, a locally owned hardware store may be driven into bankruptcy. From the perspective of neoclassical economics, the loss of the locally owned hardware store can be interpreted as a gain for the regional economy, because the big-box store brings the benefit of lower prices to the region. The owner of the hardware store will find other employment in a more efficient industry, perhaps by moving away, and the local economy will benefit by having a chain store that has cut out wholesale costs, driven down producer prices by volume purchasing, enhanced convenience by remaining open for more hours, and reduced overhead through automation and centralization.[26]

How do advocates of localism respond to such arguments about the purported economic inefficiencies of localism? In *The Small-Mart Revolution* and *The Big-Box Swindle*, the localist leaders and intellectuals Michael Shuman and Stacy Mitchell have developed in detail the economic case in favor of localism and against big-box stores. Their arguments can be grouped into three principle rebuttals to the inefficiency argument, and I have added a fourth from a slightly different literature.

The first rebuttal begins with the admission that it is true that zoning and "buy local" campaigns are in effect nontariff trade barriers or voluntary subsidies, but it points out that pro-local policies help level a playing field that includes much larger subsidies to the corporate retailers and high-tech manufacturers. For example, local governments often subsidize large corporations in order to entice them to locate in the community, but they do not offer similar incentives to small businesses that could fulfill similar retail functions or start up small manufacturing operations. As a result, one could accept the argument that "buy local" campaigns and zoning regulations that limit superstores do generate economic inefficiencies, but one could reply that the inefficiencies are valuable because they help counterbalance a situation that is heavily tilted in favor of subsidies to corporate competitors of small businesses. If we are going to talk about trade barriers on one side, then we should be fair and talk about them on all sides. If big-box stores increase expenses for city services and infrastructure, absorb taxpayer subsidies, and do not pay their fair share of taxes, then the small-business sector should be compensated so that the playing field is level.[27]

A second reply to the inefficiency argument questions the assumption that prices are lower in the big-box store. As Shuman notes, the products and associated services are often not comparable. A locally owned store may offer higher-quality product lines, better service, or special products that are especially geared to local needs. A hardware store in a neighborhood with older buildings may provide hard-to-find materials that are geared to the needs of those buildings. Rather than a simple case of two different types of stores that are selling the same goods, it is more likely that the two stores represent a bifurcation in markets. As Shuman notes, even the same product and brand may be of inferior quality in the big-box store. The argument can be generalized to other types of goods that, on first pass, may appear to be identical. For example, to many consumers locally grown food is not identical to similar food found in supermarkets. It is generally fresher and may taste better. In the case of meat and poultry, where there are rising concerns with the health of animals, consumers may be more comfortable knowing that the animals have been raised in a way that reduces the risk of disease. The local market provides different goods with different stories attached to them. Furthermore, the widespread assumption that prices are lower in big-box and chain stores does not hold up to closer scrutiny. Several studies of grocery stores and farmers' markets have shown that prices are lower in farmers' markets. Stacy Mitchell has also noted that prices tend to be lower when the big-box stores open but that they tend to rise, especially after local competition has been eliminated. This pattern is widespread enough that it has a name: price flexing. Where a big-box store has been open for more than a few years, it is often possible to find comparable goods at comparable or lower prices at a locally owned independent store.[28]

A third reply to the inefficiency argument is that it does not take into account the impact of nonlocal ownership on the general health of the regional economy. An emerging body of what might be termed "localist research" traces the effects on a local economy of spending an equivalent amount of money at a local store rather than at a large corporate retailer or restaurant. The literature is of considerable interest not only because of the empirical claims made but also because it represents the emergence of the epistemic dimension of localism from a phase of theoretical critique to empirical research. Furthermore, the research generated is often funded by localist organizations themselves; that is, to date the research has come from the movement more than from academic research communities.

In traditional economic development thought, there is a "multiplier" effect associated with a new business that has opened in the region and has created new jobs. For example, a new factory may generate only 100 new jobs, but the spending from the new jobs may generate 200–400 additional local jobs, depending on the conditions of the local economy. Similar reasoning is behind localist research on the "local economic multiplier effect," but it is based on import substitution of expenditures. The studies use a "local multiplier" to estimate the overall economic impact of spending on the local economy, much as studies of manufacturing use a multiplier to estimate the impact of a new export-oriented business on the overall local economy. The local impact studies suggest that much more of a dollar spent at a locally owned store recirculates within the regional economy in contrast with a dollar spent at a non-locally-owned business. Although the strength of the impact varies by the multipliers associated with different regional economies and industries, the studies suggest that, in general, for each dollar spent at a local retail business, the impact is two to three times greater in comparison with a dollar spent at a national or international retail chain store. Furthermore, a study of the effect in San Francisco concluded that a 10 percent increase in the market share of independent businesses would create 1,300 new jobs and increase local revenue by $200 million, and that a parallel increase in the market share of chain stores would have a similarly negative impact on jobs and revenue.[29] (See table 2.1.)

One reason why local businesses recirculate more money within a community is that a portion of each dollar spent at a corporate retailer or at a formula business (a franchise or other business for which purchasing policies are defined by a corporate headquarters) must eventually pay for the salaries of distant administrators and dividends to shareholders. However, the benefits of buying locally go beyond plugging the economic leaks of overhead and profits that flow out of the region to distant managers and owners. Some locally owned retail businesses, for example restaurants that buy from local farmers and gift stores that buy from local craftspeople, opt to buy more products from local sources. There is also some evidence that locally owned stores donate a higher proportion of revenue to local nonprofit organizations. Finally, whereas there are often tax subsidies that local governments have granted to big-box stores or tax holidays for Internet firms, locally owned businesses often pay higher taxes to the local government.[30]

Some caveats should be kept in mind when interpreting the empirical claim that more money stays within a community when it is spent at a locally owned business. If a large chain store attracts additional revenue from outside the local area, and if its gross revenue is larger than that of

Table 2.1
Local economic multiplier studies.

Study	Author	Funding	Results
Andersonville (Chicago)	Civic Economics (consulting firm)	Andersonville Development Corporation; Andersonville Chamber of Commerce; Andersonville Special Service Area #22	Local economic return of $68 out of $100 spent at local restaurants, retailers, and services, vs. $43 out of $100 spent at comparable chain stores
Austin	Civic Economics (consulting firm)	Liveable City Austin (NGO); local bookstore and record store	Local economic return of $45 out of $100 spent at the local book and record store vs. $13 out of $100 spent at comparable national book store
Maine	Institute for Local Self-Reliance	Institute for Local Self-Reliance	Local economic spending of $45 at eight local businesses vs. $14 for typical big-box store
San Francisco	Civic Economics (consulting firm)	San Francisco Locally Owned Merchants Association; Northern California Independent Booksellers Association; American Booksellers Association	Sector-dependent impacts on total local output (local vs. chain, for $100 spent): $32 vs. $19 for books, $33 vs. $20 for sporting goods, $56 vs. $43 for restaurants
Toledo	Professor, University of Toledo	Urban Affairs Center, University of Toledo; Toledo City Council; local bookstore	Local economic return of $44 out of $100 spent at an independent bookstore vs. $20 out of $100 spent at a comparable chain bookstore

the smaller stores that it displaces, then the overall positive effect on the local economy could outweigh its lower local economic multiplier. The situation is most evident when a suburb develops a strip of big-box stores just outside the city limits of a larger city. Even if the strip of big boxes displaces some local revenue in the suburb by driving some of the suburban independent stores out of business, the big boxes may more than make up for the lost local multiplier effect just by bringing in revenue from consumers who come from the neighboring city. Once the suburb has paid off its subsidies and started collecting taxes, it may be better off than before, but its improved economic condition is at the expense of retail sales in the neighboring city. The potential zero-sum relationship between neighboring cities undermines "buy local" campaigns that are restricted to a city rather than a metropolitan area, and it motivates the need to make localist efforts regional or metropolitan in scale.

Another limitation of the local impact studies is that they imply an image of an individual consumer who is spending money at a local retail store. A study of import substitution by Dave Swenson, an economist at Iowa State University, suggested that recapturing retail sales may not be the most effective way of implementing an import-substitution strategy. Swenson writes: "Much greater multipliers in a region accumulate when industries buy from one another than if households buy from local retailers." (2006: 7) His argument implies that consumer-oriented "buy local" campaigns may not be the most effective strategy if the goal is to maximize the effect of import substitution on the local economy. There may be different types of local impacts, depending on whether one is discussing business-to-business transactions or consumer-to-retail transactions. However, because independent business associations sometimes begin with consumer-oriented "buy local" campaigns and then develop into local firm-to-firm purchasing networks, in practice the two strategies may be successfully interwoven.[31]

The studies of the local impact of retail spending suggest another answer to the inefficiency argument: even when a big-box store can offer an equivalent product at a lower price, it is not accurate to say that it is a more efficient business within the broader scope of the health of a regional economy. Hidden in the lower price is the effect of the low price on local wages, benefits, taxes, and donations, and on the regional economy as a whole. In economic terms, the lower local economic multiplier of nonlocal, corporate retail businesses remains a "negative externality" for the regional economy. By correcting the negative externality of a lower economic multiplier with policies that favor local ownership, local government policies could be seen as correcting a market inefficiency rather than creating one.

A final rebuttal to the inefficiency argument goes as follows: Even if one does not accept that economic analysis provides a qualified assessment in favor of at least some degree of import substitution as a component of an overall regional economic development strategy, one should remember that localism is not only concerned with economics. There are non-economic benefits to having healthy businesses that are locally owned. A vibrant, locally owned sector of the economy means that the regional economy is less dependent politically on nonlocal businesses that may coerce governments by threatening to move outside city tax jurisdictions unless they receive preferential tax treatment, infrastructure subsidies, and other handouts. The local sector of the economy can also help inoculate communities against the lure of industries that may offer economic benefits to the region at the expense of high amounts of pollution and congestion. A vibrant, locally owned regional economy may help provide a sense of solidarity and common purpose that allows a city to resist the siren song of the next industrial brownfield or big-box development project.

Along these lines there is another strand of empirical research on localism that has been emerging: correlational studies. The classic study in this field involved a controlled comparison of two California communities, one of which had a much higher percentage of agribusiness. The anthropologist Walter Goldschmidt found that the town dominated by agribusiness had lower general living conditions, more dilapidated buildings, more concentrated power in decision making, lower community loyalty, greater social distance between social groups, lower retail trade, and fewer parks, youth facilities, social service organizations, and business establishments. Goldschmidt was widely attacked, and agribusiness interests attempted to suppress the study. In fact, publication of the study was a contributing factor to curtailment of funds for the US Department of Agriculture's Bureau of Agricultural Economics, where Goldschmidt worked when he undertook the study.[32]

Subsequent correlational studies have revealed that in counties with vibrant locally owned small businesses there is a range of general benefits for the overall quality of life. Specifically, the peer-reviewed research has shown that social capital, voter turnout, and average income are higher where there is a stronger small-business sector, and that rates of poverty, infant mortality, and crime are lower. Likewise, the construction of new Wal-Mart stores has been associated with lower levels of social capital, voter turnout, average wages, and nonprofit organizations as well as with the more predictable negative effects on existing local retail stores. The correlational studies support the argument that it is sensible to give tax breaks to locally owned businesses rather than the other way around because of the general benefits of the local business sector for the region's quality of life, including positive externalities that cannot be measured readily as economic benefits, such as voter turnout and a more vibrant civil society.[33]

Conclusion

When one raises the specter of import substitution, even in its post-mortem form as a local economic development strategy, critics who have taken a mainstream economics course will probably begin with a wry smile, then clear their throats and ask if you have heard of comparative advantage. The idea of absolute advantage is easy enough to understand with the help of a simple example: One country has a climate that makes it easy to grow apples cheaply, whereas another has a climate where it is easier to grown bananas. There are obvious advantages to trade, provided that the costs of transportation and transaction are relatively low. Comparative advantage begins with this basic assumption and shows how it is advantageous for the two countries to trade even if one country can produce both categories of goods more efficiently than the other country, as long as there is a relative difference in the cost of production between the two products. The basic mathematical proof was made famous two centuries ago by the political economist David Ricardo, who used the example of wine and textiles.[34]

Less well known is the Treaty of Methuen, signed between Portugal and England in 1703. Portugal opened its markets to English textiles, and in exchange Britain reduced its tariffs on Portuguese wine. In an eighteenth-century version of a structural adjustment policy, the treaty ended up destroying the emerging Portuguese textile industry, and food production in Portugal was displaced so that wine could be produced for export. The result was high food prices in return for foreign exchange from wine sales that were needed to pay for the textile imports. However, Britain did extend sea protection to the Portuguese empire, and Portugal was able to keep its colonies, including its prize colony, Brazil. But Portugal, de-industrialized and dependent, in effect became a subsidiary of the British empire, and Brazilian gold, which could have funded Portuguese industrialization, instead helped fund the English industrial revolution. London, not Lisbon, became the world's economic center.[35]

The story of British and Portuguese industrialization is more complicated than this short summary suggests, just as the use and misuse of comparative advantage theory as a justification for free trade is also more complicated. However, the broader point is that the gap between an economic model and the historical case can be significant. Today we are witnessing a growing gap between the neoliberal economic models that support trade liberalization and the lived experience of working people and owners of small businesses throughout the world. Although inequality between countries has declined somewhat, especially if China is included in the calculations, inequality within countries it is generally increasing. Today equivalents of eighteenth-century Portugal are everywhere—in the shantytowns of Africa and Latin America and also in the empty storefronts of once-vibrant urban neighborhoods in the United States. Likewise, the Englands of the world are everywhere, in gated communities and upper-class neighborhoods found in the global cities throughout the world. Under such conditions, it is not surprising that we might see a deep questioning of the touted benefits of free trade and corporate globalization. The argument that free trade is economically more efficient is largely irrelevant to working people who face a declining standard of living as a result of closed factories and outsourced jobs. The doctrine of valuing economic efficiency above all else may produce the tide that lifts all boats in the abstract, frictionless world of *ceteris paribus* economic assumptions, but economic efficiency means little to a worker who is unable to meet rent payments because a well-paying job has been outsourced to another country and no new job is available.

Localism as an alternative pathway in the political field is deeply engaged with the politics and economics of globalization and neoliberal ideology. Likewise, in the economic field social science research on local ownership holds out a counter-narrative of quality over quantity, equity over efficiency, and environment and community over externalities. Localist economic development policies offer a promise of better and more meaningful jobs, not to mention greater sovereignty of communities over their future, in a world where lives are often affected by decisions made in distant boardrooms. As economic jiu-jitsu, the alternative economic development strategies turn the powerful "forces" of the market against neoliberalism by encouraging the development of competitive small businesses and by developing an economic rationale for policies that would give small businesses a fair chance to compete.

3

Can Localism Be Just and Sustainable?

When evaluated from the perspective of the contribution to building a more just and sustainable society, localism is in many ways a bundle of contradictions. Local enterprises may not always be successful at providing good jobs and other opportunities for the least fortunate members of the regional economy, and they may not be paragons of environmental sustainability. However, the local sector can also be a home for entrepreneurs who have a vision of building local, living economies. To some degree the task of localist leaders is similar to that of other movement leaders: to take a heap of unruly potential and move it toward a goal of disciplined social change. The task is to take owners of small businesses who may not have been exposed to the political and economic issues discussed in the previous chapters and to help them to think through a transition of identity from "small business owner" to "community enterprise leader." For example, at one conference that I attended, a speaker compared his independent business association to a church. His somewhat tongue-in-cheek comment drew some laughter: he said the he preferred to operate a church of sinners rather than one of saints, because it was a better business opportunity.

In the previous two chapters I examined localism in the United States as a system of political thought and economic development knowledge; in this chapter I examine localism from a values perspective on the question of its potential to contribute to a vision of the good society. I explore the concern that the homegrown economy is not intrinsically just or sustainable and that the potential to build an alternative global economy based on a vast network of locally owned independent enterprises with a clear social and environmental responsibility mission is just that: a potential, realized to varying degrees in the world of actual locally owned independent enterprises. Rather than answer the question "Is localism just and sustainable?" in a monolithic and abstract way, I develop my general argument that there are, in fact, a variety of "localisms," and that in order to find opportunities to move the actual to the potential one must begin with the varieties of localism.

Lack of Concern for Justice

When considering the relationship between distributive justice and localism, a critic could advance at least four main arguments.

First, locally owned independent organizations are not inherently more just or equitable than large publicly traded corporations. Small businesses can be bastions of nepotism, sexism, and racism, whereas large corporations have human resources departments that can enforce a wide range of anti-discriminatory laws and standards. On this issue, there is no easy reply except to admit that there is tremendous variation within both the small-business sector and the large corporate sector.[1] However, there is another, more challenging criticism that emerges from the same general line of thought. A fairly well-established finding in the management literature, known as the firm-size wage effect, presents some troubling data for those who wish to claim that the small-business sector is better for workers. Various studies have shown that large firms (generally defined as those with more than 500 employees) pay higher wages than small firms (those with fewer than 25 employees). The effect remains robust even when industry type, worker category, firm age, and outlier wages such as executive salaries are controlled. Furthermore, the turnover rate is lower at large firms, and fringe benefits, such as health-care coverage in the United States, are higher at large firms. Various explanations have emerged for the firm-size wage effect, and the more recent studies in the subfield have attempted to sort out the different hypotheses. Among the more prominent explanations are variations on the claim that productivity is higher at large firms as a result of higher levels of capital, employee skills, matching of employees with jobs, managerial skills, and investment in training. However, large firms may also have more unionization, less industrial competition, and compensation for less attractive jobs. Whatever the explanation, a critic of localism can argue with some assurance that wages are, in the aggregate, lower in the small-business sector of the economy.[2]

A second major criticism of localism goes as follows: Even if there were no wage effect, a locally produced good is often packaged with an attribute of higher quality, and the poor can ill afford the double price premium. For example, local food is often packaged as organic and sold for a price premium as a kind of luxury good. Another example is a homeowner's decision to install solar panels (localist in the sense of local production of energy but not the product), which generally require an expensive investment with a long payback period. Local organic food and distributed renewable energy are examples of specialty niches with premium prices that benefit middle-class and wealthy consumers. One might argue by extension that the local economy has become an upscale niche economy that offers higher-quality goods at a price premium, including ecologically "green" goods. Locally owned independent stores are often boutiques that offer special "local flavor" experiences to tourists at "tourist prices." Localist spaces such as farmers' markets have even been described as racially privileged spaces of "whiteness" in a multi-ethnic society. Localist products are, to be brief, luxury goods.[3]

A third and related criticism is that there is a potential for localism to devolve into rich-country enclavism—that is, for communities in wealthy countries to improve their own conditions but turn their backs on broader global problems. The kernel of the argument can be found in *The Work of Nations*, where the former Secretary of Labor Robert Reich suggests that the footloose knowledge workers of the global economy have a weak sense of belonging to a particular place and may be unwilling to support domestic and local government spending on infrastructure and social services. When faced with the world's problems, they tend toward resignation and indifference, and they retreat into the enclaves of gated communities, park-like office campuses, shopping malls, and other safe zones. Reich's arguments focus on the nation-state in a global economy, but they are similar to arguments that have been raised with respect to localism. Some have argued that wealthy communities in wealthy countries, by substituting locally made products with those imported from abroad, are reducing the opportunities for low-income producers in low-income countries to reap the benefits of participation the global market. The British journalist George Monbiot suggests that working-class people in low-income countries benefit from access to global trade and would be harmed by relocalization of commerce. In other words, the import-substitution strategies of communities in wealthy countries, like the protectionist policies of those countries, can come at the expense of the export-oriented economies of poor countries.[4]

A similar argument can be found in an essay—written during the rise of the appropriate-technology movement—in which the technology theorist Langdon Winner suggested that the countercultural reformers who renounced the world of the cities and went back to the land adopted an individualistic solution to the world's problems. Although they managed to shrink their ecological footprints by developing homesteads with more sustainable agriculture and cleaner energy, their overall effect on the global economy, not to mention environmental policies, was negligible. Much the same can be said about the home-power movement, whose enthusiasts took their homes "off the grid" and sought energy from wind, solar, wood, and other sources. The subsequent growth of natural-products industries makes it possible for the wealthy to insulate themselves, at least to some degree, from a toxic environment. By greening the household but not much else, there is the potential for some people to engage in an individualistic politics of separation from the world. According to the sociologist Andrew Szasz, the "inverted quarantine" of insulation from environmental damage through green consumption can be viewed as just another iteration of a long history of attempts by the middle and upper classes in both rich and poor countries to isolate themselves from the world's problems. To the extent that localist strategies become inward looking and focus on developing the local community as a healthy and environmentally friendly place, advocates of localism can run the risk of turning their backs on the need to advocate broader solutions to the world's problems.[5]

Closely related to the problem of enclavism is a fourth argument against localism: that the growth of suburbs created political and geographical boundaries that made it easier for the middle class to escape from and ignore the problems of poor and working-class people. In the

United States, portions of the suburban middle class have turned toward a politics of green consumerism and toward improvement of the environmental quality of their suburban neighborhoods and their rural weekend retreats. Building on work by the historians Lizabeth Cohen and Mike Davis, the agrifood researchers Melanie DuPuis, David Goodman, and Jill Harrison discuss the potential for localism to exclude concern with the plight of low-income workers. For example, they argue that in California the devolution of political institutions weakened regulatory structures that would have better protected poor and working-class people (e.g., farmworkers) from pesticide exposure.[6]

Thus, four main lines of argument can be identified with respect to the potential disconnect between localism and distributive justice concerns:

• Locally owned enterprises do not necessarily offer better opportunities than large corporations for workers, the poor, and historically excluded ethnic groups.

• Locally made products are generally upscale niche products that are not accessible for people with limited incomes.

• Localism may benefit communities in wealthy countries by cutting off the poor in less developed countries from the benefits of world trade.

• The politics of government devolution and suburbanization created barriers that favored the middle class and weakened the opportunities for social justice for poor and working-class people.

Regarding the first argument, it is true that some locally owned businesses can be hotbeds of nepotism and unfair personnel practices, whereas global corporations tend to ignore differences of religion, ethnicity, national origin, gender, and so on, at least in hiring for entry-level positions in the United States. However, there are well-known "glass ceilings" in the upper reaches of the management of large corporations, where women, ethnic minorities, and even white males without the right social background find that opportunities are closed. Opportunities for advancement may be more open for members of historically excluded groups in the small business sector. For example, a study of entrepreneurs found that African-American women and men were 50 percent more likely to start businesses than their white counterparts but more likely to fail. The situation is suggestive of closed political opportunities and racial discrimination in the corporate world.[7]

There is also considerable evidence that large publicly traded corporations have continually attempted to find ways to depress wages rather than share profits with workers. The evidence is visible not only in the long history of labor struggles in the United States but also in the growing outsourcing of production. Within the United States some of the large retailers also exhibit a parallel strategy of cost savings by squeezing productivity from their workers. In those chain stores hourly workers suffer from low wages, discrimination, forced overtime, and lack of health care and other benefits. The costs of low wages and shoddy products end up being shifted onto the public sector or onto households and family networks, which ultimately have to pay for the environmental and health effects of low prices. Conversely, locally owned businesses do not face the same pressure to downsize workforces as do publicly traded corporations, and they can provide a protective shield of employment during periods of economic downturn. The protective shield is particularly evident in family businesses, where laying off an employee, perhaps a longtime friend, can be as wrenching as kicking a family member out of the household. Indeed, it is to those long-time employees and younger family members that the elder entrepreneur often turns when looking for a successor.[8]

Regarding the firm-size wage effect, caution should be exercised in applying aggregate statistical findings to a reform movement within a portion of the economy. The studies reveal that there is significant variation across industries, and that the firm-size wage effect is negligible in the retail industry, which has been the primary driving force of the localist movement. The aggregate statistics also do not separate small firms in general from small firms that are socially and environmentally responsible, which are more likely to provide living wages, good benefits, and substantial community support. Likewise, the aggregate statistics do not take into account the willingness of some people to accept somewhat lower wages in exchange for the right to own a business and control their working conditions, nor do the statistics take into account the higher levels of government subsidies and tax breaks that go to larger firms. Finally, the studies do not take into account the interaction between large and small businesses. For example, the opening of a big-box store reduces the wages of small retail stores in a region.[9]

One example of the kinds of benefits that the aggregate statistics may not capture is the "small giant" phenomenon. In a book titled *Small Giants: Companies That Choose to Be Great Instead of Big*, the journalist Bo Burlingham explored the working conditions of companies that chose to remain private and not pursue profitability growth at the expense of other goals. Some of the companies sold mainly to the metropolitan region in which they were located; others were export-oriented manufacturers. In either case, the owners of the companies decided to put the values of community support, customer satisfaction, employee well-being, and in some cases environmental stewardship above the need to show steady increases in revenue growth and profitability. The businesses had a close relationship with their home communities, and they often made significant contributions to economic development and nonprofit activity. Workers were generally enthusiastic about their jobs, the opportunities they had to participate in decision making, and the support they received for community involvement. The owners and managers knew the employees, stepped in to help them in times of crisis, and offered new opportunities for career development. In one example a food store created spin-off businesses that allowed capable and ambitious employees to find new opportunities and ownership potential. In other cases founders of companies gradually shifted ownership to employees through employee stock ownership plans, trusts, or other mechanisms. The "small giant" phenomenon demonstrates the many positive externalities associated with locally owned small businesses, including benefits that address concerns regarding social justice in a global economy.

Regarding the second argument, there is little doubt that localist goods and services have been linked to upscale market niches. However, there are also examples of local businesses that offer products that are quite affordable for low-income consumers. One example is the resale industry, which offers goods at bargain prices and also shifts waste from landfills. Furthermore, as I noted in the previous chapter, the assumption that prices are generally lower in big-box stores and supermarkets is often erroneous, especially when goods of equivalent quality are compared. Regarding local agricultural networks, there is undoubtedly a high level of middle-class participation, but the networks can contribute to efforts to build community food security. For example, some farmers' markets accept food stamps, and some community-supported farms offer scholarships for low-income residents. Farmers also donate excess produce to food banks, and the larger community gardens often have extra plots for food banks. As I will examine in more detail in chapter 5, community gardening is probably the best place to look within the range of local food and agricultural institutions to find a connection between localism and distributive justice. Again, if one recognizes that there are different forms of localism, some of which are divided along class lines, then the criticisms are best construed as challenges that deserve further inquiry rather than closing arguments that warrant a facile dismissal.

Similar rebuttals can be offered regarding the greening of energy consumption. It does not have to be configured as a luxury good, such as credits for solar panels on middle-class homes. Some affordable housing projects are beginning to incorporate energy efficiency measures and solar panels into the building design, innovations that reduce energy expenses, which are a significant part of low-income household budgets. Likewise, some utilities and nonprofit organizations offer weatherization programs for low-income households. Weatherization is not only a way to reduce energy consumption and save on energy costs; it is also a way for a regional economy to engage in import substitution. A region that engages in energy conservation replaces funds that are flowing outside the region for energy with funds flowing to contractors within the region (although some of the weatherization materials may be imported). Such strategies can also coincide with reduced household expenditures with a relatively rapid pay-back period, and consequently they may address the issue of justice much more directly than do tax credits for solar panels.

Furthermore, when the concept of justice is opened up to include not only the fates of working-class and poor people but also the general sovereignty of a community in the global economy, there are other kinds of connections between localism and justice. When retail consumption moves from Main Street to malls and superstore complexes, the enclosure of the street and urban plazas as civic spaces limits the potential for street-based political mobilization and protest that often benefit the poor.

More generally, an economy with many locally owned small businesses rather than a few large employers affords greater opportunity for "third places." Although bookstores, coffee shops, restaurants, and other places where people meet and sometimes engage in political discussion can be franchises or chain stores, they are often owned locally by small business people.[10]

Regarding the third criticism, rich-country enclavism should be recognized as a challenge that should be addressed. A perverse criticism of localism that one sometimes hears is that if everyone followed the logic to an extreme, no one would buy from nonlocal producers and the global economy would collapse. The point is ludicrous, because much of what passes for localism is actually the hybrid type of locally owned retail stores and services that sell and utilize globally produced products; those businesses are hardly cutting themselves off from the global economy. To the extent that locally owned businesses in wealthy countries seek to buy from similar businesses abroad and thereby connect the localist and fair-trade movements, they can surmount the challenge of enclavism by steering their purchases of nonlocal products away from the distant sweatshops of the global corporate economy toward small independent producers throughout the world. The development of global localism is necessary to avoid the problem of enclavism, and the project is already part of localist thinking. In general the localist literature provides a coherent analysis of the negative effects of globalization, suggestions for policy reforms from the local to international levels, and concern with how to connect the reform efforts in one community with those in others throughout the world. Like the formation of middle-class niche markets, an impassive, "us first" form of localism is a strand within the movement and a potential risk, but the diagnosis hardly applies to all forms of localism.

Finally, regarding the concern that local government boundaries are used to solidify class and ethnic divisions, and political devolution is used to weaken the mandate of federal and state governments to protect poor and working- class people, the criticism tends to paint localism with a broad brush. It would be better to distinguish between a type of localization, the devolution of political power to state and local governments and the fragmentation of metropolitan political boundaries, and the localist movement, then analyze the politics of each. Certainly, the politics of devolution and suburbanization have had negative implications for the urban poor and working-class people, especially when devolution has been accompanied by reductions in welfare programs and labor protections. However, those historical processes are distinct from the localist movement. For example, independent business associations are not geographically limited to wealthy, middle-class suburbs, but instead many associations are defined with respect to either a central city or a metropolitan region, such as greater Philadelphia or greater Boston. Furthermore, the local business networks include businesses from a variety of neighborhoods within the region, and they foster business development in urban neighborhoods as well as in suburban ones.

In summary: The criticisms of localism from the standpoint of distributive justice identify significant challenges. However, the challenges can be a basis for formulating questions about the existence, prevalence, and supporting factors of a type of localism that addresses issues of inequality and urban poverty. Locally owned businesses by definition have more at stake in the communities that they serve, tend not to leave, and give back more through participation in local politics and donations to charities such as food banks. Furthermore, by strengthening local networks of government agencies, nonprofit organizations, and small businesses, and by recovering the spaces that those organizations create for civic action, localism offers a strategy for strengthening democracy. Nevertheless, the criticisms of those concerned with distributive justice should be the basis for a more concerted attempt to develop localism throughout the commodity chain. To have a locally owned hardware store that sells the same products as are found in the big-box stores, including products manufactured under weak labor and environmental conditions in low-income countries, seems to be a recipe for exacerbating the pernicious streak identified in the third argument outlined here. An enduring challenge of localism in the twenty-first century will be to make sure that it connects a "fair-bought" local store with a "fair-made" or "fair-trade" product.

Lack of Sustainability

Another set of issues from a values perspective involves the capacity for localist politics to contribute solutions to making the world's societies more environmentally sustainable. Much of the current debate on localism and the environment involves a very specific issue: carbon emissions. I will begin with this issue, but I will argue that it unduly restricts thinking about the localism and environment connection.

Critics of localism have claimed that the shorter distance between production and consumption for local goods does not automatically mean that local goods are more environmentally sustainable. The argument that links sustainability and localism is probably most prominent among local food organizations, which suggest that by buying locally a consumer reduces the ecological footprint of consumption by lowering "food miles" (the number of miles that a food product travels from its source of production to its point of consumption). However, a growing chorus of critics has suggested that the claim that a shorter commodity chain guarantees lower greenhouse-gas emissions is not always correct. For example, a tomato grown in a hothouse in the United Kingdom that is powered by electricity from natural gas may generate more carbon than one grown under the sun in Spain, even if the latter travels by truck to the British market.[11]

If the issue were simply one of comparing different conditions of production with distance to market, then one could reply to the food-miles critics by saying that when production processes are equivalent, the local product consumes less carbon. For example, it seems intuitively obvious that a tomato raised outdoors and organically in the United Kingdom will consume less carbon than an equivalent tomato shipped in from Spain. However, additional wrinkles in the food-miles debate emerge from the possibility that local food systems entail more trips to markets by farmers and by consumers than supermarket-based shopping. Estimating how much carbon is generated by larger numbers of short trips in small vehicles versus smaller numbers of long trips in large vehicles is a complicated problem. Furthermore, differences among truck, rail, and air freight transportation for long-distance shipping are significant from an emissions perspective. To resolve the food-miles issue, one must take into account the total environmental impact of a product over its life cycle, rather than just the carbon implications of transportation distance. The complexity of measuring carbon impact has become especially important to the agricultural industry of New Zealand, which became concerned with policies in Europe that were taking long-distance transportation into account for organic food standards. One study from that country found that the total carbon impact of lamb raised in New Zealand was smaller than the comparable carbon impact of lamb raised in the United Kingdom, even when emissions from transportation were taken into account.[12]

One way to respond to the life-cycle criticism is to examine the methodology of food-miles studies and question their assumptions. For example, the localist leader Michael Shuman pointed out that the New Zealand study did not include within-nation ground transportation, which is double for New Zealand food products, because its lamb has to be trucked both within New Zealand before being shipped to the United Kingdom and then again within the United Kingdom. Shuman also noted that the study assumed coal as the electricity source for British lamb and hydropower for New Zealand lamb. Again, his arguments point to the complexity of the issue and the lack of likelihood that a single, definitive study will resolve it. In view of the significant industrial interests at stake, it is likely that there will be a proliferation of studies and an ongoing controversy regarding the variable environmental dividends for local and nonlocal food production, depending on the type of food, how it is produced, how it is shipped, and how far it travels to market. On the one hand, under some circumstances non-locally-produced food will probably have lower greenhouse-gas emissions than locally produced food. On the other hand, if other aspects of the life cycle are comparable, the smaller amount of energy spent in transporting locally produced goods to market would result in an environmental dividend, especially if the mode of transportation for the distant food were air freight.[13]

Although it makes sense to engage the detailed empirical assumptions and methodologies of food-miles studies, it would be dangerous for advocates of localism to hitch their sustainability arguments solely to the wagon of carbon and transportation. Instead, a localist would do better to step back and draw attention to other environmental issues that might lead a consumer to favor local farms and other locally owned producers. Paying attention only to the food-miles debate may result in a premature narrowing of the discussion. On the issue of local food, one might simply ask this straightforward question: Which do you want to be your neighbor, an organic farm or a factory farm? However, there are more systematic arguments that, when grouped together, provide a different type of framework for thinking about localism and the environment.

One alternative way to link localism to environmental sustainability involves feedback loops between consumers and producers. If a hog farm or a manufacturing facility pollutes the surrounding environment, the residents of the area may be well aware of the pollution. However, if the residents are not consumers of the hogs or of the products of the manufacturing plant, a point of leverage with the polluting farm or firm is lost. Furthermore, if the consumers are nonlocal, then they are not as likely to be aware of the pollution and consequently not as likely to seek changes in production practices. In other words: as economies have become globalized, consumers have become less aware of the conditions of production of the products they consume. As the political scientists Thomas Princen and Michael Maniates have suggested, more direct feedback between consumers and producers may enhance the potential to correct environmentally damaging technologies and production practices, and geographical proximity is one way to achieve the goal. If a product is produced and consumed locally, then it is more likely that feedback loops involving consumer concerns about production processes will be operational.[14]

Another type of feedback loop between localism and the environment involves local ownership. Even if a product is not consumed where it is produced, another set of feedback loops can operate if the owners of the farm or the manufacturing site live nearby. The potential influence that a community has to remediate environmentally damaging practices is likely to be greater if the firm is locally owned. For example, family members of the polluting business who live in the community may find that their social relationships in local civic and political organizations become strained. In view of the family's position in the community and its desire to maintain respect and leadership, their business practices would be more likely to be responsive to local public pressure. In contrast, if the owner of the polluting business is a large corporation with distant headquarters, it can more easily ignore the community's concerns and protests. Furthermore, if the concerns were to grow to the point that the corporation could no longer ignore them in view of the risks of brand dilution generated by bad publicity or actions of local governments, the company might threaten to move to another city. The threat of losing the company would be likely to divide the community along jobs-versus-environment lines, and the opposition could be further divided by granting a few concessions to the community and gaining publicity for the "greening" of the company in a public-relations campaign.

A third argument that links localism and the environment returns to issues (discussed in chapter 1) regarding the degrees of freedom that a closely held, privately owned firm has for investment decisions. Owners of such firms have greater leeway than the managers of publicly traded firms when deciding to invest more profits into the greening of the firm's products and production processes, even if such investments may not be the most lucrative investment option in the short term. An example is Seventh Generation, a manufacturer of green household cleaning products that went public but then bought back its publicly traded shares in order to pursue a more socially and environmentally responsible mission than its public shareholders would have allowed. Although privatization of publicly traded firms became widespread after 2000, it took place largely for reasons of making enhanced profits. Once a firm was taken private, the new shareholders could trim costs, sell off divisions, and prepare it for acquisition by another large publicly traded corporation or for a new initial public stock offering. The kind of privatization that Seventh Generation undertook is quite different from that found among private equity firms, because its goal was permanent private ownership status in order to maintain its social and environmental mission. Seventh Generation later became certified by B Lab as a "B Corporation" (that is, a corporation dedicated to stakeholder governance and social and environmental responsibility), and to date B Corporations are privately held. The experience of Seventh Generation is quite consistent with the general argument that publicly traded corporations are on a treadmill of ongoing growth and reinvestment that requires them to sacrifice social and environmental responsibility values when those values come into conflict with profitability.[15]

The primary counter-argument is that locally owned independent businesses tend to be undercapitalized. Even in cases for which there is a convergence of consumer feedback, local ownership leverage, and the desire of owners to green their production technologies, the owners may simply lack the capital to invest in the new technologies. In contrast, the publicly traded company has greater financial resources and may invest in more up-to-date and environmentally efficient technologies. The net impact on the local environment may actually be worse in the case of the locally owned company. In fact, according to the sociologist Arthur Mol, the concern that small independent firms tended to use outmoded technologies was one of the factors that led to the development of ecological modernization theory, which emphasized the importance of the greening of large industrial corporations.[16]

Together, the argument and the counter-argument suggest that two contradictory factors are at play. On the one hand, locally owned firms do not have the fiduciary responsibilities to anonymous shareholders that large publicly traded firms have, and consequently they may have more degrees of freedom that enable them to invest capital in green technologies, even when such investments may not offer the highest return. On the other hand, locally owned firms do not have the same access to capital markets as large publicly traded firms, and consequently they may lack access to capital needed for investment in green technologies. Because both factors are likely to affect firm decisions, one would have to approach the argument empirically by developing controlled comparisons to assess the extent to which locally owned firms are more or less highly polluting. For example, there is some evidence that non-locally-owned chemical plants in the United States emit more toxic chemicals than locally owned chemical plants, but the effect is complicated because the higher emissions are related to differences in the amount of chemicals kept onsite in local and nonlocal firms. However, when the plants are located in communities with a larger percentage of civil-society organizations, they emit lower levels of toxic chemicals. In turn, research by the sociologist Charles Tolbert and his colleagues suggests that higher local ownership is positively correlated with higher measures of civil-society and third-place organizations, so there may also be indirect effects of the amount of local ownership on firm behavior.[17]

The comparison of arguments and counter-arguments suggests four ways of thinking about the localism and sustainability connection. Although life-cycle analysis of energy consumption and greenhouse-gas generation is important, the food-miles controversy tends to focus the question of the relationship between localism and sustainability on a very narrow technical issue, and it is likely to lead to a proliferation of studies that will yield contradictory results. I suggest three other approaches to thinking about the relationship between localism and sustainability:

• Increased geographical proximity between consumers and producers may render producer pollution more visible and of more concern to consumers.

• Locally owned firms may be more responsive to their image in the local community and to community desire for the firms to improve their environmental practices.

• Closely held independent firms may be more able to exercise greater control over investment decisions on environmental issues than publicly traded firms, even if those decisions involve lower short-term returns than other investment options.

In short, I suggest a framework for thinking about the issue of localism and the environment that will not trap debates in the important but highly limited controversies around carbon and transportation.

Conclusion

A critic of localism would be right to argue that enhanced local ownership of a region's economy would not inherently address concerns of social justice and environmental sustainability. However, one should not jump to the conclusion that no forms of localism can be just and sustainable. Instead, one must recognize that there are various ways to conceptualize linkages between localism and justice and sustainability. The theoretical approach of this chapter has the advantage of generating a framework for considering various types of linkages and for exercising caution when one-sided arguments are advanced against localism without consideration of counter-arguments. However, once the arguments and the counter-arguments have been explored, empirical research will be necessary.

One potential weakness of the discussion in this chapter is that it has tended to leave unproblematized the definitions of sustainability and justice that were articulated in the introduction and in chapter 1. It is worth turning to those definitions again as we begin to consider how concepts of sustainability and justice might be refashioned to help clarify the issues at stake.

In *Alternative Pathways in Science and Industry*, I developed a framework for addressing the issue of localism by building on the concept of "just sustainability" as it was developed by the environmental scholar Julian Agyeman and his colleagues. One might think of justice and sustainability as two dimensions, represented by an X and Y axis. (See figure 3.1.) Pathways for change that address justice problems occupy a continuum from the remediation of rights breaches (in other words, attempts to solve social justice problems in the sense of providing basic food, clothing, and shelter to the poor) to developing new democratic institutions and processes that facilitate attempts to build a more just world. On this axis the localist movement draws attention to the goal of building new kinds of institutions, specifically those with invigorated local political and economic sovereignty, that can enable a world of just sustainabilities to develop with more facility. To some degree the axis can be conceptualized as representing an expansive concept of justice that includes distributive and procedural approaches. On the horizontal axis I suggest another continuum of environmentally oriented pathways for

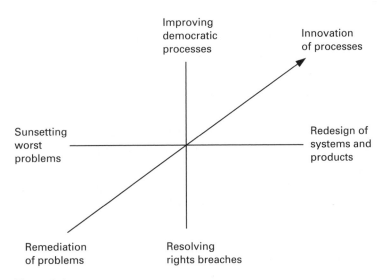

Figure 3.1
Justice and sustainability as a field of contestation.

change ranging from attempts to remediate worst practices, such as environmental justice struggles that result in cleanup projects, to more systemic approaches to design with global environmental problems in mind. As with the concept of justice, this axis also represents an expansive understanding of sustainability, in this case a range of approaches from remediation to redesign. Together, the two axes suggest a field of contested approaches to resolving problems of justice and sustainability, ranging from the remediatory to the processual. The direction of the arrow is suggestive of my assumption that building institutions that facilitate the development of the good society requires shifting the field of interventions toward the processual sides.[18]

In the chapters that follow, new empirical research is brought together with existing literatures to suggest that there are many examples of locally owned independent organizations that *do* address social justice or environmental sustainability, and sometimes both. The organizations are not always successful, and they often encounter both internal organizational and external political conflicts. Likewise, the alternative pathways of urban development discussed in the chapters that follow do not represent a utopia of a sustainable, just community. However, they provide examples of how to build a regional economy that challenges the assumptions of both the technopole model (in which the center of the local economy is a high-tech manufacturing cluster and everything else is secondary) and the enclavist utopianism of "back to the land" and communalist experiments (which seek withdrawal from the global economy). The examples represent starting points and models of a type of localism that builds environmental and/or social equality goals into organizational missions, and they reveal a variety of organizational forms that are capable of remaining economically feasible. Many adopt a nonprofit, social enterprise model that combines voluntary donations of time and money with an earned income revenue stream of sales of goods and services, but some are also for-profit businesses that are connected with the "buy local" campaigns of the independent business associations. As a group, the examples suggest some starting points for understanding a strand of localism that goes a long way toward addressing the criticisms that were explored in this chapter.

4

The Politics of Local Retailing

Independent business associations have become the focal point of mobilizations to shift regional economic development priorities in favor of greater consideration for the small-business community. As big-box stores have proliferated, independent businesses have come together to articulate the benefits that they provide to the communities in which they are located. Since the mid 1990s, independent business associations have launched an increasing number of "buy local" campaigns, which urge consumers and businesses to shift some purchases and other transactions to locally owned retail stores, banks, credit unions, manufacturers, services, and farms. However, the "buy local" theme is often only one among many that can be found articulated in the associations. In my experience with one such organization, some members join because they are concerned with figuring out how to survive and prosper as small businesses in a global economy, whereas others are more concerned with developing a more sustainable and just regional economy. The range of goals and motivations is reflected in the various names of independent business associations. Some call themselves an independent business alliance or business council, others use the phrase "sustainable business network," and yet others use the phrase "local first" in their name. In this chapter I will provide a background on the current wave of "buy local" campaigns and independent business associations, then I will explore the role of justice and sustainability goals.

Historical Background

On first glance the most recent wave of "buy local" campaigns appears to repeat the oppositional politics that emerged during the 1920s, a decade when the number of chain stores in the United States grew from 30,000 to 150,000. Retail consolidation was particularly strong in the grocery industry, where chain stores achieved about 40 percent of the market share of sales. The Great Atlantic and Pacific Tea Company (A&P) was the Wal-Mart of the day, with 15,700 stores in 1930 and a ranking as the country's fifth-largest industrial corporation. As Richard Schragger has noted, the figure of 15,000 stores was not surpassed until 2003, the year that the Subway chain broke the previous record, although via franchising rather than direct ownership. As in the present era, the chain-store phenomenon of the 1920s and the 1930s was not limited to grocery stores; many other markets were touched, including the pharmacy, restaurant, and automotive care industries.[1]

Although the figures are impressive, the chain stores of the 1920s and the 1930s were much smaller than the big boxes that arrived in late twentieth century, and the market share of the chains in most of the retail industry remained much lower than today. Nevertheless, an anti-chain-store movement emerged, and reformers convinced 26 states and dozens of cities to impose taxes on chain stores. In some cases the taxes were severe enough to affect chain stores' profitability, and the stores responded to the threat by challenging the laws in the courts. The legal battles eventually ended up in the US Supreme Court, which upheld the laws but also limited them. In 1936 Congress responded to the wave of public concern by passing the Robinson-Patman Act, which prohibited price discrimination. Two years later, Wright Patman (D-Texas) and 75 other representatives proposed additional legislation that would have placed a national tax on chain stores and would have effectively driven them out of business. However, the chain stores had been mobilizing to improve their labor relations, recruit farmers for support, and develop public-relations campaigns that touted the benefit to consumers of low prices. They won a referendum in California that reversed the state's chain-store tax, convinced voters in Utah to reject a chain-store tax, and defeated the Patman proposal in

Congress. "Though A&P would be subject to a damaging anti-trust lawsuit in the 1940s," Schragger notes, "no new states adopted chain-store taxes after 1941, and a few allowed theirs to lapse, or repealed them." (2005: 1081)[2]

Partly as a result of the anti-chain-store movement, the chains held less than 25 percent of the overall retail market from the 1920s through the 1950s. The relatively low and stable market share suggests that industrial consolidation is less a natural outcome of the impersonal forces of markets than a result of government policies that shape the potential for consolidation. A change in the federal tax code in 1954 allowed commercial real estate investors to take large deductions for property depreciation during the early years of their investment rather than averaging the deduction over 40 years. The depreciation rates were so high that some investors could pay for construction costs with rental income, avoid taxes on the income by deducting the front-loaded depreciation costs, and then use the cash to build again. A flood of investment into commercial real estate followed. The private-sector investment coincided with the huge federal government investment in the interstate highway system and the suburbanization of society, and consequently retail began to grow rapidly in suburban shopping centers. In 1962 Wal-Mart and Target were launched, and by 1967 chains had one-third of the retail market. By the 1980s many other retail chains had been launched, among them Toys "R" Us, Home Depot, and Circuit City. By the end of the century independent stores held less than 20 percent of the market share in a wide range of the retail industry, including supermarkets, pharmacies, and bookstores. Furthermore, as the suburban markets became saturated, the chains colonized previously forsaken market segments, such as small towns and old urban neighborhoods; they also moved aggressively into foreign markets.[3]

In the late 1990s a second movement against chain stores emerged. Retail consolidation had affected a wide range of businesses, including restaurants, coffee shops, supermarkets, and stores that sold toys, sporting goods, hardware, stationery, electronics, books, music, and clothing. Although proposals for a "big-box sales tax" were introduced in Maine and in Minnesota, in general the second movement adopted a strategy that differed from the "tax the chains" approach of the first movement.

Some local and state governments responded to retail consolidation by requiring community impact analyses for big-box and shopping-center projects, by passing zoning ordinances to limit the size of retail spaces, and by limiting formula businesses such as franchises. Furthermore, independent business associations appealed directly to the individuals, businesses, and governments in campaigns to "buy local," if not always, at least occasionally or as a first choice (hence the slogan "local first"). In the process, the new campaigns of independent business associations tapped local, place-based identities to encourage consumers to think of shopping as a civic activity rather than as a narrowly construed economic activity.

The present-day "buy local" movement is less oppositional and more pro-alternative than the anti-chain-store movement of the 1920s and the 1930s. Of course, the oppositional politics that were characteristic of the early movement have not disappeared. For example, numerous mobilizations have occurred in communities across the country to stop the construction of Wal-Marts and other big-box outlets. However, in general today's "buy local" campaigns are closer to the politics of what I have termed "technology- and product-oriented movements," or movements to develop alternative technologies and products such as organic food, renewable energy, green chemicals, and community currencies. Here, the alternative product has less to do with its design than with its provenance and the ownership of the store from which it is bought. Consequently, the "buy local" movements represent an amalgam of an ideal typical "technology- and product-oriented movement" and anti-globalization, pro-democracy movements. Although the "buy local" campaigns implicitly encourage avoidance of big-box stores, they stop short of organized boycotts. In today's retail environment a call for a complete boycott of big-box stores and chains would probably be self-defeating, because factors of convenience and availability make shopping in such stores almost unavoidable for most families. Rather than call for a consumer boycott of the chain stores, the independent business associations have adopted the double strategy of encouraging consumers to shift some purchases toward locally owned independent businesses and city governments to place limits on the growth of large retail spaces and formula businesses. "Buy local" campaigns also encourage a community-based identity that bridges class, ethnic, and other divisions that can often weaken a community and its civic life.[4]

Although independent business associations can unite communities across political and ethnic divisions, they can also face internal divisions based on issues of mission, especially regarding the importance of social and environmental responsibility. Locally owned independent businesses are for-profit organizations, and the degree to which individual business owners wish to incorporate the triple-bottom-line thinking of profitability, social responsibility, and environmental sustainability into their business decisions is highly variable. It is likely that, in order to sell consumers on the value of buying locally, small businesses will increasingly need to link themselves to the politics of ethical consumption and the category of consumers known as "lifestyles of health and sustainability." For those consumers, the price of products is less important than their provenance, that is, the social and environmentally responsible pedigree of both the product and the retail outlet. However, ways can also be found to link the lifestyles of health and sustainability issues to lower prices, such as occurs in the resale industry.[5]

How important are social and environmental responsibility goals in the movement to support locally owned independent businesses? To begin to understand and assess this complicated question, I will follow three strategies. In the next section I will present an overview of independent business associations in the United States on the issue. Next I will discuss specific examples drawn from some of the associations. In the third section I will examine a segment of the retail industry where sustainability and justice goals are prevalent.

The Missions of Independent Business Associations

Independent business associations have proliferated in American cities partly because chambers of commerce usually are dominated by large publicly traded corporations and by the service companies that work directly with those firms. To review, in the United States there are two main alliances that support locally owned independent business associations: the American Independent Business Alliance (AMIBA) and the Business Alliance for Local Living Economies (BALLE). AMIBA grew out of the efforts of locally owned businesses in Boulder, Colorado, to encourage patronage and discourage the growth of chain stores. Success in Boulder led to the creation of the national organization, which provides information and services to independent business associations across the country. AMIBA affiliates tend to use the term "independent business alliance," and AMIBA describes the goal of its affiliates as "helping maintain unique community character, ensuring continued opportunities for entrepreneurs, building local economic strength, and preventing the displacement of locally-owned businesses by chains." Notice that issues of environmental sustainability and social justice are not listed as central goals; AMIBA is focused on supporting locally owned independent businesses.[6]

BALLE has a slightly different pedigree and set of organizational goals. Although its co-founders support independent business associations in the cities where they live, BALLE emerged from the Social Venture Network, an association of business owners and investors who advocate the development of socially and environmentally responsible businesses. During the early 1990s, Judy Wicks worked with members of the Social Venture Network to develop social and environmentally responsible businesses in Philadelphia. When she became chair of the Social Venture Network, she developed the "local network initiative" to build "local living economies" of socially and environmentally responsible businesses. She saw a need for a new organization to support such initiatives, and at the 2001 meeting of the Social Venture Network, she and Laury Hammel, the owner of several health and recreation clubs in Massachusetts, founded BALLE.[7]

It is clear not only from statements made by Wicks that were analyzed in chapter 1 but also from BALLE's mission statement that social and environmental responsibility goals are central to the organization: "We envision a sustainable global economy made up of Local Living Economies that build long-term economic empowerment and prosperity through local business ownership, economic justice, cultural diversity, and environmental stewardship."[8] To some degree the definition of "local business ownership" is left up to individual affiliate networks, so there is variation. Furthermore, at the annual conferences that I attended, many participants were from nonprofit organizations and government agencies. The concept of local living economies is meant to serve as a bridge across diverse organizations that share a common purpose. Like AMIBA, BALLE focuses on locally owned independent businesses, but unlike AMIBA, BALLE is more concerned with the local ownership issue as a means toward the end of building sustainable and just economies. As a result, the affiliate networks of BALLE tend to use terms such as "sustainable business network," "socially responsible," or "local first" in their organizational titles rather than "independent business alliance."

To better understand the issue of local ownership in relationship to sustainability and justice goals, I analyzed the mission statements of all AMIBA and BALLE affiliates. Focusing on formal mission statements is only one way to assess the social and environmental responsibility goals of the organizations. In practice, organizations may operate at variance from their missions, and there may be groups of member businesses who work on sustainability or justice issues, but their work may not be visible in the mission statements of the associations. Nevertheless, the analysis of mission statements provides one valuable source of information on how the movement for locally owned independent businesses is related to social and environmental responsibility. When I conducted the analysis in 2007, the websites of the two umbrella organizations had functioning links to 19 AMIBA affiliates, 36 BALLE affiliates, and four associations affiliated with both organizations. Although both umbrella organizations had considerably more affiliate organizations and were growing rapidly, the analysis focused only on that set.

All of the 19 AMIBA affiliates for which information was available focused on local independent ownership and its benefits to the community. Environmental or social justice goals did not appear in the mission and goal statements. The same was true for the four organizations that were affiliated both with BALLE and with AMIBA. BALLE's affiliates were much more diverse organizationally. Its affiliate networks included chambers of commerce (generally of small cities, where the chambers were concerned with the small-business sector), statewide associations of socially responsible businesses, neighborhood business associations within large cities, metropolitan-level sustainable business associations, and "local first" organizations. In the organizational mission statements, the term "local" was not always clearly defined as referring to locally owned independent businesses.

I then categorized the BALLE affiliate organizations into four groups based on the degree of concern for sustainability and justice issues and the extent to which they focused on independent business issues. (See table 4.1.) About 10 percent of the organizations were dedicated to socially and environmentally responsible (SER) businesses at a state or local level. Those organizations were primarily concerned with sustainability and/or social responsibility, and they appeared to accept as members organizations that were not locally owned independent businesses. Another small group was primarily concerned with neighborhood, downtown, or local business development. The group included chambers of commerce, downtown or neighborhood business associations, and a community development corporation. Again the issue of locally owned independent businesses was not primary, but one could presume that most of the businesses affiliated with this group of organizations were

Table 4.1
BALLE network affiliate missions, 2007 (*N* = 40).

Organizational type	Percentage of all affiliates	Equality or social responsibility goals	Sustainability goals	Goals of supporting locally owned independent businesses
Socially and environmentally responsible business associations	10%	x	x	
Chambers, downtown business associations, etc.	22.5%	Some		x
Independent business associations	25%			x
Comprehensive	42.5%	x	x	x

locally owned and independent. Sustainability goals were either absent or very minor, but poverty remediation and economic development considerations were present. The third group, which included the four organizations co-affiliated with AMIBA and six others, was primarily oriented toward locally owned independent businesses, and sustainability and social responsibility goals were either absent or not well articulated. The largest group consisted of what might be considered "comprehensive" organizations in terms of consistency with the mission of the umbrella organization BALLE. They were oriented toward local businesses, often specifying local ownership and independence. Sustainability goals were generally prominent, and several associations also mentioned some variant of a goal of economic justice, affordability, or benefits for all citizens. Although the comprehensive group is a minority, it is the largest group, and presumably the other organizations have chosen to affiliate with BALLE because they agree with the concept of bridging local ownership with social and environmental responsibility goals.

Although a different analyst might come up with a slightly divergent breakdown and categorization, the general conclusion would probably not change: the local business movement is divided on the issue of social and environmental responsibility. AMIBA is more much vigilant about the issue of local ownership and independence, but social and environmental responsibility concerns are absent from mission statements. BALLE reveals differences among organizations that emphasize social and environmental responsibility but not local ownership and local business development, those that emphasize local ownership and/or economic development with little concern explicitly mentioned for environmental responsibility, and those that emphasize a comprehensive set of goals. Based on my experience working with a group that became a BALLE affiliate organization, I have come to the conclusion that such issues of organizational definition represent an ongoing conversation for nonprofit associations that wish to bridge local ownership and social and environmental responsibility. Although in the Pacific Northwest and in New England the bridge between the local ownership mission and social and environmental responsibility goals may be built with relative ease, it is likely to be built with more difficulty elsewhere. In my experience, locally owned independent businesses can be rallied with ease, and with some passion, under the banner of loss of sales to big-box stores and the desire to motivate consumers to support local businesses. However, getting them to take the next steps—greening their practices, looking at social and environmental issues in product sourcing, and examining how to improve their own labor practices and the region's inequalities—is likely to prove more difficult for the small businesses that are not already in a green market segment. Leadership can come from the member businesses that have already shifted toward social and environmental responsibility, and gradual education can slowly move the other businesses along. However, the issue of relative emphasis between local and green/blue goals is likely to permeate the independent-business movement for some time to come.

Another issue worth considering with regard to the variety of mission statements and goals is the somewhat obscure but significant legal difference between two types of nonprofit organization. Under the US federal tax code there are many flavors of nonprofit organizations, but the two most relevant tax-code designations are 501(c)(3) and 501(c)(6). The 501(c)(3) designation is for organizations that have a charitable, scientific, or educational mission and provide a general public benefit for a designated geographical area. Contributions to a 501(c)(3) organization are deductible as charitable contributions, less an amount specified for services provided, and organizations that receive the designation may pursue grants from charitable foundations—a feature that can open up many opportunities for financial resources. The status is consistent with a broad organizational mission that includes local sustainability, poverty reduction, and other programs with charitable and/or educational purposes. However, such organizations must restrict lobbying activities, and consequently business associations that wish to pursue local procurement policies, zoning changes, and other policy reforms may find the 501(c)(3) designation limiting. Furthermore, if such organizations have members, the government may frown upon restrictions on the limitations of membership to a category of individual or organization, such as independent business owner.

The 501(c)(6) designation is for nonprofit, membership-based business associations that promote their industry and wish to engage in lobbying activities. Contributions are not tax deductible as charitable contributions, but businesses can usually deduct membership fees as business expenses. 501(c)(6) status is appropriate for independent business associations, but it is not entirely clear how to define organizations that wish to support the local business sector and also to pursue a variety of public educational and charitable goals having to do with environmental sustainability, economic development, and the alleviation of poverty. As a result, an organization's legal designation can affect decisions about its mission. Some of the BALLE affiliates are 501(c)(3) organizations, some are 501(c)(6) organizations, and in a few cases network leaders have set up sister organizations, one a 501(c)(3) and the other a 501(c)(6) organization. Classification is a subject of ongoing discussions within and among networks in the movement.

Organizational Choices

To better understand the tradeoffs that can occur with respect to environmental and social justice goals, I developed three case studies based on interviews with leaders of the AMIBA affiliate in Austin and the BALLE affiliates in San Francisco and Philadelphia. In each of the three cases I was able to gain a somewhat more detailed perspective on how the organizations encountered tradeoffs among sustainability, social responsibility, and local/independent goals.

The Austin Independent Business Alliance (AIBA) emerged from a campaign to stop the construction of a Borders Bookstore on a street corner where two landmark independent businesses were located: BookPeople and Waterloo Records. The independent stores used the slogan "Keep Austin Weird" and argued that the city should not subsidize the construction of the Borders store. Their campaign was successful, and in the place of the proposed Borders store a flagship store in the Whole Foods chain opened. Because the Whole Foods chain is headquartered in Austin, and because the new Austin store did not compete directly with the two independent stores on the same street corner, many considered the new store acceptable. If a chain store had to be built on that corner, their thinking went, the flagship store of a publicly traded corporation that was headquartered in Austin was one of the most acceptable choices.

Since then AIBA has pioneered innovative programs oriented toward locally owned independent businesses. One program, Connecting and Linking Independents with Commercial Developments (CLIC), has shown that consumers want independent businesses in new shopping centers and has connected real estate developers with independent businesses. Another program, Independent Business Investment Zones (IBIZ), uses signs, brochures, and advertising to draw the attention of consumers to neighborhood business districts. The business districts also sponsor "first night out" events, in which businesses stay open late and offer special attractions for shoppers.[9]

Although the focus of AIBA is on such support programs, some of the founders and members of AIBA were concerned with environmental issues, and at one point the organization joined with other groups to oppose plans to construct a Wal-Mart above the Edwards Aquifer. The aquifer has a special meaning in Austin because it feeds Barton Springs, a landmark green space that is considered to be the soul of the city. Although there is widespread support for preserving and protecting the aquifer and the springs, some local businesses were uncomfortable with the idea of remaining members of a business association that took political positions on issues not directly related to the interests of small businesses. Another local business association (Choose Austin First) emerged, and one newspaper report characterized it as more conservative than AIBA. Since that time, AIBA has not taken stands on politically sensitive issues, and the two associations have reached out to each other. More generally, as Melissa Miller, executive director of AIBA noted, the point is that some local businesses "do not want to be affiliated with an organization that endorses politically sensitive campaigns that have nothing to do with creating opportunities for small businesses."[10]

Social and environmental responsibility issues have also been controversial in some of the BALLE affiliates. In Local Exchange (once the BALLE affiliate in San Francisco), differences in perspectives emerged between members who emphasized a local orientation and those who emphasized an environmental orientation. As Don Shaffer (at the time of my interview the executive director of BALLE and the head of Local Exchange) noted, the retail stores tended to emphasize the "buy local" goal, whereas businesses in other industries, including restaurants and hotels, were more interested in greening their business practices. Eventually the new BALLE affiliate for San Francisco, the San Francisco Locally Owned Merchants Alliance, coalesced around the themes "local" and "independent." In contrast, one of the model affiliate BALLE organizations—Sustainable Connections of Bellingham, Washington—has managed to keep the politics of sustainability connected with the "buy local" theme and, in the process, build a large and successful 501(c)(3) organization. The identity issue of the local networks has to be solved locally, and it depends greatly on the composition and values of the founding members.[11]

A somewhat different controversy occurred in the Sustainable Business Network of Greater Philadelphia, the founding BALLE affiliate. One group sought the endorsement of the organization for the repeal of a business tax that was harmful to small businesses, but another group asked for an endorsement of the same tax on the ground that the proposed repeal would have a negative effect on city services. Caught between two understandings of justice (one oriented toward the development of locally owned small businesses, the other oriented toward services that were particularly beneficial to low-income residents), the Sustainable Business Network faced a difficult decision. The leaders studied the issue and ultimately decided not to take a position on it, but in the process they began to develop a mechanism for evaluating public policy issues in light of the organization's goals and vision. "Instead of just taking a position," said Leanne Krueger-Braneky, the network's director, "we will evaluate an issue in light of our mission and our vision. We may take positions on some issues if they are in line with our mission and vision, but the decision is not to take a public position unless there is a really clear match."[12]

In view of the diversity of political viewpoints that will be found in any association of locally owned independent businesses, it would be a recipe for deep organizational conflict if an organization's leadership were to take political stands on issues that do not directly represent the general interests of the members as local owners of independent businesses. Clearly, endorsements of proposals for neighborhood independent-business districts, local government procurement policies, and zoning regulations that favor small-business development would likely be prime candidates for widespread support among members. In contrast, opposition to a new manufacturing facility or big-box store would likely be more controversial, unless the facility promised few general economic benefits and raised a widespread perception of a threat to destroy neighborhoods and generate substantial pollution. Support of small-business development in low-income neighborhoods is, in my experience, much less controversial, although it remains to be seen how central this issue will be as the movement of local independent businesses develops. In 2008 BALLE announced an "economic justice initiative," which promised to make the issue more prominent among its networks.

I suspect that as independent business organizations proliferate and become more involved in local politics, they will tend to select local issues of environmental and justice policy only if a good case can be made for their positive or negative effect on a wide range of local businesses. As the Austin case indicated, where the organization is focused on the theme of independent businesses, some local businesses are likely to worry about being associated with an organization that takes environmental or other political stands that could alienate customers. In contrast, to the extent that the definition of the association tilts toward an environmental or economic development message over a local business message, the organization would be more able to define political positions on those issues that have widespread consensus. In either case, there is ongoing potential for tension between the independent ownership side of the local business movement and the social and environmental responsibility side. The possibilities for tension are evident at various scales: within local businesses as they undergo internal discussions about their goals, within local business associations as they establish missions and programs, and between the two umbrella organizations (AMIBA and BALLE). In this sense, the case studies are consistent with the variation and divergences found in the analysis of mission statements, but they provide a perspective on how the issues can appear in everyday processes of organizational decision making.

Reuse Centers

Although some of the BALLE affiliates indicated concern with social justice issues, it can coexist uneasily with the sovereignty goal of supporting local businesses and certainly with the environmental mission of some of the associations. The tradeoffs among laudable organizational goals are real and should not be ignored, but one should also not give up once the potential for conflict or tension is recognized. If one accepts that such tradeoffs are part of the difficult politics of building an alternative economy, one might then look for sites where the goals can coexist with considerably less tension. My strategy has been to focus limited research resources on understanding where those opportunities already exist. The agrifood scholar Julie Guthman and colleagues suggest that in the case of local agricultural networks, there are some mechanisms for mediating the conflict between farm security and food security, such as food stamps at farmers' markets and low-income scholarships for community supported agriculture farms. To date, those mechanisms appear to be poorly developed and lacking in adequate governmental support, but they can be analyzed for their challenges and potential. I would add that in the resale industry, and in the reuse segment within that industry, there are very favorable opportunities for organizations to explore the convergence among the three goals.[13]

The resale industry includes retail businesses that sell used clothing, books, furniture, and other household items; nonprofit charitable organizations such as Goodwill and Salvation Army; flea markets and rummage sales; and yard or garage sales. Because the resale industry removes from the waste stream objects that could end up in incinerators or landfills, and because it provides goods at low prices (generally through nonprofit organizations, independent stores, and the informal economy), it is an example of local business ownership for which social and environmental goals may be addressed with relative facility. Some smaller cities organize town-wide yard sale days, and some cities have business districts where antique and "junk" stores can be found, but in general the potential of this industry is unrealized. American cities have not yet made concerted efforts to bring together used-goods stores into a used-goods retail district, where shoppers could go to buy clothing, books, furniture, appliances, building materials, and a wide range of other goods at prices and quality that beat those of the big-box retail outlets.

Our case studies focused on one segment of the resale industry: reuse centers—that is, stores that sell used home and building supply materials, such as doors, windows, toilets, sinks, cabinets, wood, and appliances.

Some reuse centers also have spinoff operations, such as deconstruction (the hand-based dismantling of building interiors and even whole buildings) and furniture remanufacturing from used wood. Reuse centers can be either nonprofit or for-profit enterprises, and they may explicitly embrace environmental goals, distributive justice goals, or a mixture of the two. We completed case studies of some of the best-known reuse centers in the country, located in Austin, Baltimore, Berkeley, Burlington (Vermont), Oakland, Pittsburgh, and Portland (Oregon).[14]

Regarding the sustainability side, about one-third of the solid waste in the United States is construction debris, and most of that is from renovation and demolition rather than new construction. By developing a market for construction debris from renovation and building deconstruction, reuse centers provide a model of how to reduce the local solid waste stream. The larger reuse centers, such as the Rebuilding Center in Portland and Urban Ore in Berkeley, were saving 4,000–6,000 tons of materials from landfills per year. Some of the organizations also sponsored community recycling events. For example, the Construction Junction in Pittsburgh joined with other local environmental groups to host monthly collection events for specific types of goods, such as appliances, tires, and electronics.[15]

Another environmental benefit of reuse centers is that they draw attention to the upstream issue of product design and sustainability. Much of present-day sustainable product design is focused on energy efficiency across the product life cycle, and another strand of product design focuses on materials substitution to decrease toxicities in the manufacturing, use, and disposal of a product. Reuse centers have the potential to draw attention to another aspect of sustainability in product design. For example, in my interview with the Habitat for Humanity Re-Store in Austin, I learned that their deconstruction operation was finding that more recent buildings, with their glued and prefabricated components, were more difficult to dismantle and reuse. To the extent that the growth of reuse centers begins to draw attention to the need to develop a new building design that facilitates dismantling (a consideration that is left out of green building standards such as Leadership in Energy and Environmental Design), it could have some effect on concepts of "green buildings" that go beyond the current emphasis on energy efficiency.[16]

Reuse organizations offer at least four social benefits: affordable home supply materials, donations to low-income housing organizations and families, worker training and potentially worker ownership, and neighborhood development. On the first issue, reuse centers provide a clear case of a significant savings for purchases from local, independent retail that challenges the argument of critics that the local green economy is more expensive than the nonlocal chains. Often prices in reuse centers are 70 percent below new retail prices for similar household objects and materials, sometimes even 90 percent lower. In our visits to a variety of the stores across the United States, we saw and met a diverse range of buyers, often including students, African-Americans, and Latinos. Even when the buyers are professional contractors, there may be benefits for their renters. For example, one apartment owner at Portland's Rebuilding Center told me that by using materials from the reuse center he was able to make repairs and upgrades at a low cost and pass on his savings in lower rental rates. Often reuse centers were located in or near low-income neighborhoods, and they provided an accessible and affordable source of home supplies for those neighborhoods.[17]

Another major social benefit of reuse centers is the donation of materials to low-income renters and homeowners. The Habitat for Humanity Re-Stores are a primary example. The Austin Re-Store served not only as a source of low-price goods for renters and homeowners throughout the city but also as a warehouse for materials for use in their home construction projects. Another example is the Loading Dock in Baltimore, which has supported more than 2,000 low-income and moderate-income families; it also has donated materials to about 8,500 local organizations, including soup kitchens, low-income housing groups, senior citizens groups, and day-care centers. Another example is The Reuse People, which put together a drive to gather materials to help flood victims in Mexico, and the organization continues to donate building materials to a variety of nonprofit organizations, including some that channel the materials to developing countries. It also sells surplus lumber to a company that builds affordable housing in Mexico.[18]

A third social benefit of reuse centers comes from their hiring and training practices. The larger centers have staffs of 30–40 employees, and from what I was able to ascertain in interviews they generally provide good benefits and job rotation so that employees gain well-rounded job training. Reuse centers often hire from the urban neighborhoods in which they are located, and several of those that we visited had significant percentages of Latino and African-American employees. The nonprofit organizations sometimes also receive contracts for job training, and the deconstruction work in particular helped employees obtain valuable construction skills that led to better jobs in the construction and contracting industries. For example, during the 1990s ReCycle North in Burlington received grants from the US Department of Housing and Urban Development for job training, and subsequently it received funding from the state government for its training programs for the homeless and unemployed. ReCycle North and Austin's Re-Store also provide work for people who are completing community service for the criminal justice system. Another possible benefit for employees is ownership. Although worker-owned reuse centers are not common, an experiment in worker ownership was underway at the ReBuilders Source reuse center in the South Bronx.[19]

A fourth social benefit of the reuse centers is neighborhood development. In Austin, the Re-Store's Brush with Kindness program refurbished existing homes and made neighborhood improvements such as community gardens, and the Habitat for Humanity chapter built homes that met the city's rigorous green building standards, which in turn resulted in energy savings for occupants. More generally, the reuse centers themselves can become sites of activity and revitalization in otherwise desolate neighborhoods. For example, Portland's Rebuilding Center became a significant component in the revitalization efforts for the area surrounding Mississippi Street in the northeast section of the city, Urban Ore also anchored redevelopment in West Berkeley, and the Construction Junction helped restore the Union Baptist Church as an element in a broader neighborhood revitalization effort in Pittsburgh. A crucial part of the revitalization efforts is creating opportunities for home ownership, as occurs with the Habitat for Humanity reuse centers and as can also occur when there is funding available from community development corporations and other affordable housing organizations.[20]

We found many instances where the distributive justice goals of reuse organizations coexisted well with environmental goals. In some organizations the environmental goals were more prominent; in others the economic development side was more prominent. However, all the owners and managers whom we interviewed saw their organizations as having both environmental and social dividends even when such goals were not an explicit part of the organizational mission. There were a few instances when environmental and equity goals may have come into conflict. One problem was accepting items that might be of benefit to low-income customers but posed environmental problems, such as old appliances. Should a reuse organization opt for a strong supply of cheap, used appliances, or should it discard some of the most energy-inefficient items? Although many organizations carried used appliances, some refused to accept the more environmentally inefficient ones. For example, ReCycle North dismantled and recycled old energy-inefficient refrigerators, and the Loading Dock of Baltimore did not accept appliances that were more than 5 years old. The Loading Dock generally accepted only multiple-pane windows; it accepted single-pane windows only if they had historic value. Also problematic are older toilets, which have large tanks and use large quantities of water. One reuse center came up with an ingenious low-tech solution: add a brick to the water tank.[21]

More generally, reuse centers also urge us to think about the utilization of waste as a form of import substitution that can be an element of a localist economic development strategy. Increasingly, private waste contractors charge homes and businesses to have their garbage hauled to landfills, which have become more and more distant as a result of the closure of local landfills. Likewise, most recycling programs end up selling waste to distant remanufacturing companies, some of them abroad. Unlike landfilling and remanufacturing in distant locations, reuse centers generate jobs locally. Of course, they do not solve the overall problem of solid waste, because reuse centers are capable of converting only a portion of the waste stream into consumer products. However, like the broader resale industry, reuse centers draw attention to a way of configuring local retail that reduces overall consumption and waste, saves consumers money, and retains profits in the community.

Conclusion

In this chapter I have used three different approaches to the problem of assessing the justice and sustainability dimensions of local businesses in the retail industry: reading the mission statements of independent business associations, interviewing local business association leaders about how such issues and conflicts emerged in their organizations, and analyzing the issues in reuse centers based on our case studies. The method is consistent with my overall thesis regarding localism: that an analysis of its potential, shortcomings, and challenges must take variation into account. The views of critics who wish to describe localism as unconcerned with environmental and justice issues are not confirmed by this method. However, the critics do point to issues that are far from resolved. My analysis does not present an entirely rosy picture in which environmental benefits, support for the small-business community, and social justice converge without conflict. Instead, it suggests that convergence tends to occur in a segment of BALLE organizations (the "comprehensive" affiliates), but not necessarily in all local affiliates of that national organization and (at least from the perspective of mission statements) not at all in AMIBA chapters. The convergence can also be found in reuse centers, and perhaps more generally throughout the resale industry, although we did not generate any new research on the broader industry. Even where there is evidence of convergence, there can be tensions or simply divergences within an organization. For example, some reuse centers emphasize the environmental side of the organization, whereas others emphasize the anti-poverty side.

A central challenge for owners of locally owned independent businesses is to bring the together the goals of environmental sustainability, local ownership, and distributive justice into a coherent whole. The challenge should be justified not only on moral or political grounds but also in terms of organizational strategy. Local retail already suffers from a perceived tradeoff between supporting locally owned independent businesses and benefiting from the advantages of shopping at big-box stores. To some degree the idea that prices are higher in small retail stores is mistaken, but independent business associations will have to use aggressive marketing to overcome the perception in the minds of consumers. Furthermore, many small businesses are not open evenings or weekends, and shopping locally may involve multiple trips unless local businesses are located in clusters such as those now being organized in Austin. Although Internet-based purchasing from locally owned independent stores will be able to mitigate inconvenience and the perception of higher prices to some degree, independent business associations will have to find some other way of distinguishing themselves from corporate retail. Merely selling green products is not likely to work. As corporate retail "goes green," it creates consumer tradeoffs between the green and the local, and ultimately both corporate retail and local retail will shift toward greener products. The distinguishing feature of local retail could be its mix of local ownership and greener products in *addition* to a concern with the social justice of a regional economy, as occurs to some degree in the reuse centers that we studied. Equality goals can take many forms, among them better benefits and living wages for employees, transition plans that convert small businesses to employee-owned enterprises, and hybrid for-profit and nonprofit organizations that have community development and job training goals. Those are the elements of a form of retail localism that could probably distinguish it in the long term from its corporate competitors, which in their ongoing race for higher and higher profits will tend to squeeze workers' wages and benefits, avoid investment in low-income neighborhoods, and dedicate only minuscule portions of their profits to low-income development programs.

5

The Challenges of Urban Agriculture

Although food and agriculture account for only a small percentage of the total gross domestic product of the United States, it is often in regard to food that people understand localism. We ingest food into our bodies, and it is closely linked to how we feel in the short term and how healthy we are in the long term. Local produce often tastes better because it is fresher than nonlocal produce found in supermarkets, and knowing where one's food comes from can be reassuring in an era of heightened concern with food safety. Furthermore, by supporting regional farms or by growing food in a community garden, people can directly contribute to building green spaces, local social networks, and the region's overall quality of life.

For those reasons, food and agriculture have been one of the primary sites of localist thinking and action. There is a growing popular literature on people who have tried to "eat local," some of whom even eat only foods grown and raised within a 100-mile radius of their homes. For people who live in a cold climate, the challenge of eating locally is feasible only during the warm months, although for the purists it is possible to eat mostly locally even in the winter by relying on canned goods and food that can be stored for long periods of time. As with the "buy local" campaigns of retailers, the point of the "100-mile challenge" is not to shift all purchases to food grown within 100 miles, but to explore what the implications are for the local economy and for one's lifestyle if some consumption is diverted to locally grown products.[1]

Localism in the food industry has considerable internal variation and diversity, including class divisions. The linkages between local farms and consumers via farmers' markets, retail food cooperatives, community-supported agriculture, and locally oriented restaurants are based on middle-class consumers and small farmers, whereas community gardening, urban nonprofit farming, and food security work focus on the needs of urban working-class and poor people. Those differences suggest the need for methodological caution in making generalizations from one part of the local food industry to the industry as a whole. Furthermore, because of the importance of food for localism in general, it is possible to mistake patterns observed in the food industry for localism as a whole. Although food is undoubtedly important to localism, such "agricentrism" should be taken with a grain of salt, and again a methodology that attends to the diversity of localism both within the food industry and outside it can help avoid the tendency to overgeneralize that is sometimes found in the scholarly literature.

Localism Studies and the Food Industry

Owing to the significant presence of rural sociologists, geographers, and interdisciplinary food studies scholars, the literature on food, agriculture, and localism is relatively well developed. One topic of research that may have general implications for the study of localism is work that documents tradeoffs between localism and sustainability. For example, agrifood researchers Brandon Born and Mark Purcell warn of a "local trap," or the assumption that local food production is automatically more sustainable. Likewise, other scholars have argued that agricultural localism can adopt a "defensive" or "parochial" posture that emphasizes supporting local farms and maintaining cultural boundaries between a place-based community and its outside. The defense of local farms and pride in local food and recipes is not automatically linked to concerns with food quality and environmental sustainability. This issue appears to be parallel with the differences discussed in the previous chapter regarding the mission statements of independent business associations; in other words, the literature here suggests that there are varying degrees of convergence and divergence between sustainable food and local food.[2]

From a historical perspective, localism and organic food production were more closely linked during the 1970s, and they became increasingly disconnected in subsequent decades. The history of Cascadian Farms, which the journalist Michael Pollan has described as a transition of the small hippie farm to a subsidiary of General Mills, is an exemplar of the integration of organic food production into the mainstream food industry. Although there are other examples of small family farms—even some with "back to the land" and countercultural values—that became part of the large-scale, corporate, organic industry, agrifood researcher Julie Guthman's detailed work on the history of organic agriculture in California suggests that other historical trajectories were also important. The rapid development of industrial organic agriculture in that important agricultural state occurred when conventional farmers converted land to organic production in recognition of new market opportunities. Her history may not generalize to other parts of the country, but it does caution us against assuming that present-day organic agriculture emerged from a differentiation of large-scale, industrial organic farms from small-scale family farms with countercultural values. Nevertheless, the bifurcation thesis is of general interest in the study of localism because it reminds us not only that the localism-sustainability connection can be tenuous but also that it can change. Furthermore, it reminds us that global corporations can easily disaggregate a complex of values that link localism and sustainability by selecting in favor of green production while leaving behind the politics of local control, just as they have done by selecting green production and leaving behind fair labor practices.[3]

Another important cluster of studies by agrifood researchers that has general implications for the study of localism is the critical analysis of the link between agricultural localism and distributive justice. Most of the discussions have focused on the problems that emerge when the concept of justice in the agrifood field is limited by a focus on the problems of the family farmer. In a comparative study of "buy local food" campaigns with "buy union," "buy black," and "buy American" consumer campaigns of the past, Patricia Allen and E. Clare Hinrichs suggest that the emphasis on local provenance in "buy local food" campaigns deflects the attention of consumers away from distributive justice concerns. David Goodman and Michael Goodman view the development of local labeling and attention to local provenance as new forms of intellectual property or brand identity that allow local farmers to extract higher rents. More generally, E. Melanie DuPuis and David Goodman suggest that localism should be redefined based on a concern with both local and global inequalities. They and other agrifood scholars have identified other categories of distributive justice that tend to become marginalized when the focus is on justice for family farms. For example, there appears to be little concern in middle-class agrifood networks with the problems of farmworkers and non-farming neighborhoods affected by factory farms, pesticide drift, and agricultural waste products. Another justice consideration, generally not discussed in the agrifood literature, is the threat that the growth of direct sales via farmers' markets and farm stands can pose for locally owned retail stores, so we could add the economic effects on locally owned independent retailers as well. There is also the concern with how the suburban-to-rural configurations of localism may deflect attention from the food security issues in the low-income, urban neighborhoods. In short, just as agrifood researchers have clarified some of the tensions that have emerged between local and sustainable food production, so they have noted similar tensions between local agricultural networks and economic justice considerations.[4]

In this chapter I will adopt a strategy similar to that of the previous chapter for the study of reuse centers. The conclusion that there are significant disjunctures and tensions, along with some convergences, among local ownership, environmental, and social justice goals in local agricultural networks appears to be empirically accurate for the range of institutions studied in the agrifood literature, namely small farms, farmers' markets, community-supported agriculture, and locally oriented food retail, mostly in the North America and Europe. However, a more complete understanding of the relations among localism, the environment, and social justice in the context of local food requires an analysis that steps out of the confines of a rural framework so that urban agriculture (or, more accurately, horticulture) is considered as a more central part of the discussion. For that reason I have chosen to focus on community gardening as another aspect of localism, food, and agriculture, because there is greater synergy among the three types of organizational goals. Like reuse centers, community gardens are sites where the potential positive connections, in addition to their challenges and limitations, can be explored. Furthermore, because community gardens exist as a network of informal voluntary organizations, formal nonprofit organizations, and local government agencies, the study of community gardening provides an opportunity to understand better how localism functions in a civil-society context and how conflicts and partnerships between civil society and the local state operate. By exploring such organizational and political issues, it is possible to examine how the politics of neoliberalism affect and are affected by this aspect of the local food industry.

There is a small scholarly literature on community gardening in the United States that includes some excellent historical overviews and good case studies. For example, the historical work of Malve Von Hassell and Laura Lawson is consistent with the general argument that the study of localism should attend carefully to its high degree of variability. They have shown that the motivations behind the ebb and flow of support for community gardens from local and national elites varied significantly, from concerns with food provisioning for the poor in the early twentieth century to general food provisioning in the form of Victory Gardens during World War II. Their research dates the present era of community gardening to the urban activism of the 1960s, when a mixture of civil rights, grassroots community development, and environmental concerns led to a new wave of gardening.[5]

An important finding in the literature on community gardens that is consistent with the historical studies and relevant to the broader discussion of justice, sustainability, and localism is that the motivations for joining community gardens are not always centered on food production. In a study of community gardens in San Francisco, the geographer John Ferris and his colleagues delineated gardens based on leisure, education, food production for sale, crime diversion and work training, healing and therapy, ecological restoration, and other goals. In some cases, community gardening is linked to nutrition education and promoted by the Women, Infants, and Children Program of the American federal government in a manner reminiscent of government promotion of community gardening in the early twentieth century. A survey of the reasons for starting community gardens in the United Kingdom also indicated that food provisioning was only one motivation among many. Education, community development, leisure, skills and training, health issues, and protection of an area all ranked higher. The researchers also found that the motivations changed over the history of a garden. A similar study in upstate New York found that health benefits, the taste of fresh food, and the enjoyment of the open space were more important considerations than providing a source of food, but food provisioning was a positive motivation for 55 percent of the respondents.[6]

One might conclude from the surveys that community gardeners are not primarily concerned with food provisioning, and therefore that community gardens should not be considered when examining the relationship between food and justice in the distributive sense of gaining more food for the poor. However, justice for poor and working-class people includes many issues other than food security. For example, the upstate New York study reported that the development of a community garden led to a more cohesive neighborhood that developed a neighborhood association and a "neighborhood watch" program for crime prevention. The neighborhood also organized to keep a large supermarket from leaving, and it developed a park with a playground. Likewise, a study of low-income community gardens in Philadelphia concluded that the gardens led to stronger neighborhood ties that in turn led to a better ability to address urban problems. In low-income neighborhoods in New York City, gardens became centers of neighborhood activity, including community gatherings, children's activities, health fairs, voter registration drives, and community activism. Of course, the record is mixed; owing to the high crime and theft of food in some neighborhoods, some gardens have restricted access, and in some cases a few individuals have taken control of the supposedly shared, quasi-public space.[7]

The research presented here builds on the existing literature by focusing on environmental and justice goals in urban community gardens and urban nonprofit farms. I did not have the resources to study all major community gardening programs in the United States, so I and the graduate student researchers focused on the gardens in the Northeast, Midwest, and West. We examined a range of cities with different climates, land values, and rates of poverty. We conducted interviews of representatives of community gardens in Boston, Cleveland, Denver, Detroit, Philadelphia, Portland, Sacramento, San Francisco, and Seattle. We also compiled a case study on the city of New York based on existing research and documents, which were extensive, and we identified urban farms that were the basis of additional inquiry into the relationship between localism and social justice.[8]

Sustainability, Justice, and Community Gardening

In general, community gardens are examples of sustainable horticulture, and city governments increasingly recognize their value as part of an overall strategy of improving both neighborhoods and urban green spaces. Many community gardeners utilize composting and refrain from using synthetic pesticides and fertilizers, and consequently there is generally a fairly close connection here between local control of food production and sustainable horticultural methods of production. Where the gardens occupy old brownfields (such as abandoned building lots), city governments or university extension services sometimes provide the resources to test the soil and to remediate it where it has proven toxic. However, in unofficial "guerilla" gardens such assistance is not always available, and there is a risk of importing soil-born toxins into the food if the people do not use raised beds with new soil. In Denver, Portland, Sacramento, and Seattle, we learned that the large immigrant populations sometimes used conventional fertilizers, and community gardening programs attempted to educate them in more sustainable practices. However, those cases appeared to be exceptional, and in general community gardening coincided with relatively sustainable methods of horticulture. Although usually not certified as organic (the certification process would generate an unnecessary expense for food that is produced mostly for consumption by the gardeners), the gardens were using techniques that were considerably less toxic than conventional agriculture and often less toxic than organic standards allow. The very visible tension of the "local trap"—that is, the tradeoff between purchasing produce from locally owned farms and purchasing produce grown with sustainable or organic techniques—is much less prominent in community gardening than in small farms that sell to local markets. Already, then, there is reason for caution in interpreting one side of local agricultural networks as an exemplar of food localism as a whole.

With regard to the issue of justice, one of the primary problems facing community gardens is land tenure. In the de-industrialized cities of the

Northeast and the Midwest, many community gardens began as informal occupations of vacant lots. Often the city owned the property as a result of a foreclosure for nonpayment of taxes, and city government programs eventually legalized some occupations by providing leases for the gardens. In Cleveland the city formalized the relationship through its land bank program, which leased empty lots to gardeners. However, even where city governments officially recognized the informal occupations or otherwise leased land to gardeners, they retained the right to revoke the leases when land values rose. In cities where land values were very high, most of the community gardens were located on public lands or on lots held by land trusts and nonprofit organizations. As I will discuss in the next section, many present-day arrangements are the results of intense political struggles over a city government's right to sell its land and the citizens' right to use city-owned land. The conflict is important because it draws attention to the general localist concern with sovereignty in the sense of local ownership. In this case the "local" of local ownership is defined as a neighborhood's access right to a green space as well as its right to demand that public lands not be privatized.[9]

Although the sovereignty issue is central, community gardening is also directly concerned with distributive justice. Information about the class and ethnic composition of community gardens was not easy to obtain, but in the cities that we studied the urban middle class was not the primary beneficiary. For example, in Cleveland and Denver about 80 percent of the community gardens were in low-income neighborhoods, and in Cleveland about two-thirds of the gardeners were Latino or African-American. Even in relatively affluent Seattle, 37 of the city's 70 community gardens were in low-income neighborhoods, and 16 were located on public housing land. In most of the other cities community gardens also could be found on public housing land. In addition to the food provisioning benefits of community gardening, our research supported earlier studies' suggestions that community gardens developed neighborhood networks, reduced crime rates, promoted public health, provided a setting for food education, and otherwise enhanced the civic culture of a neighborhood.[10]

In addition to serving low-income neighborhoods directly, community gardens often contributed to broader urban food security networks. In

Seattle some of the gardens had plots specifically dedicated for food banks, and community gardens as a whole donated about 7–10 tons of food per year to food banks. In Cleveland gardeners had an "adopt a family" program, and in Philadelphia the food security organization Philabundance helped run a community garden that provided food to the hungry. Programs with creative names—Lettuce Link, Share the Harvest, Produce for People, and so on—connected the harvest of community gardens to homeless shelters and food banks. Portland had a Food Policy Council, an advisory group for the city government that drew together a wide range of stakeholder groups. Sacramento had a food charter, which affirmed the right of all citizens to be free from hunger and included community gardens as an integral part of the overall strategy for food security.[11]

Although community gardens combined local sovereignty in the sense of land tenure rights with distributive justice in the form of food security and neighborhood empowerment, they did not always do so equally. In some cases there were conflicts between longstanding members of community gardens and new members, and we occasionally heard complaints that longstanding members took up more than their fair share of plots. In some cities there were waiting lists for people who wanted to garden but could not obtain a plot, and San Francisco had developed a policy to ensure fair treatment of those on waiting lists. However, by far the greater social justice problem confronting community gardens was attempting to preserve them when confronted with renewed interest in the land from developers. The smaller squatter gardens, which appear to be disproportionately held by the poorest citizens, were the most vulnerable. Larger, more established, and "better-connected" gardens were better able to mobilize resources to ensure their longevity and protection. Nonprofit organizations that faced difficult decisions as to where to invest limited resources tended to select the larger gardens first.[12]

Leaders of community gardening initiatives were often frustrated by the lack of resources available to them from city governments, and some of them bemoaned the failure to utilize community gardening more thoroughly as a mechanism for achieving goals of both enhanced sustainability and justice. However, the shortcomings are not a good reason to ignore the potential of community gardening as a localist institution in which various practices oriented toward building a more sustainable and equitable society can converge. Certainly, the convergence occurs with much less tension in community gardens than in the networks of suburban consumers and small farmers that have occupied most of the attention in the agrifood literature on localism.

Neoliberalism, Gardeners, and Governments

In addition to drawing out tensions among local ownership, environmental, and social justice goals, the agrifood literature has developed a broader critique of the politics of localism. The agrifood scholar E. Melanie DuPuis and her colleagues argue that "relocalization appears to be not in resistance to neoliberal globalization but an intrinsic part of it," and consequently "localism is not an 'innocent' term" (2006: 256–257). Because neoliberal policies have led to "upscaling of power and . . . downscaling of responsibility," localism represents a "dangerous political bargain [that] can lead to the dismantling of hard-fought rights for state protection" (ibid.: 256–257). DuPuis and colleagues suggest that the focus of localism on developing local markets plays into two neoliberal tenets : deregulation and reliance on market.[13]

The critique of DuPuis and colleagues brings out two related issues regarding localism and neoliberalism. First, to the extent that localist politics do not involve political mobilization directed at the federal government level, localism may fall prey to the devolutionary politics of neoliberalism, which shifts responsibility for social welfare and environmental protection to state and local governments and often does so without providing adequate funding and authority. Second, to the extent that localism involves shifting political action from government to the private sector via the politics of consumption, localism can fall prey to the privatization politics of neoliberalism. For example, middle-class consumers may think that they are doing something politically valuable when they board their hybrid vehicles and head to the farmers' market to buy food from a local organic farmer, or when they stop at the food coop to buy fair-trade products from a cooperative in Latin America, but are they fooling themselves? In other words, to the extent that socially responsible consumption comes to displace political action from a government orientation toward a marketplace orientation, the politics of localism involves a reproduction of two main tenets of neoliberalism: devolution and privatization.

An analysis that links neoliberalism and localism can be taken only so far before it runs into other political strands within the localist movement, such as liberalism and even radical political thought. As I argued in chapter 1, complex political phenomena such as "buy local" campaigns cannot be reduced easily to expressions of existing political ideologies. On the one hand, there is a way in which the tag of neoliberalism can be affixed to the campaigns, because they shift political attention from states to markets. However, as I noted in the previous chapter, "buy local" campaigns are often connected to other kinds of political activity. One could interpret the campaigns as market-based jiu-jitsu within a neoliberal order that is part of a broader strategy that also includes government-oriented reforms at various geographical scales. In other words, one could argue that the consumer subsumes the citizen, and therefore displaces political action, but from another perspective one could argue that the citizen subsumes the consumer, and therefore treats consumption as one more avenue for political action. One should exercise caution in making blanket statements about the politics of localism, especially regarding its relationship with neoliberalism. Although the analysis of DuPuis and colleagues might be applied to the middle-class green consumers who populate farmers' markets, can their analysis be extended to community gardens? Are community gardeners also captured by the logic of neoliberalism, or is something else going on?

Certainly, the politics of food security within the United States have undergone a localization process (again, as I suggested at the outset, a historical change that should be distinguished from localism as a movement), and the localization of food security was at least partly caused by the devolution of welfare-state responsibilities from the federal level to the state and local levels. Indeed, we found that some cities used federal Community Development Block Grant programs to support community gardening efforts, and in this sense community gardening has benefited from the devolutionary politics of neoliberalism. Furthermore, the devolution of welfare-state responsibilities has been accompanied by their privatization, in this case the shift of food security responsibilities from government at any level to networks of government agencies, individual donors, corporate benefactors, and nonprofit food banks. One might conclude that community gardening is a neoliberal's dream response to the problem of hunger and welfare: if you cannot get it from a food bank, then grow your own food, but do not come crying to the federal government, because hunger is no longer our responsibility.[14]

However, the analysis of the relationship between neoliberalism and community gardening would be seriously flawed if it were to stop at the recognition of the links among urban agriculture, food insecurity, and the devolution and privatization of the welfare state. Instead, it is necessary to delve into the complex relationships of conflict and cooperation that can occur between governments and community gardeners in the context of general trends in which neoliberalism has become an influential political ideology. This perspective makes it possible to find ways in which localism can also be a target of neoliberal policies and configured as an anti-neoliberal political movement. Perhaps the best example is the case of community gardening in New York City under Mayor Rudolph Giuliani.

During the 1970s, in what the geographer David Harvey describes as one of the first experiments in neoliberalism, New York City went bankrupt, was refused assistance from the federal government, and was forced into accepting budget cuts that broke unions and cut social services. In retrospect, Harvey suggests, those events might be compared with the structural adjustment programs that were later forced on developing countries that defaulted on their debts. The resulting decline in land values literally created the space for community gardens to grow, often in the gaps between buildings on vacant land or on lots destroyed by arson. Many community gardens that emerged during this period in New York and in other de-industrializing cities were unofficial "guerilla" or squatter gardens. The gardeners then lobbied the city for formal recognition, and in 1978 the city created Operation Green Thumb, which offered leases for gardens. However, the leases were revocable, and the stage was set for a struggle over land rights. Although the city claimed legal sovereignty over the land in the sense of a right to sell it, the people who had occupied the land came to see themselves as having another type of sovereignty over the same land: the right to ongoing use.[15]

Giuliani, who became mayor in 1994, included privatization as one of his goals, and in 1999 he put 114 community gardens up for public auction for sale to real estate developers. The community gardeners mobilized various forms of resistance, and, as the geographers Christopher Smith and Hilda Kurtz argue, they also mobilized at broader levels of geographical scale than their local neighborhood networks. For example, they formed citywide coalitions, used the Internet to bring in sources of support from the outside, and prevailed upon New York State's Attorney General, Eliot Spitzer, to file a lawsuit against the city. In response to the growing opposition movement and with the intent to split it, the Giuliani administration reframed the issue from the neoliberal politics of privatization and real estate development to the liberal politics of affordable housing for the poor: the community garden lands would now have a new use. At the last minute two land-trust organizations purchased the gardens, and another round of the many battles that would occur in many cities between development interests and public-use interests for the space of community gardens drew to a close.[16]

In this case, community gardeners mobilized to oppose a neoliberal political program, and, as Smith and Kurtz argue, their mobilization strategically employed various levels of geographical scale, from the neighborhood to citywide coalition politics to the state government and even out-of-state supporters. Although one might argue that the result (ownership of the gardens by nonprofit organizations) still represented a type of privatization, the outcome was quite distant from the original prospect of private ownership by real estate developers, which would have entailed destruction of the gardens. The outcome preserved the civic function of community gardens as green spaces that grow relationships, food, and, occasionally, grassroots politics. The actions of the community gardeners can hardly be described as reproducing neoliberal politics. Rather, in this case community gardeners were clearly opposed to the neoliberal policies of their mayor. In other words, this case may be another example of the politics of "reflexive localism" that DuPuis and colleagues have sought to articulate for localism.[17]

How widespread is such an oppositional relationship between community gardeners and urban governments? Our research can only begin to answer the question, but we uncovered several similar conflicts between gardeners and city governments' plans to privatize the land for development. For example, during the 1970s and the 1980s, federal Community Development Block Grants allowed the city of Boston to fund the Revival Program, which paid for the costs of starting community gardens. However, by the 1980s the city faced financial deficits, and the Boston Natural Areas Fund purchased many of the Revival gardens. In 1986 a community garden in Chinatown was bulldozed for low-income housing, and in other parts of Boston developers were converting single-family homes into condominiums and driving up land values. Although no intense public conflict comparable to the one in New York occurred in Boston, a grassroots housing and gardening coalition emerged in recognition of the growing threat that development posed to community gardens. The coalition developed a consensus for preserving gardening and building low-income housing in the South End neighborhood. With support from the city and assistance from the Trust for Public Lands, the South End/Lower Roxbury Open Space Land Trust was formed. The solution of nonprofit ownership via land trusts became a model for other cities, including New York.[18]

Different types of conflicts and solutions emerged in other cities. In Sacramento the state government decided not to renew the lease on the 30-year-old Ron Mandela Community Garden. The gardeners protested the decision to no avail, and in 2003 the police arrested gardeners who had chained themselves together under an apricot tree in the garden. Ignoring the negative publicity that came from repression of the civil disobedience, the state government went ahead and constructed a building on the site, but it left a small portion of the land for a garden or a green space. Two other community gardens in Sacramento were also lost to housing developments. Those events spurred action from community gardeners, and eventually the Capital Area Development Authority donated land to the city for the first community garden on city land. A few years later, the city government hired the leader of the Sacramento Area Community Gardens Coalition to become its first community gardens manager. By 2008, Sacramento had five community gardens. This case draws attention to a resolution of the conflict that involves moving gardens from one government-owned property to another.[19]

Even in Seattle, where environmental considerations have a powerful presence in urban politics and where the city government dedicates five and a half staff positions to community gardens (known locally as P-Patches), conflicts can emerge. An example is described by Ray Schutte, president of the P-Patch Trust:

> The city was going to sell Bradner Park to develop it into condominiums. The activists said "no" and developed a plan to turn it into Bradner Gardens Park with a P-Patch, and the Trust had an involvement with it. People were at Parks Commission meetings, lined up out the door to speak, filling the hall at city council, in the press, and on TV.

Not only did the park remain in city hands; it was renamed Bradner Gardens Park. Furthermore, a new city ordinance barred the city from selling park land unless it first found another property of equal value in the neighborhood. In another case, the city opted to replace a large community garden with a golf course, but it found other land for the garden, and the leader of the garden with whom I spoke seemed satisfied with the outcome.[20]

In Portland, Oregon, another city with a strong reputation for concern with environmental issues, the city government mandated in 2005 that all departments rank their priorities of expenditure as a first step in finding a solution to a fiscal crisis. When news reached the public that the Parks and Recreation Department had ranked community gardening as its lowest priority, Friends of Portland Community Gardens mobilized substantial opposition to the plan. Although community gardens were not threatened directly, as had occurred with Mayor Giuliani's planned auction, Portland's city council responded to the public outcry by mandating that community centers, pools, and community gardens be exempted from budget cuts.[21]

Even in Cleveland, a city that has many abandoned lots, pressures on public land from developers has emerged, albeit much later than in Boston or New York. In 2006 a community garden on West 117th Street was removed in order to build a Target store, and gardening advocates noted with some concern that five other gardens had been lost to development during the preceding 5 years. In response to the emerging threat, gardening advocates mobilized, and the city council passed the country's first ordinance to designate community gardens as a separate zoning category that would require a public process for replacing them.[22]

In brief, our case studies suggest that, although Mayor Giuliani's plan to auction off more than 100 community gardens was the most dramatic and widely publicized example of the attempted sacrifice of community gardens to development interests, city governments continually weigh the relative costs and benefits of privatizing publicly held land on which community gardens rest. The strength of the mobilization of community gardeners in New York and in other cities suggests that a city development official may want to think twice before threatening a large and established community garden. In cities (e.g., Denver and Seattle) where there is a good working relationship between the community gardening advocacy organization and the city government, the city generally finds an alternative site for the gardeners. However, where there is no such relationship, or where there is only a weak umbrella organization, gardeners may find themselves on the losing end of a development battle. For example, a community gardening leader for Detroit told us that if there was a conflict between development and gardening, the city's planning department generally opted for development. Likewise, in Los Angeles community gardeners lost one of the largest urban "farms" in the country; after 3 years of protests, the gardeners were evicted and the land was bulldozed.[23]

Support from City Governments

So far this analysis has brought out the potential conflict between city governments and gardeners over what the geographer Lynn Staeheli and her colleagues refer to as different concepts of land rights and what I suggest might be viewed as one aspect of the general concern with sovereignty in localist politics. In the examples discussed above, the localist concern with sovereignty in the sense of local ownership and control coincides fairly closely with the social justice and environmental goals of preserving green spaces, growing food in sustainable ways, and improvements in low-income neighborhoods. However, our research also suggests that the relationships between gardeners and city governments are quite variable and not always conflictual. Usually there is at least one department within a city government that provides some support to community gardening, often in cooperation with a university-based extension service and in partnership with nonprofit organizations.

Because the city may give with its left hand of neighborhood or parks departments and take away with its right hand of economic development offices, the relationship between community gardening organizations and city governments is complex. A few examples provide some sense of the variation, the strengths, and the weaknesses of the partnerships that have evolved.[24]

Boston has one of the most developed organizational fields for community gardening. There are several well-established nonprofit organizations that support community gardening in the city. In 1997 eleven of the organizations came together under the umbrella of Garden Futures to ensure baseline support for all gardens regardless of ownership, and in 2002 Garden Futures merged with the Boston Natural Areas Network. Given the high property values in the city, the Boston organizations have helped to secure land tenure through land trust organizations. As in other cities with high land values, most of the community gardens are located on land controlled by the nonprofit trusts or on public land, including schoolyards, parks, and public housing land. The city government supports community gardening through its Department of Neighborhood Development, which administers Community Development Block Grant funds that allow conversion and capital improvements of gardens. The Parks Department also partners with the city's Environment Department to administer a small grants program that assists with garden maintenance and to maintain a resource guide. However, Betsy Johnson, both a local gardening leader and the former executive director of the American Community Gardening Association, noted:

The Parks Department does not help us, aside from their small grant program for community gardens. They've given out up to a total of $25,000, I think. Last year it was less than $10,000, and this year it must be less than $5000. . . . The South End Land Trust manages as many open space parcels as the Parks Department does in the Lower Roxbury and South End neighborhood, and we get no tax dollars for operations.

As a result of the limited support from the Parks Department, the gardeners have had to rely on support from the nonprofit sector and their own fundraising efforts.[25]

In Seattle there is much more extensive support from the city government—arguably more than in any other American city. In general the city government has worked closely with the nonprofit support organization, the P-Patch Trust, to relocate land that is targeted for development. In 2000 the city council increased its support of community gardening by adopting the P-Patch Strategic Plan, which includes the goal of adding four new gardens per year. Seattle's community gardening program was originally located in the Health and Human Services Department, but it was transferred to the Neighborhoods Department, which maintains a staff to assist community gardens. The Parks Department had been unfriendly to community gardens, but by 2005 its plans for park development included community gardening.[26]

In Philadelphia there is no department of neighborhoods, but under Mayor John Street (mayor from 2000 to 2008) the Neighborhood Transformation Initiative promoted green space improvements, a program that was subsequently discontinued. Philadelphia's strong nonprofit organizations, including the Neighborhood Gardens Association/A Philadelphia Land Trust, have linked the development of community gardens with neighborhood revitalization and urban greening efforts. Since 1974, Philadelphia Green, a project of the Pennsylvania Horticultural Society, has supported the development of community gardens as part of its broader mission of urban greening and horticultural development. Philadelphia Green also has organized neighborhood associations to work with the city's Recreation Department to help them maintain and improve parks; one type of improvement is building gardens on parkland. In 2003 and 2004 the city contracted with Philadelphia Green to develop programs to clean up and maintain vacant lots, to develop general greening programs in targeted neighborhoods, and to assist in citywide greening for streets, parks, new community gardens, and commercial corridors. In general, substantial nonprofit support and partnerships with the city have helped make community gardening a vibrant part of the city's improvements of empty lots and existing green spaces.[27]

Portland's and San Francisco's parks departments have played more prominent roles in providing support for community gardening than their counterparts in Boston, Seattle, and Philadelphia. Most of the community gardens in Portland are on land controlled by the city's Parks and Recreation Department or on the grounds of public schools. The city government also pays for one full-time staff person and has a budget of about $200,000 for community gardening. Although the extent of support was higher than in other cities, it was still inadequate to meet the long waiting lists of people who wanted to have a community gardening plot, and the gardeners have had to mobilize on occasion to maintain political support. Two advocacy organizations have been influential. Friends of Portland Community Gardens was founded in 1985 in response to threatened budget cuts, and Growing Gardens provided educational programs for children and youth, as well as assistance to home gardeners and some community gardens.[28]

In San Francisco, squatter or guerilla gardens are rare (because of the high value of the land), and most of the gardens are on land owned by the city's Parks and Recreation Department or other public land. For many years the city government contracted with the nonprofit San Francisco League of Urban Gardeners to manage community gardens. By the early 2000s the city contract of about $1.6 million allowed the organization to employ 70 teenagers and 50 part-time and full-time staff in its job training programs. In 2004 the city decided not to renew the contract for various reasons, including alleged participation of the organization in a political campaign and lack of successful job training. The city then took the management of the gardens back into its Parks and Recreation Department, and a new organization, the San Francisco Garden Resource Organization, emerged to advocate for community gardening. The voters also approved a ballot proposition that called for the city to set aside $150,000 in annual funds for community gardens.[29]

In summary: City governments' support for community gardens ranged from providing full-time staff and other resources (as in Seattle) to nearly token support (as in Detroit). Likewise, support from the nonprofit sector ranged from a variety of well-developed and well-networked organizations including land trusts (as in New York and Boston) to a small association of community gardeners (as in Sacramento). City governments generally provide some support for community gardens, but the amount of financial support and the type of city government department that is involved vary widely. (See table 5.1.) In San Francisco and Portland, the parks departments have taken on the responsibility of stewardship of community gardening, whereas in other cities the responsibility has fallen more to neighborhood or community development departments. Public schools sometimes welcome community gardens onto their

Table 5.1
City government departments and community gardens.

	Neighborhood department or division	Parks and/or recreation department
Boston	Block grants	Small grants program, resource guide, gardens in some parks
Cleveland	Block grants, assistance program, land bank program	
Denver	Grant for seeds and transplants	Parks master plan, rental of land
Detroit		Seedlings assistance
Philadelphia	Neighborhood initiative in mayor's office, block grants	Park maintenance partnerships, gardens in some parks
Portland		Dedicated staff, half of gardens in parks
Sacramento		Dedicated staff, gardens in some parks
San Francisco		Dedicated staff, gardens in >40 parks
Seattle	Dedicated staff	Gardens in 20 parks

land, and other departments also sometimes play a role. For example, in Cleveland police officers have organized several gardens as part of their community watch programs, and Portland has a Food Policy Council in the Office of Sustainable Development.[30]

Parks departments tend to view community gardening with some ambivalence. Parks department leaders often worry that adding maintenance of community gardens to their busy schedules can cause a "mission drift" away from the main goal of recreation. At first it may be difficult to build partnerships with parks departments, but it is possible to convert opposition or recalcitrance into support, especially if the parks department leaders see benefits from community gardens in park safety and maintenance. Ray Schutte, the president of the P-Patch Trust, commented on how the relationship has changed in Seattle:

Up until very recently the Parks and Recreation Department was unfriendly toward P-Patch. When building a new park, they never thought of putting in a P-Patch, even though it is a multi-use property. Now they often think about using a portion of the park as a P-Patch, and they're even thinking about using a portion of the parks' funds to buy a property and turn it into a P-Patch. In the last three or four years this adversarial relationship has really changed. We kept a very friendly relationship with them. Several new parks have been developed by community groups that include a P-Patch within them, such as the Trolley Hill Park. The gardeners share a tool shed with the Parks Department, and they help maintain the park. So the symbiotic relationships developed, and they've come to accept that a P-Patch is an acceptable use.[31]

The case studies suggest that community gardening leaders do not turn their backs on the government and try to seek social change only through the market and nonprofit sector; instead, they continually press city governments to enhance services and to include community gardening in plans and budgets. The politics of localism in this case appear to be closer to liberalism, in the sense of advocacy of government-oriented service provisioning, than to neoliberalism. Furthermore, in view of the increasing use of parks, schoolyards, public housing yards, and other public lands for community gardens in cities with high land values, one might even make the case that community gardening is to some degree an example of local socialism. However, public ownership is only one avenue for securing land tenure for community gardens; nonprofit organizations have stepped in to provide a mixture of both advocacy and (in the absence of government service provisioning) some services. The role of the nonprofit sector relative to the government is quite variable.

One might argue that even if community gardening organizations are heavily involved in government-oriented politics, they operate only at the level of local governments, and consequently on that ground they play into the devolutionary politics of neoliberal localization. However, the American Community Gardening Association (ACGA) addresses policy issues at the federal level. For example, when in 2007 the United States Farm Bill (a large piece of legislation that is passed every 5 years that allocates money for farmers and agricultural programs) was undergoing reauthorization, the ACGA called for its members to support efforts to include community gardening in the Farm Bill. The ACGA also worked closely with the Urban Agriculture Committee of the

Community Food Security Coalition, and it provided general information to local community gardening organizations on local policy interventions, such as how to develop a community gardening ordinance.[32]

In conclusion: Community gardening in the United States has been
affected in numerous ways by neoliberal policies. The rise of food insecurity, the availability of federal Block Grant programs, the decline of
employment opportunities, and the degradation of urban neighborhoods
are all effects of policies that reduced the federal government's responsibilities for the poor and encouraged the trade liberalization that facilitated de-industrialization. Community gardening operates in a neoliberal
political environment, but it would be a distortion to claim that this type
of localism is an expression of neoliberalism. Rather, community gardening presents a coherent vision of how to link the goals of local sovereignty, sustainability, and distributive justice, and it does so by constantly
working with (and occasionally against) governments to demand greater
support, including the use of public lands for gardens.

Urban Farms

Community gardening by no means exhausts the range of urban agriculture in the United States. Backyard private gardens far outnumber public
community gardens, and developers are beginning to realize that shared
private gardens, such as rooftop gardens in high-rise condominiums and
gardens for residents in new housing developments, increase the value
of the real estate and the speed with which it sells. Another form of urban
agriculture is the entrepreneurial, for-profit urban farm, which often
occupies a highly specialized product niche that may include food
processing. Yet another form of urban agriculture, and one that often
addresses issues of food insecurity and community development, is the
nonprofit urban farm.[33]

While doing background research for this chapter, I visited two successful urban farms. One was the Zenger Urban Agricultural Park,
located on 6 acres of city-owned land in the southeastern part of Portland, Oregon, where it preserves one of the remaining green spaces in
the city. A nonprofit organization manages the former dairy farm and
supervises multiple uses: part of the land is leased to a local farmer, who

adds the produce as part of her community-supported agriculture subscription; a youth program provides educational tours for schoolchildren; and part of the land is used as a community garden for low-income immigrants. The organization also provides "scholarship" (pro-bono) shares in the farm produce for low-income families. A similar nonprofit farm, the Soil Born Urban Agriculture Project, operates in Sacramento on leased land and land owned by the city government. Supported by community-supported agriculture (CSA) shares and grants, the farm offers educational programs for middle-school and high-school students; it also has an apprenticeship program for college students and graduates who wish to become farmers. The two founders of the farm also helped to develop a farmers' market in a low-income neighborhood.[34]

Not all such projects are successful, as my visit to the Alemany Youth Farm in San Francisco revealed. Located next to the Alemany Housing Project, the 4-acre urban farm served low-income youth from the housing project and from other neighborhoods. At its peak in the early 2000s, the farm had a budget of about $500,000, employed 30 teenagers at wages above the mandated legal minimum, and offered them training in sustainable agriculture and access to classes at the City College of San Francisco. One measure of success was the fact that many of the teenagers who ordinarily would not have gone to college finished the program and went on to college. At its peak the Youth Farm received national and international attention, but it was overgrown with weeds when I visited it. A particularly sad sight was the greenhouse, which was emptied of plants and showed signs of use for illicit activities. The farm became defunct as a result of the restructuring that occurred when the city government revoked its contract with the San Francisco Urban League of Gardeners. Without the funding for youth jobs, it was impossible to attract low-income teenagers and to keep the farm running. It was also hard to attract middle-class residents who lived up the hill from the site, because they were afraid of crime. (The farm was adjacent to the public housing project.) However, by 2007 there was an effort by "guerilla gardeners" to revitalize the site, and the city's Recreation and Parks Department was discussing a lease agreement with the local residents.[35]

In other cities that we studied, there were also examples of urban farms. In Boston, a shelter for pregnant and homeless women called the

ReVision House runs a one-acre organic farm that provides residents and members of the CSA with fresh food. The farm has an internship program that helps young mothers to develop basic job skills and knowledge of organic farming, and it offers educational programs for local youth. Boston's Food Project provides training for more than 100 youths at its lots in the city and at its 31-acre farm in Lincoln. Food is sold through membership shares and farmers' markets, and some is donated to local shelters. Another example is the nonprofit organization Denver Urban Gardens, which operates the 130-acre DeLaney Community Farm in the city of Aurora. The farm offers CSA shares (including scholarship shares) and educational programs. In Detroit, a partnership between the Capuchin Soup Kitchen and the Gleaners Community Food Bank launched the Earth Works Urban Farm, which offers CSA shares, food for the hungry, and educational programs for schoolchildren.[36]

As a type of local food organization, the nonprofit urban (and suburban) farm is situated somewhere between the community garden and the small, locally oriented, for-profit rural farm. Like the community garden, the nonprofit farm often mixes missions of community development, education, and food provisioning for the food insecure, but like the for-profit farm, the nonprofit farm derives a significant portion of its revenue stream from sales. The sales can include CSA membership shares and direct sales to nonmembers of fresh food and processed products such as jams and cider. But the social enterprise also operates like a traditional nonprofit organization in that it also derives revenue from voluntary work, small donations, and grants.[37]

In view of the appeal that a revenue stream from sales of produce has for a nonprofit organization, it seems likely that we will see more nonprofit urban farms in the future. A range of organizational forms is likely to emerge: independent organizations that, like the Zenger Farm, include community gardening on some of their land as part of their mission; community gardening organizations and other nonprofit organizations that, like those in Boston and Denver, expand into farming; and coalitions of food-security organizations that, as in Detroit, come together around a shared urban farm project. As the projects develop, the boundaries between an urban farm and a community garden are likely to become increasingly blurry. This was already the case for the Alemany

Youth Farm and for community gardens that hosted youth training activities and sold some of their products.

As land values increase and central cities are redeveloped, the era of informal land tenure on vacant and abandoned lots will draw to a close in Detroit, Philadelphia, and Cleveland, much as it already has in East Coast and West Coast cities where land values are high. Community gardening will continue to undergo formalization under the protective wing of either land trusts and other nonprofit organizations or city government departments. In either case, the neighborhood dimension of community gardening as a meeting ground for social interaction, fresh food production, recreation, and politicking is likely to begin to interact more with formal organizational goals that frame community gardens as opportunities for youth programs, neighborhood development, local sustainability, and educational activities. The winning of land tenure on a city park, in a schoolyard, or on land owned by a nonprofit organization may come with a *quid pro quo* of assisting the city and nonprofit organizations in their missions. Community gardens may be reframed as not only great places to grow food, develop neighborhoods, and green the city but also great places to teach children multiplication (using rows of vegetables) and to develop job skills for teenagers. Those skills can include record keeping, observation, and analysis, but they might also be expanded to include the entrepreneurial activities that are more characteristics of nonprofit urban farms. Although one cannot predict that community gardening in the future will begin to approximate the nonprofit urban farm, the structural conditions are in place for such a transition to occur.

Conclusion

The forms of urban agriculture studied here occur largely in civil society, including informal associations (gardens) and formal organizations (nonprofits), but community gardening programs also involve substantial interaction with local governments. Furthermore, nonprofit farms have one foot in the world of sustainable local agricultural networks (the world of farmers' markets, small farms, CSA shares, retail food coops, and locally oriented restaurants), but they fare better on labor issues than some of the locally owned for-profit farms. The problems raised by agrifood researchers for the local agricultural networks do not extend well to the case of urban agriculture. The tradeoff between sustainability and localism—so evident in many farmers' markets, where local, fresh food may be conventionally grown and consumers can be faced with the choice between local and organic—is much less evident in the world of urban agriculture, which is all local and, as our interviews indicated, mostly sustainable in the sense of using composting, organic fertilizers, and nontoxic pest-control methods. Likewise, much more than the for-profit independent retail industry but closer to the reuse centers studied in the previous chapter, the case of localism in the urban setting exhibits much less tension between localist and social justice goals. In fact, the cases reviewed here, combined with the examples of reuse centers discussed in the previous chapter, suggest that it may be easier to find an approximation of sustainability, justice, and local ownership in the nonprofit sector than in the small-business sector. The gray zone between nonprofit charitable and environmental organizations and for-profit independent retail businesses and farms—that is, the growing sector of nonprofit social enterprises and for-benefit social businesses—also deserves further attention from social scientists who study the potential linkages among localism, sustainability, and justice.

Another conclusion from this chapter is that tacit participation in the politics of neoliberalism, such as by turning to markets rather than to governments for political solutions, is much less evident in a field that is largely one of voluntary, civil-society activity. In the case of community gardening, the politics have tended to be situated in the traditional liberal frameworks of requesting resources from governments—mostly local but, through the umbrella organization, also federal—and demanding that governments under the spell of neoliberalism live up to their purported democratic mission of representing the people rather than development interests. A research strategy that attends to the varieties of localism, even within the field of agrifood localism, offers significant benefits for building general theories of localism.

6

Local Energy and the Public Sector

In the United States, the "appropriate technology," "home power," and "back to the land" movements left a legacy of off-grid power production, experiments in distributed renewable energy, and green building innovations. Some of the projects associated with the movements involved local ownership and import substitution, but in general they remained relatively small and specialized. In this chapter I focus on another side of localism and energy, one which has greater promise for achieving a significant effect on aggregate consumption and can address issues of sustainability and inequality. In the first section I will explore three models of localism and grid-based electricity: public power, community choice, and the energy-conservation utility. In the second section I will examine the greening of public transportation, specifically bus transportation, and its connections with localism. Because at the local level most electricity and public transportation is supplied through government agencies or heavily regulated public utilities, the industry is much more oriented toward the role of government than the retail and food industries. As a result, this chapter helps to develop a better understanding of how localism works in the public sector.[1]

Localism and Electricity

The peer-reviewed literature on local ownership and electricity is less well developed than the literature of the agrifood field. The largest cluster of research involves the practical problem of why there is so much grassroots opposition to wind farms and what kinds of intervention might increase public support. A common assumption is that opposition groups are primarily worried about the visual impact of wind farms, especially when the planned sites are located in scenic areas, such as Cape Cod. Also often cited is local concern with environmental impacts of the projects, such as the effects on birds and, for aquatic wind farms, on marine life. The public policy analyst Jeremy Firestone and his colleagues found that opponents can name a variety of concerns, including possible negative effects on property values, bird deaths, electricity rates, and, for wind farms on marine sites, marine life, fishing, and boating. In the Cape Cod case, opponents said that their opinions might change if they were to have new information that indicated that electricity rates would not increase, marine life and fishing would not be harmed, jobs would accrue to the area, and the region would benefit directly from the electricity production. Surprisingly, only 4 percent of the respondents mentioned climate change when giving a reason for or against the wind farm proposal.[2]

The Dutch psychologist and energy researcher Maartin Wolsink has noted the paradox that public support for renewable energy is high, whereas local acceptance of wind farms is much more difficult to obtain. His analysis is significant for the broader study of localism because his research led him to link the problem of wind farm opposition with local ownership and control. In a comparative study of acceptance in Europe, Wolsink et al. found that the implementation of wind power plans was affected not only by planning and financial support but also by the relative strength of landscape protection organizations and local ownership patterns. In Spain, Scotland, England, and Wales, the wind industry is dominated by large corporations, whereas in Denmark, Germany, and the Netherlands local ownership and a history of stronger energy activism plays a greater role. The researchers suggested that local ownership may counterbalance the opposition raised by landscape and conservation organizations. The research is important not only because it draws attention to the role of local ownership in facilitating large-scale renewable energy projects but also because it suggests that support for local ownership may trump resistance from the segment of the environmental movement and local communities that is most concerned with landscape preservation.[3]

Other studies also suggest that local ownership, control over site location, and citizen participation in a planning process that is perceived to be fair have consistently affected local acceptance of new wind farms. Where local ownership is declining, opposition may increase. For example, in Denmark the decline of local, cooperative ownership and the increase in the scale of wind farms have contributed to increased opposition to wind power. A study from Denmark found that there was a preference for offshore wind farms over on-land farms, where the locally owned wind farms were historically placed. In a study of wind energy in South Wales, support was higher among older males, who were often former coal miners with beliefs more favorable to local and worker ownership. In Japan, environmental and ownership considerations were primary factors that favored increased support for community wind energy. One mechanism used to garner support was to name each turbine and to have investors' names inscribed on wind towers. Although not as well established as in Europe, in the United States community wind power has been gaining ground in Massachusetts and in some of the midwestern states.[4]

In view of the importance of wind energy as a cost-competitive source of renewable energy on a potentially significant scale, the research that links acceptance of wind farms to local ownership suggests that as the growth of wind energy continues, local ownership may emerge as a significant factor in energy development. However, there is very little research on localism and energy as a general topic. This section will fill the lacuna by examining public power agencies, community choice programs, and energy-conservation utilities. I selected for case-study research three public power utilities that were widely recognized for their reputations for environmental leadership, the city with the most advanced model of community choice, and the state with the oldest energy-conservation utility.[5]

The majority of electricity service providers in the United States are municipally owned (public) and cooperative entities, but most of them are very small. Popular during the Progressive Era, the number of public utilities peaked in the early 1920s. Today investor-owned utilities represent only a minority of electricity service providers in the United States, but they are concentrated in cities with large populations, and they serve the majority of American consumers. The dominance of investor-owned utilities in the United States can be traced back to lobbying efforts by for-profit electric power corporations. The National Electric Light Association, an industry group that supported private power, lobbied against "socialist" approaches to electricity generation and transmission and supported research and policies in favor of privatized electricity. As a result, the investor-owned utility with public regulation emerged as the dominant form of electricity generation and service provision. Although public regulation limited profits to a "just and reasonable" amount, by the 1920s interstate holding companies were siphoning off profits through the use of management fees. The failure of some of the holding companies during the Great Depression made it easier for President Franklin Roosevelt to achieve passage of legislation that regulated the utilities at a federal level and to gain support for the construction of federal hydropower projects and rural electricity cooperatives. Although investor-owned utilities have dominated electricity distribution and generation, public power held about 25 percent of the market share as of 2000.[6]

In 1996, consistent with the general climate of neoliberalism, the American electricity industry underwent "deregulation." As the historian Richard Hirsh has noted, the term is a misnomer because the industry remained highly regulated. Under the new regime of "restructuring" (the alternative term that Hirsh favors), generators were allowed to use the transmission lines of other companies in order to sell electricity to remote customers. Once electricity competition went into effect, generating companies found that they could make high profits by selling electricity to utilities on the open, interstate market. By 2000, many states faced spikes in prices for electricity purchased on the open market. In California price caps on customer charges created a bind for utilities: they had to purchase electricity on open markets, but because of the price caps they could not recuperate the costs by passing them on to consumers. As a result, the utilities were paying more for some of their electricity than they were charging for it. Pacific Gas and Electricity declared bankruptcy, and the state experienced blackouts. Similar problems occurred in other states.[7]

The price gouging that occurred with the creation of electricity markets was one factor that caused some cities to buy out their utilities and shift to public power. In many cases "public power" merely means public ownership of local transmission and distribution, but it is possible for public power organizations to invest in generation capacity as well. Some of the larger cities own generating capacity, and a few of the larger public power departments and agencies have become leaders in the transition toward greener electricity. Overall, about 20 percent of the electricity provided by public power utilities is from renewable sources, in comparison with 7 percent for investor-owned utilities. The difference is largely explained by the greater access to hydroelectric sources, including those of the federal government. However, even when the hydroelectric sources are not counted, the public power utilities provide twice the percentage of renewable energy as investor-owned utilities, and public power utilities do not have the renewable energy tax credit advantages that investor-owned utilities have.[8]

A pure type of localism for public power agencies, a form that is comparable to locally grown food with local inputs for local consumption, would be achieved only if an agency were to have control over its generating capacity and the power were to come entirely from local sources. As in food production, local energy production is not necessarily green; the energy source could be coal from a local mountain. However, in practice there is considerable interest in renewable energy sources, including hydropower, wind, and solar power. I studied three public power agencies or departments that had reputations for leadership in green electricity: Austin Energy, Sacramento Municipal Utility District (SMUD), and Seattle City Light. All three had programs that supported distributed renewable energy, such as rooftop solar installations, and were investing in wind energy, either via ownership or contracts. Seattle City Light and SMUD also owned substantial hydroelectric generating capacity.[9]

Because solar power remains expensive and new sources of hydropower are environmentally controversial or unavailable, wind energy is the most attractive source of new renewable energy. However, wind is plagued by a number of problems, including intermittency. To solve the intermittency problem for wind, SMUD was considering using wind-powered pumps to move water upstream after it had run through hydroelectric generation facilities. In contrast, there is little potential for hydropower as a storage mechanism for wind energy in Texas, and Austin Energy was investigating a distributed storage system that uses plug-in electric hybrid vehicles. In addition to the intermittency problem for wind energy noted above, representatives of all three agencies cited transmission congestion as a significant hurdle to bringing more wind resources on line more rapidly.[10]

Although all three public power agencies were leaders in the development of renewable energy sources, only Seattle City Light, a department of the city government, could claim that it had achieved the status of the country's first "carbon-neutral" electricity provider. In 2007, partly because of the department's efforts, the city of Seattle claimed to have met the Kyoto Protocol targets. Given a mandate from the city council, the city department was able to achieve carbon neutrality because of its significant hydropower resources and its purchases of carbon offsets for its relatively small percentage of grid-supplied electricity from fossil fuels. Although both SMUD and Austin Energy had several model programs, during the early 2000s they were also investing in new natural gas plants. They viewed the choice of continued fossil fuel as necessary in order to meet growing demand and (in the case of Austin Energy) to replace older, less efficient power plants. Although natural gas is much cleaner than either coal or oil as a source for electricity, the decision to invest in natural gas suggests that even the most environmentally oriented public utilities face difficult choices in making the transition to renewable energy sources while also providing customers with reliable and affordable electricity.[11]

Seattle City Light was founded in 1902, that is, during the Progressive Era growth spurt in public power. The city department added hydroelectric power capacity throughout the twentieth century; it also purchased hydroelectric power from the federal government's Bonneville Power Administration. To achieve carbon-neutral status, the department has continued to increase its wind power purchases; it has also generated offsets through conservation programs and purchases of biodiesel for the city's other vehicle fleets. There are many complicated issues involved in determining what exactly is "carbon-neutral" and "green" energy; among them are the environmental problems and greenhouse-gas emissions associated with hydroelectric dams. Furthermore, there would probably be questions about how to count the use of biodiesel as carbon offset credits. According to the representatives of Seattle City Light whom I interviewed, the biodiesel offsets were the least preferred of the three programs, and the municipal department instead made extensive investments in energy conservation. With a staff of about 70 and a budget of more than $20 million, Seattle City Light's energy-conservation efforts were among the largest in the United States.[12]

By investing in energy conservation, Seattle City Light has been able to reduce growth in energy consumption by its customers. As a result, the department will not be forced to develop new hydropower facilities; instead, it will focus on upgrading existing facilities and mitigating the environmental effects of its existing facilities. The investment in mitigation earned Seattle City Light environmental awards and certification from the Low Impact Hydropower Institute. It will be able to continue to sell excess capacity to the grid, and consequently it will have a revenue stream for ongoing investment in conservation and related measures both within Seattle City Light and in other city departments. Finally, the use of hydropower, wind, and other renewable resources will protect customers from future rate volatility.[13]

Turning from environmental to social goals, Seattle City Light helps low-income customers in a variety of ways. First, it keeps rates low for customers. Before the electricity crisis of 2000, the department advertised that it had the lowest rates in the country, but it was severely affected by shortages caused by droughts and the spillover effects from the energy crisis in California. Consequently, wholesale rates spiked, and customer rates had to be increased. Even so, rates remained much lower than for customers of investor-owned utilities. Low-income customers were exempted from some rate increases, and programs were available for low-income, senior, and disabled customers to apply for price reductions of up to 50 percent. Various other low-income assistance programs were available, and the Seattle's Department of Housing also offered weatherization support for low-income residents. More generally, public power agencies offered benefits to low-income and restricted-income customers by converting to renewable energy resources with fixed long-term costs, a change that will reduce future rate increases that will come with the growing scarcity of natural gas. Furthermore, when a city is able to control its energy generation, it is better able to remediate environmental justice problems by closing down the most polluting plants and replacing them with conservation, renewable energy, and cleaner fuels such as natural gas.[14]

Although Seattle is the envy of many cities with environmental ambitions, not everything is perfect there. Environmentalists have raised concerns with the effects of hydroelectric dams on environmentally sensitive species such as salmon, and Seattle City Light has put in place programs to address those concerns. A looming but not yet pressing problem is the threat that climate change poses to the production of electricity via hydropower. The glaciers that feed the rivers are melting, and since the late 1990s most of the years have been drier than usual. Another potential problem is that the federal government may force public power agencies to separate transmission and generation activities. If the regulatory change were to occur, it would dramatically undermine the revenue streams of the organization and consequently the ability of the city department to pursue its sustainability and low-income programs. Another potential problem is that state government renewable portfolio standards and other mandates, which are generally viewed as important legislative steps in building a transition to greener electricity, could pose problems for public power providers such as Seattle City Light if the mandates were to place specific targets on types of renewable energy or conservation.[15]

Notwithstanding actual and potential problems, cities that have local ownership of their electricity generation and transmission are in an enviable position for a variety of reasons. In addition to being able to build synergies among energy sources, as Seattle and Sacramento are doing with wind and hydropower, they are able to control emissions from local power plants and to shape the broader transition to renewable energy sources. They can also decide how to use profits from electricity sales to develop conservation, weatherization, and low-income assistance programs. In view of the advantages, why are more cities in the United States not considering municipalization? One reason is that investor-owned utilities have fiercely resisted the attempts. Even where the campaigns for public ownership have been successful, city governments have faced high capital costs and steep learning curves when attempting to make the conversion. Furthermore, city governments that convert to public power can incur significant debt, and consequently they have an incentive to maintain or increase revenue, which in turn favors increased power consumption rather than conservation.

In response to the difficulties of converting from private to public power, a new form of local electricity governance has emerged that enhances local control within the framework of competition among electricity service providers. Led by Paul Fenn, at the time the director of the Massachusetts Senate Committee on Energy, Massachusetts passed the country's first "community choice" law in 1996, just as energy competition was being implemented nationally. Since then several states have passed "community choice" legislation, which empowers city governments or larger units to aggregate consumers and purchase electricity from electricity suppliers as a unit. Consumers are allowed to opt out, but if they do not exercise the option (and most do not), they are added to the aggregation. By combining local electricity customers into a block contract, city governments are in a position to negotiate a better price for their residents and, if they choose, to mandate a cleaner energy mix.[16]

In San Francisco citizens were angered by the power outages and price hikes, and in 2001 reformers floated a ballot initiative to gain voter approval for municipalization. As in other cities, the investor-owned utility outspent the grassroots campaign by several magnitudes, and the initiative failed that year and again the next year. However, other ballot initiatives did pass, including Proposition H, which authorized the city to issue revenue bonds for renewable energy and energy conservation. Another victory took place in 2002, when the state government approved community choice legislation that Paul Fenn, who had since relocated to California, had authored. In 2004 the California Public Utilities Commission issued a statement that allowed community choice programs to start up. By combining the city's revenue bond authority with community choice legislation, the stage was set for a powerful new model of locally controlled and owned renewable energy.[17]

In an interview, Fenn, who was trained as an intellectual historian, recognized that community choice legislation was in tune with a neoliberal regulatory environment that emphasized privatization and devolution. He noted that in many cities people were heavily concerned with environmental problems and strongly supportive of renewable energy, so the combination model of revenue bonds and community choice had great potential for success in the current policy environment. Although he supported devolution, he was critical of the lack of financial support for cities and the "corporate control" of the economy. The model of community choice with city revenue bonds was one way to strengthen local finances as well as local ownership. He was also attentive to the possibility that community choice could be configured to address the needs of working-class and poor people. For example, his plans for the San Francisco transition to renewable energy included new unionized jobs for construction and closure of the polluting plant located in the low-income neighborhood of Hunter's Point. If all went as planned, and as of 2008 the process continued to move forward, San Francisco would use its revenue bonds to support the construction of 150 megawatts of capacity in a wind farm outside the city, 107 MW of energy conservation and efficiency reductions, and 104 MW of distributed generation, including 31 MW of rooftop solar. The new energy sources would represent about half of the city's average load, and much of it could be achieved in a few years. The scale of the transition is even more impressive when one considers that many other cities in California were exploring community choice.[18]

In contrast with public power, which can saddle a city government with huge debts and the need for new areas of expertise, with "community choice" the city government only acquires debt associated with bonds for new renewable energy construction projects that are built by the electricity service provider. The city government specifies in its terms of bid contract that the electricity service provider is responsible for building renewable energy projects and conservation programs with capital provided by the city through its bond authority. The contract enhances local ownership and control over the city's energy sources, reduces both greenhouse-gas emissions and overall growth in electricity consumption, generates new jobs through public works projects, and potentially contributes to the San Francisco Bay Area's emerging status as a green technopole for renewable energy technology. In other words, the transition will combine some of the best features of both import substitution and export-led growth, or localism and the high-tech manufacturing cluster.

A third model of localism and grid-supplied electricity production is the energy efficiency utility. The previous two models of local ownership in electricity also support energy efficiency and conservation, and the energy efficiency utility can be combined with public power, community choice aggregation, or even investor-owned utilities. In many ways energy conservation is the purest form of sustainable localism, because it substitutes imports with non-consumption, and it also provides cost savings to the consumer over the long term. Programs can also be configured to address justice issues by mandating that a percentage of revenues be spent on energy conservation for low-income households and small businesses. Many investor-owned utilities are required to implement energy efficiency programs, but the programs run into conflict with the profitability goals of the utilities' owners, who benefit from continued growth in energy consumption. Even public power utilities can be caught in the conflict between the goals of increased energy conservation and enhanced revenue from growth in energy sales. As a result, electricity efficiency programs nationwide have achieved less than 10 percent of what is considered possible, and so far they have not been able to reduce growth in overall consumption. One strategy to increase the effectiveness of energy-conservation programs is to shift the energy efficiency responsibilities to one utility. The effect is to aggregate energy-conservation programs across a state and to achieve economies of scale in energy-conservation program expenditures. The idea of a conservation utility need not be limited to energy conservation; it could also be applied to water conservation, automobile use reduction, and so on. In the case of energy efficiency utilities, the aggregated utility is funded by a small charge on the customer's energy bill.

Efficiency Vermont, established in 2000, is the first statewide energy efficiency utility in the United States. It is operated by a nonprofit energy organization that won a competitive bidding process for a performance contract with the state's Public Service Board. Although Efficiency Vermont is a public utility, it does not sell energy. Rather, its purpose is to provide advice, energy savings programs, and help with financing for all customers within the state. The utility views the positive economic effects of retaining energy expenses in the state as a primary benefit of its work, and its 2007 report notes that the net effect of the approximately $20 million annual budget and $20 million in participant expenditures is another $40 million in net savings.[19]

Even with a relatively small annual budget, by the end of 2007 Efficiency Vermont had leveraged its resources to save about 56,000 megawatt-hours in annual electricity consumption and $300 million in foregone energy expenditures counted over the lifetime of the installations. It had become, in effect, the fourth-largest utility in the state, and it was meeting 6.5 percent of the state's electricity needs. Although the number of electricity customers in the state was growing, the utility was able to offset the state's load growth. The utility's estimated cost to save one kilowatt-hour of electricity was about three cents, or roughly half the cost of purchased electricity at the time. The utility also achieved nearly complete participation from major lighting and appliance dealers in the state.[20]

Efficiency Vermont provides assistance to a wide range of energy consumers in the state, including homes, small businesses, ski resorts, dairy farms, government facilities, schools, and builders. State guidelines determine the percentage of the budget that is spent on assistance for low-income families. At one point about 40 percent of the utility's budget was spent on small businesses, many of which were locally owned, and increasingly the utility has achieved participation from larger customers as well. One of the primary mechanisms of assistance is providing reviews of current electricity consumption and making recommendations on how to reduce consumption, but the organization does more than provide expertise and consulting. The utility also provides links to stores that sell energy efficiency products, encourages retailers to offer those products, and helps connect customers to contractors who specialize in energy efficiency installations. Although not all retailers and installers are locally owned independent businesses, many are, and consequently the utility helps stimulate import substitution through a second channel of supporting the local retail and service industries. The utility also provides coupons and incentives for purchases of energy efficient appliances and compact fluorescent lighting, and it helps customers find financing for more substantial innovations.[21]

The three models discussed in this section show how local ownership operates in the public sector and the electricity industry. The models are of some general value in qualifying the understanding of localism as merely a private sector or civil-society activity, a conclusion that one might draw from the previous two chapters. Even community choice aggregation, which is made possible by electricity restructuring and a political climate that enabled privatization and competition, succeeds by linking together a network of federal, state, and local government regulations, legislation, and voter initiatives. All three models offer ways to achieve greater energy conservation, which like the reuse center is a form of localism that not only involves import substitution but also facilitates a reduction in consumption. Localism in the energy industry need not be green, and in both the cases of Sacramento and Austin I was surprised to learn that two of the most well-known green public utilities were constructing new natural-gas-fired plants. Although both plants would be locally owned, the natural gas was clearly not, and as a result this form of public sector energy localism is only marginally green (depending on the fuel source that it replaces) and hybrid (local ownership of generation, but nonlocal ownership of fuel sources). There can be many good reasons for a public power utility to select natural gas, including the cost of distributed solar, rapid growth in population and demand, lack of available wind energy (caused by construction delays and transmission problems), the need to close plants with higher amounts of pollution, and the political goal of keeping electricity rates under control. It is difficult to second-guess or criticize managers of such a volatile industry, and it is worth recognizing that they see such decisions as short-term investments inside a long-term strategy of transition to much higher levels of locally owned renewable energy and energy conservation.

Localism and the Greening of Public Transportation

Public transportation, like reuse centers and community gardens, is an example of a type of localism where sustainability and justice goals can come together. Compared to the automobile, urban public transportation is not only more energy efficient but also relatively inexpensive and disproportionately used by low-income residents and ethnic minority groups. Indeed, civil rights groups and transit activists have reframed the public funding of highways versus public transportation, and within the latter commuter rail versus bus transportation, as issues of "transit justice." The long history of civil rights and racism in the United States has been deeply linked to transportation, from the 1896 *Plessy v. Ferguson* case (which involved an African-American rider on a whites-only rail car in Louisiana), to Rosa Parks and the Montgomery bus boycott during the 1950s, to the transit-justice activism of bus riders in Los Angeles, Boston, and other cities during the 1990s.[22]

The greening of public transportation has also become an environmental justice issue. The increasingly well-documented health effects of diesel exhaust have accompanied a politicization of the emissions standards for urban diesel buses and the siting of urban bus depots. In Atlanta, Boston, Los Angeles, New York, and San Francisco, grassroots groups have protested the unequal distribution of diesel-based air pollution from urban buses, and in some cases they have demanded, and even won, concessions from urban transit agencies to shift to new fuel sources that have lower emissions. During the 1990s, the mobilizations coincided with two other developments: the natural gas industry was lobbying city governments to convert from diesel to natural gas, and the federal and California governments were developing regulations to require urban bus fleets to reduce emissions.[23]

To a large extent the public debate over the greening of public transportation in the United States since 1990 has centered on the issue of diesel fuel versus compressed natural gas (CNG). Both are fossil fuels, and in a world of increasing prices for both petroleum and natural gas—not to mention issues of peak oil, peak gas, greenhouse-gas emissions, and energy independence—neither can be a long-term solution to the problem of energy and public transportation. As a result, part of the debate centers of which type of bus and fuel design offers a better bridge technology to a future of electrical and/or hydrogen-based transportation that one hopes, in the long term, will be supported mostly by renewable energy. Some cities have opted for CNG, some started down a path toward CNG conversion before shifting back to diesel, and others firmly stayed on the diesel path. The debate is complicated because the technology and regulations are changing very rapidly. A complex brew of health effects research, grassroots mobilization, design innovations in bus technology, fuel industry lobbying, and government regulations has created the context for what I call the "object conflicts," or definitional struggles, that have emerged around the question, "What is a clean bus?" In this section I will consider each of those factors in a little more detail. Each of the arenas of contestation are fields of action across variable sociopolitical scales, where the effects of outcomes in one field reverberate on others.[24]

Health research has increasingly pointed to the risks of lung cancer, asthma, and other diseases associated with exposure to diesel exhaust. By 1990, the National Institute for Occupational Safety and Health and the State of California had separately declared diesel exhaust to be a carcinogen, and continued documentation over the subsequent two decades from government units such as the National Toxicology Program and the Environmental Protection Agency confirmed the determination. Similar statements were issued at an international level. The International Agency for Research on Cancer reviewed the literature and declared that diesel exhaust was a probable carcinogen, and a 1996 report by an international body sponsored by the World Health Organization and several other organizations conducted a similar appraisal on the carcinogenicity of diesel exhaust and recommended actions to reduce exposure. In the United States, California became a center for research and policy directed at diesel emissions, which were estimated to contribute approximately 70 percent of the cancer risk from air pollution in that state. A report from the California Air Resources Board noted that diesel exhaust contains 41 toxic air contaminants as defined by the State of California.[25]

A second field that affected decisions on the greening of urban bus fleets was regulatory policy at the federal level of government. The Clean Air Act of 1990 allowed the EPA to take steps that led to the Clean Fuel Program, which developed an emissions target for new fleet purchases beginning with the 1998 model year, identified 22 non-attainment cities in terms of air quality, and mandated that those cities purchase clean-fuel fleets. The goal was for fleet purchases of clean-fuel vehicles to reach 30 percent in 1998, 50 percent in 2000, and 70 percent in 2001. However, in 1998 a report by the Natural Resources Defense Council accused the EPA of backpedaling on its own goals in several ways: weakening the emissions standards, delaying implementation, and allowing most non-attainment regions to opt out by demonstrating equivalent reductions through other programs. Although the mandates were weakened, they did pressure urban transit agencies to consider switching to CNG or liquid natural gas (LNG) as a cleaner fuel. One reason was that fleet purchases are a long-term investment and the predicted future trend was toward regulation in favor of cleaner fuels.[26]

A third field of action was the growth of environmental justice mobilizations to "dump dirty diesel." In New York and Boston the groups achieved changes from the state government, in San Francisco the groups worked through the city government and city-level voter proposition system, and in Atlanta and Los Angeles the groups operated through the courts. At issue was both the quality of diesel bus emissions and the health effects of bus idling on the low-income neighborhoods where bus barns were located. In Los Angeles the transit justice issues also included the unequal funding of bus transportation and the commuter rail system, and in 1996 the court transferred decision-making authority to a "special master," a court-appointed person who had authority to override the decisions of the transit agency. In Los Angeles and other cities environmental justice advocates generally pushed for a transition from diesel to CNG. When new, emissions-controlled diesel technologies became available, the groups in San Francisco and Boston were more flexible in their approach, whereas in Atlanta and Los Angeles the environmental justice groups remained more firm advocates of a continued transition to natural gas.[27]

In 2000, the EPA issued new standards set to begin with the 2007 model year. Those standards were scheduled to drop allowable emissions of nitrous oxides, particulates, and non-methane hydrocarbons. The EPA also reduced sulfur content in highway diesel fuel by 97 percent from 500 to 15 parts per million, with a stepped phase-in from 2007 to 2010. The diesel industry struggled to meet the new standards, and the low level for nitrous oxides presented an especially critical design challenge. The federal standards were complicated by California state-government standards, which were more stringent. In 2000 the California Air Resources Board mandated that transit agencies had to commit either to a diesel or an alternative fuel path by 2001. Forty-eight transit agencies across the state opted to pursue the clean diesel path, among them the

Alameda–Contra Costa Transit District of the East Bay and Muni of San Francisco, whereas 28 agencies, including Los Angeles and Sacramento, opted for the alternative path, mostly CNG and LNG. The California Air Resources Board also enacted nitrous oxide standards more stringent than those of the EPA, but it subsequently harmonized down to the federal standards.[28]

As diesel bus manufacturers struggled to meet the new standards, a series of tests that compared various types of diesel and CNG bus technologies revealed contradictory information. Diesel buses with ultra-low sulfur fuel and catalytic converters, especially when combined with hybrid-electric technology, significantly reduced emissions. Because diesel buses cost less than CNG and much less than hydrogen technology, fleet managers could argue that a decision to purchase clean diesel buses represented the greener alternative because it allowed the more rapid retirement of older, dirty buses. As clean diesel became available, some fleets that had tested CNG began to shift back to diesel. For example, Boston, Cleveland, New York, and Washington returned to diesel after having tested CNG. Other cities, including Oakland, San Francisco, and Seattle, had simply waited for cleaner diesel to emerge. For fleet managers, "clean diesel" represented a significant advantage on many accounts, including the up-front cost of the vehicles, saved costs on depot and other infrastructure conversion, and general accumulated knowledge about operating a diesel-based bus fleet. A study by the Greater Cleveland Transit Authority, which had used both diesel and CNG buses, found that the fuel costs for emissions-controlled diesel and CNG in 2003 were equivalent, but the labor and parts costs were significantly higher for CNG. Taking into account the difference in purchase price, fuel, labor, and parts, the Cleveland agency concluded that a CNG bus was about 20 percent more expensive to operate per mile than an emissions-controlled diesel bus. Likewise, a comprehensive survey of transit agencies using CNG, conducted by the National Renewable Energy Laboratory and published in 2002, found that most fleets reported higher costs for CNG than diesel, but a few fleets experienced lower CNG fuel and maintenance costs. The study suggested that transit agencies with large CNG fleets and a high degree of training were more likely to experience the lower CNG costs. Even the Los Angeles

Metropolitan Transportation Authority, with its large CNG fleet, noted that although fuel costs were equivalent for CNG and diesel, annual maintenance costs were 15–20 percent higher for CNG. Another study, written for the natural gas industry, admitted that another drawback for CNG was a lower range and payload than diesel but argued that reliability and fuel economy problems had been overcome by the late 1990s.[29]

To give a little more detailed understanding of the complexities of the factors behind the transition to cleaner fuels in urban public transportation, I will focus on the decisions at Metro Transit of King County, which includes the city of Seattle. During the 1990s the city council had pressured the agency to shift to CNG, but it resisted the political pressure. Although the natural gas industry strongly supported the conversion in Seattle, as in other cities, the transit agency had several concerns, including the conversion costs, the refueling time, risk to workers from potential explosions in converted bus depots, the higher marginal cost of CNG vehicles, and the inadequacy of the gas infrastructure pipelines to handle the nocturnal refueling load. After an election that shifted the political composition of the city council, the new council backed away from the proposal.[30]

In 2003 Metro Transit attracted national attention for its test and purchase of more than 200 60-foot hybrid-electric diesel buses. The purchase earned the agency the distinction of having the largest fleet of such buses in the country and an award as the National Clean Bus Leader from the Environmental and Energy Study Institute. Although the cost of each bus was about $200,000 more than a standard, emissions-controlled diesel bus, the agency's tests revealed that maintenance reductions and fuel savings allowed them to recuperate the marginal cost within eight years. Because the wear-and-tear on the engine was lower, the agency expected to keep the buses for 16 years rather than for twelve years, which is the expected lifespan of the standard diesel bus. The reduced need for maintenance allowed the agency to downsize its workforce of mechanics by 10 percent, and consequently it was able to recuperate some of the marginal cost of the hybrid buses through savings in labor costs. Through careful planning and coordination with the union, the agency was able to reassign all positions.[31]

From the perspective of localism and economic development theory, the shift toward hybrid-electric technology is a type of import substitution based on energy conservation. Money flowing out of the region for fuel expenses is retained within the region as fuel savings. As the technology shifts to plug-in electric hybrid vehicles, an additional import substitution is available to the extent that the electricity can be provided by local sources, such as the local hydropower and wind resources available from Seattle City Light. A third type of import substitution is also possible but not realized in the Seattle case: the shift toward the manufacture of the buses locally. The shift is probably not feasible in the case of hybrid electric vehicles because of the huge investment required to start up a new firm in the globally competitive market. However, the city of Chattanooga did sponsor a local manufacturing venture for its small, downtown, electric circulator buses, a product for which global competition is much lower. Although the company ended up failing, probably because of a decision to diversify outside its niche product area, it provides an example of yet another way in which urban transportation can be linked to import substitution and local ownership.[32]

Another innovation in the transit agency that involves import substitution is the use of biodiesel, which was funded by Seattle City Light. The use of a 5 percent biodiesel blend meant that in 2005 the agency purchased about 500,000 gallons of biodiesel per year. From a fleet management perspective, the shift to biodiesel was of limited value. Although the emissions benefits of biodiesel were significant for older buses, for the new, emissions-controlled diesel buses the benefits were negligible. Furthermore, if Metro Transit were to use a higher percentage of biodiesel, such as 20 percent, the bus manufacturers would void the warranty on the buses. Although the purchase of biodiesel did help spur the state's biodiesel industry, in the Pacific Northwest demand for biodiesel was substantial enough that it was not always easy to purchase the biofuel in the quantities that the fleet required. Finally, at the time the price for biodiesel was not competitive with diesel. In combination, the reasons made the use of biodiesel relatively unattractive, even though its use was helping to build the local biodiesel industry.[33]

As David Morris, vice president of the Institute for Local Self-Reliance, notes, biofuels can be configured to be made from locally owned farms and locally owned refineries. However, Morris also notes that there has been considerable consolidation in biofuels refining, and the trend for biofuels refineries is probably away from local ownership or at least toward partnerships between farmers and nonlocal investors. Furthermore, fleet managers are wary of becoming dependent on biofuels, with their potential for price volatility and their unreliable supply.[34]

In general, the development of greener urban bus fleets provides one pathway in which sustainability and justice goals can be brought together under the mantle of local ownership. As in the case of public power and energy-conservation utilities, the form of local ownership is a government-based department or public agency rather than a for-profit small business, an informal association, or a nonprofit organization. The justice goals include resolving the unequal effects of urban air pollution and uneven availability of transportation. However, conflicts within justice goals can occur if the downsizing of fleet staffs is done in a way that results in job loss or if public funds are diverted from bus transportation to commuter rail. In Seattle the two types of public transit are under different agencies, an arrangement that prevents the diversion of public funds to commuter rail that has occurred in other cities. When both bus and rail transit are under the same agency or at least linked by a single funding stream, the two types of public transportation can become aligned with class and race divisions in society. For example, in Los Angeles the Bus Riders Union has regularly criticized the city's investment in rail, which it sees as largely benefiting middle-class commuters at the expense of the city's bus system. Such tradeoffs can rapidly become a tinderbox in the context of America's history of transit racism and the prominence of urban buses in the civil rights movement. One middle ground, which agencies such as Alameda–Contra Costa County Transit are developing, is bus rapid transit, which uses traffic signal control and station design to provide some of the benefits of urban light rail at a fraction of the cost and with much lower disruption to neighborhoods during construction.[35]

The examples discussed here suggest how justice and sustainability goals can be brought together when configuring urban public transit systems, but there can also be difficult tradeoffs. Hybrid-electric diesel, CNG, and hydrogen buses all cost more than conventional emissions-controlled diesel buses, and fleet managers must negotiate the goals of increasing bus service and improving the environmental impact of each bus. Furthermore, although the percentage of petroleum in the energy source of urban public transit is declining, the gradual shift from emissions-controlled diesel to hybrid-electric diesel to plug-in hybrid-electric diesel with biofuel blends will still rely on petroleum as a significant source of energy. As a result, urban transportation in the United States faces a conversion problem that is similar to that of electricity: a system that remains mostly based on fossil fuels in a world where burning greater quantities of fossil fuels poses severe environmental risk, not to mention price and supply volatility. Although federal transportation funding could be shifted toward the expansion of public transportation and its greening, the fleet managers with whom I spoke were generally disappointed in the level of federal funding that was forthcoming. For example, Jim Boon, the manager of vehicle maintenance for Metro Transit of King County, noted:

When we first started the hybrid program, there was no state or federal funding. It was our feeling that if we wanted to show a reduction in emissions and fuel consumption, the federal government should help reduce the $200,000 delta that we were paying per bus. We did get a $5 million earmark, but that was from our senator, who earmarked the funds in the transportation budget. The entire purchase was $160 to $170 million, so $5 million doesn't buy that much. We're just not seeing the support from the Federal Transit Administration. We hear that they're happy that we're doing this, but they're not offering to help. They offered a lot of subsidies and grants for natural gas, but they haven't done the same for hybrids.[36]

Conclusion

The study of local ownership in the electricity and public transportation industries provides a dramatically different perspective from the retail and agrifood industries. Although conservationist, general environmental, and environmental justice organizations have been involved in the politics of the greening of electricity and public transportation, there is little evidence of a localist movement, such as the "buy local" movement or the community gardening movement seen in the previous chapters. For cities that already have public power, and certainly for public transportation agencies, there is no need for a localist movement, because the primary organizations are already locally owned and controlled. In some cases, the existence of public power is a legacy of political battles and social movements of prior generations. The closest approximation to a localist movement in the electricity industry today is mobilization that has occurred in support of public power and community choice in cities that have investor-owned utilities, such as in the struggles in California to shift San Francisco to public power and then later to community choice. Otherwise, the driving force for change is often coming more from the professionals within the organizations who champion transitions to more sustainable energy sources and configure programs that ensure the distribution of the benefits to low-income users. The cases discussed in this chapter provide another reason why it may be better to think of localism, at least the forms discussed in this chapter, as comprising a series of alternative pathways for change that may sometimes, but not always, approximate a social or reform movement.

Another difference between localism in the retail and agrifood industries and in the electricity and transportation industries is that public ownership plays a significantly greater role. Although the shift toward regulated competition of the electricity industry during the 1990s reshaped the landscape of electricity markets, the political change also created opportunities for new regimes, such as community choice. When combined with municipal bonds to shift ownership to local distributed-energy sources, community choice operates within the neoliberal landscape to recreate publicly owned electricity. In other examples—public power, government-sponsored efficiency utilities, and public transportation—localism in this industry is one in which public ownership has widespread public acceptance. To some degree the acceptance of public ownership is a result of general patterns of provisioning municipal services in the United States. Historically, police, fire, water, and waste have been controlled by city governments. If one wishes to find a credible site for public ownership in the United States, local electricity and transportation may be better places to start than the nationalization of large fossil-fuel companies.

Localism in the electricity and transportation industries is also different from the other industries in its potential to scale up rapidly. Through public debt financing arrangements, surcharges on consumer energy bills, and regulatory policy changes at the state and federal government levels, it is possible to finance significant investments in energy conservation and the greening of existing energy and public transportation systems. Although the locally owned systems discussed in this chapter may not be as well funded as they could be, they do have access to capital at levels far beyond what is generally available for the small retail businesses and the local agricultural and community gardening networks. The other fields of localism studied so far are much more limited by lack of access to funding.

Local electricity and transportation also address environmental and social responsibility goals in a different manner from local ownership in the other two industries. Although the resale centers and urban gardens address environmental problems, they do not provide solutions to the increasingly visible problem of greenhouse-gas generation. Localism in the electricity and transportation industries can also address significant areas of low-income household budgets through low-income energy assistance programs, reduction of future price increases that is the result of renewable energy investment, and increases in public transportation availability. Because of the unequal burden of air pollution across class and ethnic divisions, the greening of electricity production and urban bus fleets also has positive environmental justice implications. In the energy and transportation industries, localism has received scant attention and study but may have greater potential than in other industries.

7

Localism and the Media

Like the retail, agriculture, and electricity industries, the media industry in the United States is dominated by large corporations. Furthermore, the industry has become highly consolidated; the number of corporations that controlled the majority of media outlets in the United States fell from 50 in 1983 to 28 in 1987, 23 in 1990, 14 in 1992, 10 in 1997, and 6 in 2000. Again, it would be simplistic to attribute the trends to greater efficiencies and economies of scale. The industry is heavily regulated, and its historical trends are driven by changes in regulatory policy. In synch with the restructuring of the electricity industry during the mid 1990s, the Telecommunications Act of 1996 also had a dramatic effect on the broadcast media industry. During the decade that followed, new levels of media consolidation were achieved.[1]

Defenders of corporate media have noted that if one examines the media industry as a whole, overall levels of consolidation have not declined since the 1970s. In other words, if one takes into account the emergence of new industries and sources of news—cable television, satellite radio, the video rental industry, and news and information via the Internet—rather than any particular media industry, then the emergence of new forms of media has exerted a counterbalancing effect on the consolidation trends. Furthermore, the recent waves of consolidation in the electronic media are by no means new for the media in general. For example, the growth of the Gannett and Knight-Ridder chains of daily newspapers during the late twentieth century was not so much a new pattern as a shift away from the dominance of the Hearst and Scripps chains. Likewise, radio ownership was heavily centralized during the 1930s, but it became more localized after the advent of television during the 1950s, and then a new wave of consolidation occurred during the 1980s.[2]

Although it is true that media consolidation varies over time and across industries, the defenders of media consolidation tend to gloss over some of the crucial differences between earlier forms of consolidation and the pattern that emerged during the 1980s. For example, although there were newspaper chains earlier in the twentieth century, during the half century after World War II newspaper ownership in the United States went from 80 percent local ownership to about 80 percent ownership by corporate chains. Furthermore, the existence of huge, vertically integrated media conglomerates with vast holdings across a wide range of media industries is also new. There may be many channels of news and entertainment, but the venues that reach the largest audiences tend to select stories that are compatible with the neoliberal politics of the corporate owners. The perspectives of social movements, the voices of ethnic minority communities, and political perspectives incompatible with the corporate owners tend to be filtered out or reduced greatly. Furthermore, the new forms of media consolidation have been associated with lower amounts of locally oriented programming, participation by the community, and diversity in media content. As corporate media became more influential, they weakened regulatory protections in favor of minority rights and political participation. For example, during the 1980s the demise of the Fairness Doctrine allowed media conglomerates to adopt an editorial viewpoint on a political issue without a legal obligation to allow the opposing viewpoint to be heard. Likewise, the rule that required stations to report coverage of the ten most significant community issues was suspended. Both the consolidation of ownership and the relaxation of rules contributed to the increasing dominance of neoliberal politics in the mainstream media. As a result, there may be many channels, but the opportunities for local perspectives, minority voices, and radical (or even liberal) political discussion have declined.[3]

Protecting a democratic society from the threat of concentrated media ownership is by no means a new topic. As early as 1927, broadcast regulations were introduced to protect what became known in media law as "localism." In the media industry the term has a different meaning from its use in this book. Media "localism" is the legal doctrine that protects news content and programming that serve the needs of local communities. As the localism doctrine developed, the law mandated that broadcast studios be located in the geographical communities that they served and that they provide some programming that contains local content, such as local news. Because of the focus on local programming content and service, the idea of "localism" in media policy and law tended to sidestep the more controversial issue of local ownership. However, the issue of local ownership was not completely lost, and consequently there is some overlap between the doctrine of media localism and more general localist politics in the United States. For example, until 1984 regulatory policy followed the "rule of sevens": a corporation could own no more than seven television stations, seven AM radio stations, and seven FM stations. By 1994, the rule had been relaxed to a limit of 12 television stations and 20 radio stations. The Telecommunications Act of 1996 lifted the limit on stations and allowed a single company to reach up to 35 percent of the national television market. For broadcast radio the changes caused a dramatic centralization of programming controlled by megacorporations such as Clear Channel. As a result, ownership issues became more prominent in discussions of media localism. In 2004, a Federal Communications Commission report on ownership and local coverage found that locally owned television stations added five minutes more local news coverage than similar news owned by networks or nonlocal corporate entities. Because of the importance of local news for a functioning local democracy, the issue of local ownership of the media has become an increasingly visible part of the longstanding discussions of media localism.[4]

In this chapter I will focus on a meaning of localism in the media that is consistent with the way the term is used throughout the book: locally owned and independent media. I will first look at the history of media-reform efforts in the United States by returning to the controversies of the 1920s and the 1930s, when commercial media became a target of concern analogous to those voiced against the chain stores of the era. After reviewing the background of media-reform efforts, I will look at three types of independent media: alternative national media that have a political agenda consistent with the localist movement, independent community media, and Internet-based news developed by small organizations outside the orbit of the media conglomerates. Finally, I will examine how media ownership and consolidation may affect coverage of the "buy local" movement.

Historical Background

The first major media-reform movement in the United States during the twentieth century confronted a rising tide of commercialism in the newspaper industry. During the late nineteenth century, reformers responded to the increasing business orientation of the media by forming their own media, and the groups also joined forces to form the National Reform Press Association. However, the sensationalistic stories of the commercial media brought about increased circulation and advertising revenues, and the alternative media were displaced. Ongoing reform efforts steered clear of the issue of press ownership, but they did achieve the passage of the Newspaper Publicity Act of 1912, which required the news media to list owners and to distinguish paid advertising from news. The mainstream press held off additional reforms by wrapping itself in the flag of the First Amendment and developing professional standards for journalistic objectivity.[5]

As with print media, the issue of commercialism was central for reform efforts in the electronic media during the first half of the twentieth century. In the late 1920s labor, educational, and religious organizations formed a coalition to protest the commercialization of radio that was encouraged by the Radio Act of 1927. Had the organizations been successful, they might have achieved a moratorium on the development of commercial radio. As with the newspaper reformers, the coalition was no match for the commercial radio industry, which not only had superior financial resources but also offered programming that was often more popular with listeners. As a result, by the mid 1930s the reform coalition was in disarray, and the number of noncommercial radio stations had dropped to under 40, in contrast with about 130 in 1925. The Communications Act of 1934 represented an additional victory for commercial radio, but it also set the stage for some policy protections in favor of media diversity and locally oriented programming.[6]

After the defeat of the reform efforts, commercial radio absorbed and transformed the opposition movement by developing a doctrine of co-operation with educational media. Commercial radio stations provided limited funding and air time for educational programming, and educational broadcasting slowly regrouped. However, it was not until the late 1950s, when post-Sputnik concerns with science education mounted, that advocates of noncommercial programming found another political opportunity. Government funding began in 1962, and, following rapidly on the heels of a Carnegie Foundation report in 1967, the federal government created the Corporation for Public Broadcasting and, a few years later, National Public Radio. Although public broadcasting was specifically defined as non-instructional, in many ways it was heir to the educational broadcasting and noncommercial radio of the 1920s and the 1930s. The development of public television and radio during the 1960s was a response to ongoing concern with the limitations of the commercial model of broadcast media, and it also responded to calls for programming diversity that had emerged from the civil rights movement. By providing limited government funding for the noncommercial model, support for public broadcasting also deflected attention from any efforts to place restrictions on commercial media.[7]

Because public broadcasting lacked an endowment and independent revenue sources, from its inception it was hostage to Congressional and presidential scrutiny for stories that were considered politically sensitive. For example, after a critical public radio report on banking and the poor, President Richard Nixon vetoed funding. Given the high partisan scrutiny and the need for continued government funding, public radio and television in the United States have tended to avoid airing positions from either the far right or the far left. Instead, the model has been one of a mainstream political debate, as occurs during the PBS News Hour, with almost no air time given to radical criticisms in either the socialist or communalist tradition. Since the 1980s public subsidies have been reduced, and public broadcasting has sought increased corporate sponsorship, underwriting of specific programs, and quasi-advertising. In the eyes of some critics, public broadcasting has become merely highbrow commercial media. To the extent that one can identify oppositional action in this industrial field that is continuous with the anti-commercialization politics of the late 1920s, it is the continued mobilization in defense of the autonomy of public broadcasting. For example, in 1999 media-reform advocates formed Citizens for Independent Public Broadcasting, an organization dedicated to forming a public trust for public broadcasting to reverse the commercialization process. Likewise, in 2005 activists opposed the censorship of liberal public broadcasting journalists such as Bill Moyers.[8]

In 2002 a new wave of media reform coalesced around Free Press, a nonprofit organization that networked half a million activists concerned with media bias, violence, concentration of ownership, and net neutrality. Especially relevant from the perspective of localism, Free Press has advocated stronger anti-trust regulations that would limit media consolidation. The organization also advocated support for "public media," a term that includes not only public radio and television but also community radio, local low-power FM, public access cable television, independent publications, community Internet, and other forms of media that serve a broad public benefit rather than shareholder profits. Free Press also supported the "Stop Big Media" campaign, which marshaled opposition to changes in Federal Communications Commission policy that have favored corporate consolidation of the media and have undermined longstanding policies of media localism. The campaign advocated a range of policy reforms, including increased "local control" of the media. As a result, localism has now become an important component of the new wave of media-reform action.[9]

If the history of the earlier media-reform movements is any guide to the future, then the current wave of opposition movements will face a difficult battle to reverse the consolidation of corporate ownership in the media industry. To the extent that media reform has become increasingly focused on the question of concentration and ownership, reformers face the delicate problem of building public support by getting sympathetic media coverage from commercial media organizations, which in turn have little interest in reporting their proposals. Reformers may utilize the Internet and alternative media, and they may play print media against electronic media, but in general they face a severe problem in getting their message heard. Furthermore, elected political officials are afraid to antagonize a consolidated, corporatized media industry that holds direct sway over opinion formation and voter preferences. The movement will require a long, steady strategy of building grassroots support and cultivating independent, noncorporate news sources.

Alternative National Media

The opposition movements outlined in the previous section have coexisted with parallel reform efforts that have focused on building alternative, noncommercial media that are independently owned and are politically opposed to increased corporate control of the economy. Two primary examples are alternative media with a national scope and community media. I use the term "alternative" here to refer to a range of political positions from the liberal to the radical to the localist, a diverse body of viewpoints that is generally united by its opposition to neoliberalism, corporate control of politics, and militarism.

In this section, I focus on the national, independent, alternative media because they are among the few venues among the national media where there is consistent discussion of issues such as corporate ownership of the media, the value of media localism, the effects of globalization, and alternative forms of economic ownership. I am less concerned here with exploring the politics of such publications than the problems that have emerged with independent ownership for a media organization that intends to have a national audience and to develop content that challenges the power of large publicly traded corporations. To explore the issue, I will focus first on the national press publications, then discuss briefly some of the problems that have emerged with similar ventures in radio and television.

The alternative national press includes noncommercial publications that have survived from previous generations of political reform movements, such as *The Nation* and *The Progressive*; the post-1960s political and cultural magazines *In These Times*, *Mother Jones* (successor to *Ramparts*), *Ms.*, and *Z*; environmental magazines such as *E: The Environmental Magazine*; and pro-localist magazines such as *Yes!* In contrast with the noncommercial right-wing press, large corporate advertisers and economic elites have tended to shun the liberal, radical, and localist press because of its anti-corporate message. In some cases, wealthy individuals have stepped in to fill the void—there was for a time a "rich kids" network of wealthy heirs who came of age during the 1960s and supported some of the liberal and left national press organs—but their resources were limited and were best used to get new projects off the ground rather than provide ongoing support for unprofitable enterprises.[10]

Although some nonprofit organizations have been able to fund sophisticated magazine-like newsletters based largely on membership dues and donations, when magazines attempt to achieve high levels of circulation and to compete in commercial markets, they generally need to adopt a commercial model that is based on revenue from advertising. In most magazines about 90 percent of the revenue is from advertising, and only about 10 percent comes from subscriptions. However, access to mainstream corporate advertising not only is limited but can also be intentionally withdrawn. For example, *Mother Jones*, a liberal-socialist American magazine for which I worked directly and indirectly in the late 1970s, ran into financial problems as a result of its high-profile exposés. The investigative journalist Mark Dowie broke the national story on the Ford Pinto, a passenger car with a defect in the bolts near the gasoline tank that caused explosions in accidents when the vehicles were hit from behind. The magazine also published a highly acclaimed article on smoking and nicotine addiction. Those and other stories led to a withdrawal of advertising not only from specific firms but entire industries, a process that those of us who worked at the magazine at the time referred to as "the boycott by Madison Avenue." Automobile and cigarette firms pulled their advertising, and the liquor industry—the third of the triad of big advertisers at the time—followed on their heels. More generally, even if a magazine does not face an advertising blockade from large corporations, it can be driven out of business by litigation from companies that have been the target of investigative stories. Furthermore, the general lack of advertising revenue from more conventional corporate sources left many of the alternative national magazines with an inverted revenue structure; in other words, they earned the bulk of their revenue from subscriptions. As the green economy developed in subsequent decades, some of the magazines were able to capture advertising revenue from the natural foods and health products industry, consumer electronics manufacturers, and socially responsible investment firms. However, even with the growth of advertising from the new sources, the inability to capture advertising revenues from mainstream consumer products firms severely restricted the ability of the national alternative magazines to scale up and shift to a commercial model in which the bulk of revenue is based on advertising.[11]

The inversion of revenue sources from advertising to subscriptions drove many of the alternative national magazines to nonprofit status. This transformation is important because it appears in other media industries, and nonprofit organizational status may end up being the most economically feasible organizational form for local independent ownership in the media industry. Most of the major alternative national magazines in the United States that have survived for any length of time have published under the umbrella of nonprofit organizations. The use of nonprofit organizational status is legally complicated and, as I learned when consulting for several of the magazines when President Ronald Reagan came to office, subject to tax audits during periods of hostile presidential administrations. However, nonprofit status is widespread among literary, academic, and political publishing companies, and the nonprofit model can be successful if carefully developed, as the publication of larger magazines such as *Mother Jones* and *Ms.* indicates. Nonprofit organizational status also provides the opportunity to build up endowments and to encourage direct donations from wealthy supporters. The educational functions of 501(c)(3) organizations also create opportunities for training a new generation of journalists and generating content at a relatively low cost. Although this model first appeared in the alternative magazine industry, by 2008 it was beginning to appear as well in the local newspaper industry, where the commercial model had dominated. With the growth of the Internet and the decline of advertising revenue that print publications faced, there was a new trend toward the growth of nonprofit local electronic newspapers.[12]

Although the nonprofit model is clearly important for the maintenance of alternative print media, the model has some shortcomings. Perhaps the most significant is the tradeoff between board and staff control that often occurs. One or more large donors may share the organization's political vision but also exercise substantial control over a group of board members.

Even in the absence of a single deep-pockets donor, when a publication develops a board that is based on securing organizational finances rather than representing the staff, a shift occurs in the governance of the organization. Organizations with democratic governance and staff members who work either for below-market wages or on a volunteer basis will tend to develop conflicts between the staff and the board or between staff and administrators who represent the board.[13]

Similar issues can be found in history of Pacifica Radio, which is the only national liberal-radical radio network in the United States. Operated by the Pacifica Foundation, a nonprofit organization, the network emerged out of the peace movement of the 1930s and the 1940s. It eventually grew from its San Francisco Bay Area beginnings to include more than 100 affiliate stations in the United States and Canada. The organization's history is punctuated by crises that provide some insight into the difficulties of developing and sustaining alternative broadcast media in the United States during the twentieth century. One of the most severe crises occurred after the New York station aired an exposé in 1962 by a former agent of the Federal Bureau of Investigation. Government repression followed rapidly and included Red-baiting, threatening not to renew licenses, and requiring station members to take loyalty oaths. Although the repression largely backfired on the federal government, it divided the radio network, led to the resignation and firing of important staff members, and resulted in a strike. A second major conflict occurred a decade later, when attempts to increase programming for minority communities in New York and the San Francisco Bay area led to another series of pitched battles between the staff and the board. A third major conflict began in the late 1990s, when the central board attempted to institute greater control and diversity of programming at two of the radio stations. Although the board eventually lost the conflict, the organization was saddled with a substantial debt, and public access to core programs such as Amy Goodman's "Democracy Now!" (also a nonprofit organization) was lost temporarily.[14]

In television, there is no alternative national broadcast network comparable to Pacifica. Until the development of cable and satellite television in the 1980s and the 1990s, the prospect of creating an alternative television "network" was prohibitively expensive. After more than 10 years of work in cable and other television venues, in 2000 Free Speech TV became the first 24-hour alternative television network available by satellite TV. By 2003 the nonprofit organization's programs reached 11 million homes and 70 public access cable stations. In 1999 broadcasting also became available through satellites for the organization that became Link TV, and by 2008 it had reached 29 million homes with documentaries, foreign news, and other sources of information not usually available on television. Another organization, OneWorld TV, provides web-based video news and features based on the affiliates of OneWorld. net, an umbrella organization that links together groups dedicated to using "people's media" in the interests of social justice. All three sources of television and video are nonprofit organizations.[15]

Too little information is currently available, and too little time has passed, to examine patterns of development and transformation for the alternative television projects. The general lesson for the broader study of localism is that most of the alternative media with a national audience have been established as nonprofit organizations. Having a nonprofit status not only gives the organization the financial room to develop a noncommercial revenue model but also protects the organization from acquisition by commercial media conglomerates. However, the addition of large donors to the board of directors can lead to professionalization and the adoption of more businesslike procedures, which in turn may affect staff morale, organizational structure, and even news and feature content. The history of alternative media suggests a general lesson for all activists who wish to use the nonprofit model as a vehicle for their organizations: a deep problem of the nonprofit model of independent media ownership is that conflicts tend to develop between a movement-oriented staff and a professionalizing board.

Community Media

Consideration of independent, locally owned, and locally-oriented media raises some interesting questions. Many communities are conservative politically, and one would expect that an increase in local ownership of the media, especially if the ownership were concentrated among local elites, would lead to more conservative political content. In this section

I will focus on one segment of independent, locally owned, and locally oriented media: those that tend to be supportive of the localist message of concern with the corporate domination of the economy and the need for renewed local ownership. The term "community media" will be used to refer to this segment of locally owned, independent, locally oriented media, including alternative newsweeklies, community radio, micro-broadcasting, minority-owned radio, and public access television.

The history of community media has some significant differences from that of the alternative national media, among which is the higher prominence of for-profit enterprises in the newspaper industry. During the 1960s social movement activists established a wave of underground newspapers, largely as an expression of dissatisfaction with coverage in the mainstream media of the Vietnam War, the civil rights movement, and the counterculture. In 1967 five newspapers formed the Underground Press Syndicate, and the organization soon grew to include other newspapers. Although some of the underground newspapers began as purely voluntary, noncommercial ventures, the weeklies that survived adopted a commercial, for-profit framework with revenue generated from advertising. The primary source of advertising revenue was the small local-business sector that was serving the baby boomer demographic group. For restaurants, theaters, clothing boutiques, and other locally owned independent retail and service businesses, the newspapers served as inexpensive and targeted vehicles to reach a valued segment of the local market. In my experience of reading dozens of such newspapers over the decades, the otherwise critical eyes of the alternative weeklies tended to look through fairly rosy lenses when covering local independent businesses, a proposition that I will examine more systematically later in this chapter. Instead, the alternative weeklies directed their investigative energies and exposés toward big media (including the regional dailies), local political machines, and large corporations.[16]

The alternative weeklies brought about several important changes in the conventions of journalism. They engaged in journalistic experimentation such as longer feature stories, in-depth labor coverage, coverage of alternative music and arts scenes, sex and romance advice, discussions of recreational drug use, and highly critical investigative stories about local governments and corporations. The weeklies also offered greater opportunities for amateur and part-time writers than the mainstream press, and in some cases careers launched in the alternative weeklies later transitioned into the mainstream press, which were influenced by the topics and styles of the alternative weeklies. In addition, many of the alternative weeklies were completely free; that is, they did not seek revenues from home delivery subscriptions or newsstand sales.

In 1978 owners of a group of alternative weeklies formed the Association of Alternative Weeklies, and by 2008 the association had about 130 members and a readership of more than 25 million. As circulations grew and owners aged, the organizations underwent changes. They retained their alternative flavor, but revenue increasingly came from the cigarette and the sex industries, which were especially interested in reaching the youthful demographics represented by the papers. During the 1990s the alternative weeklies also underwent some consolidation, but mostly through the development of chains that grew up from within the industry. The *Village Voice*, which managed to be both a locally oriented and a national alternative newspaper, built up one of the two alternative newspaper chains. Its chain tended to be more decentralized and more to the political left than the Arizona-based New Times chain, which some have claimed has significantly weakened the critical political content of alternative weeklies that it acquired, such as the *LA Weekly*. In other cases, small chains of alternative weeklies were purchased by larger corporate entities, such as the purchase of Alternative Media, Inc., by Times Shamrock.[17]

The professionalization that occurred after acquisition resulted in changes of form and content of coverage, and the innovations in both journalistic style and organizational structure have, in some cases, given way to patterns that are more in alignment with the mainstream newspaper industry. For example, staff members at the *East Bay Express* reported that after acquisition the policy of editorial openness to amateur writers, which allowed non-editorial staff to contribute some writing and feel much more a part of the paper, was lost; the idiosyncratic feature stories of 6,000–12,000 words on the daily lives of the working-class people were cut down; and investigative stories were limited. The complaints provide some details on the kinds of changes that can accompany corporate acquisition of the alternative weeklies.[18]

At an extreme the evolution of the alternative weekly began to approximate the weekly entertainment guide that many daily newspapers issue in direct competition with the weeklies. The daily newspapers also showed increasing interest in acquiring the alternative weeklies. In 2000 a task force of the Gannett chain, the largest newspaper chain in the United States, targeted weeklies as a way to reach the elusive 25–34-year-old readers. The goal was problematic, because the demographics of the alternative weeklies were floating upward as the Baby Boom generation aged. By 2002 the average reader's age had risen to 46, and the weeklies were struggling with the same issue of reaching the younger cohort. As the chains entered the market with their weekly entertainment guides, there was additional filtering out of critical political content that was parallel to some of the changes that the alternative weeklies faced after acquisition.[19]

The consolidation process that has occurred with local alternative newspapers has a parallel in the history for community and minority radio stations. As noted above, radio became somewhat more localized during the 1950s, when network programming migrated to television. Furthermore, in the wake of the 1960s social movements, the number of community radio stations grew from a half-dozen licensed stations in the early 1970s to more than 170 stations in the mid 1990s. Often led by volunteers, the smallest community radio stations had precarious financing that made them especially vulnerable to elimination. In the early 1990s the umbrella organization, the National Federation of Community Broadcasters, began pushing stations toward the goals of increased audience share, paid hosts, and greater homogeneity of programming. The Corporation for Public Broadcasting funded the "Healthy Station Project," which encouraged stations to accept greater national programming from public radio. The public corporation also developed a list of stations targeted for defunding because of their small audience size and independent programming. Pressure to increase listening audiences by reducing local content in favor of syndicated content continued for local stations that were affiliated with National Public Radio, and in 1996 the divisions became explicit when the grassroots stations held the first Grassroots Radio Conference as an alternative to the National Federation of Community Broadcasters.[20]

In addition to supporting licensed community radio, the Grassroots Radio Conference also supported microbroadcasting, or low-power FM broadcasting that generally can only reach a neighborhood or small city. Streaming over the Internet was another, legal option for small broadcasters, but in the 1990s the potential audience, especially among the urban poor, still tended to use broadcast radio. Consequently, even though microbroadcasting was often on legally contested grounds, it remained central to the grassroots forms of locally owned community radio. Again, public radio was not supportive. During the 1980s the Corporation for Public Broadcasting and the National Federation of Community Broadcasters requested that the Federal Communications Commission limit low-power noncommercial FM broadcasting on grounds of "spectrum scarcity." In the wake of federal regulations that made low-power community stations illegal, a microbroadcasting movement sprang up and engaged in legal battles with the Federal Communications Commission over the constitutionality of the agency's suppression of the "pirate" stations as a form of free speech. After a decade of struggle, in 2000 the Federal Communications Commission created a low-power FM service that began licensing noncommercial, low-power stations (10–100 watts) throughout the FM band. National Public Radio and the National Association of Broadcasters (the commercial broadcasters' trade association) lobbied Congress, and later that year Congress passed a rider to an appropriations bill that changed the technical requirements from the FCC's two-band buffer to a three-band buffer. In effect, the requirement of a larger buffer ended up restricting low-power FM mostly to rural stations. The new regulations ended up not legalizing microbroadcasting but instead splitting the movement between those who sought legal recognition and those who believed that low-power FM was constitutionally protected free speech that did not require licensing.[21]

Although community radio and microbroadcasting often included programming oriented toward ethnic minority communities, minority-owned radio represents a third category of locally oriented programming. After court rulings and activism over content diversity during the 1970s, the Federal Communications Commission developed preference policies for ethnic minority ownership via the licensing process. Although the changes were helpful, minority radio stations faced discriminatory practices by advertisers. Furthermore, changes in the Commission's policies after 1984 discouraged minority ownership, and the rapid consolidation of the radio industry after the 1996 telecommunications reforms had an additional negative effect on minority ownership. Total market share of stations owned by ethnic minority groups during the 1990s was below 4 percent of all stations, a figure that can be compared with about 12 percent minority participation in print and electronic newsrooms or with 30 percent of the population that is represented by African-Americans, Latinos, Asian-Americans, and Native Americans. Consolidation of ownership has also been shown to be related to a decline in the diversity of programming, and blame for the decline of local, minority news coverage has been directed not only at a radio conglomerate but at the African-America network Radio One.[22]

At a local level, television has opened up somewhat to independent, local programming and control through government-mandated public access channels. Public, educational, and government (PEG) channels are supported by funding from city franchise agreements with cable television firms. The community-based stations air content generated by community groups, individual volunteers, educational institutions, government agencies, hospitals, and other nonprofit or civil-society organizations. Because cable companies tended to resist support for PEG channels, and local party politics sometimes weakened attempts to present a united front to the cable companies, negotiations to develop new PEG channels have sometimes failed. Still, the number of public access stations has grown, as has funding from the private foundations, governments, and telecommunications firms. Programming appears to have remained largely under local control, and there was not yet significant interest from commercial television in capturing this still small portion of the market.[23]

In summary: The history of locally owned community-oriented media for print, radio, and television suggests the difficulty of maintaining long-term local ownership in the context of industrial consolidation. The for-profit model of the alternative weeklies was subject to high levels of consolidation, and the changes in ownership affected the content of the publications. However, even nonprofit and voluntary community radio stations were not immune from consolidation pressures, because some were absorbed by the National Public Radio system, which tended to replace community-based programming with syndicated content. The incorporation process into corporate media chains or national public radio is less evident in microbroadcasting and public-access community television, probably because the audience size is still negligible. The examples of community media suggest again that the nonprofit model may be essential for success and longevity, especially in broadcast media, but even nonprofit status cannot serve as a complete buffer against large national media corporations.

Lessons for the Internet

The Internet promised to democratize information by providing a new type of media that was decentralized and interactive. Much as had occurred with radio during the 1920s and the 1930s, during the 1990s the commercialization of the Internet displaced the first, noncommercial wave of pioneers. Unlike the history of radio, the noncommercial sites remained available for public consumption rather than being swept away. The process is similar to the consolidation of print media, in which alternatives have survived but with smaller circulations and limited political influence.

In its early days the Internet provided a fertile ground for local, non-commercial, voluntary experiments known as community networks, community informatics, and community computing. The first development, the San Francisco Bay Area Community Memory Project of the 1970s, was an outgrowth of 1960s social movements, whereas the Free Nets of the 1980s and the early 1990s focused more on free access, especially for low-income users. As costs of access dropped and private firms took over service provisioning, the community networks developed into public access centers, large websites, or a combination of both that provided information on various aspects of a city or region. In order to attract users, the sites had to be dynamic and to have constantly changing content. As a result, the informal voluntary networks ran into increasing competition from three kinds of sites: those run by the local media and non-governmental organizations; those with a local orientation that were run by major corporations, such as the America Online Digital Cities sites; and those sponsored by city and regional governments. By the first decade of the twenty-first century even well-known models such as the Seattle Community Network faced an uncertain future, and advocates of community networks increasingly called on local governments for support for this new form of public space. One option has been to establish the community network as a nonprofit organization or to set up a foundation for support of the project; however, as in the case of other nonprofit media organizations, the option has led to conflicts between volunteers and board members.[24]

The political potential of the role of the Internet to provide an alternative source of news information, particularly news that has been blocked or underreported in the mainstream media, has become increasingly evident. One example is the Indymedia or Independent Media Centers (IMC) movement, which began as a website for media activists during the 1999 Seattle demonstrations against the World Trade Organization and attracted more than 500,000 viewers per hour at its peak. Within a few years the Indymedia movement had quickly grown into an international movement with about 100 local groups around the world. The basic premise of the organization is that anyone can publish a news story, and accuracy judgments are left up to the reader and other writers. The premise is combined with the anti-globalization stance of most of the writers, and in practice the editorial groups of local Indymedia groups exercise some control over content. The Indymedia movement has the advantage of relatively low costs in comparison with print media, but Internet-based publishing is hardly immune from cost pressures that arise when increases in traffic require higher bandwidth. So far the Indymedia movement has survived based on the volunteer work of a committed core of activists, but it has been less successful at developing network-level planning and coordination. The movement also has a long-term problem similar to that faced by Pacifica and community radio stations: adjusting the core activist group, which is largely white and male, to ethnic and other changes in the community's diversity. As with community radio, IMCs also face the problem of balancing the need for editorial quality with a goal of editorial openness. One would expect that as the scale of traffic and news increases, voluntary and charismatic efforts would

undergo routinization through the formation of formal nonprofit organizations, and subsequently board and staff conflicts that occupied other
alternative media would emerge. The transition to a formal organization
has occurred in some centers, such as the one in Urbana-Champaign,
which is also the first IMC to gain formal nonprofit status.[25]

Perhaps the greatest potential for independent media is the proliferation of news oriented websites, blogs, podcasts, videocasts, and social
networking sites. As of 2005 a few blogs topped 100,000 hits per day;
in other words, their daily "circulation" reached the scale of the national
alternative magazines, and their influence on national political events
was widely recognized. However, before becoming too celebratory of the
potential of the Internet to undo a century of media consolidation, a few
limitations with respect to the localist potential should be listed. Most
of the "independent" media sites on the Internet are topically narrow
and geographically broad, rather than localist in the sense of providing
information on local communities or the localist movement. Furthermore, many of the sites with the highest number of downloads have a
commercial component based on advertising or other forms of business
sponsorship. The commercial model opens this form of communication
to the same processes of consolidation and content selection that occurred
elsewhere in the history of the media. Another caveat is that as the
Internet makes the transition from the silent era to the talkies, the loss
of net neutrality could set up a two-tiered system that further marginal-
izes independent news and information sources.[26]

Media Coverage of Localism

Because the message of building support for locally owned independent
enterprises could be threatening to corporate-owned media, one might
expect that corporate media would be sources of negative press coverage
of localism, whereas the alternative national media, community media,
and independent, Internet-based news sources would offer more positive
coverage of localism.

A possible example of such divergence is coverage of the 2005 "Buy
Local Philly" campaign run by the Sustainable Business Network of
Greater Philadelphia. As the campaign got underway, the *Philadelphia*

Inquirer published a critical article by the business columnist Andrew Cassel, who claimed that buying from locally owned independent businesses was not different from buying from "Christians" or "white people." The "buy local" campaign had cited the local economic impact research, but Cassel called the claims bogus. His article received numerous replies on local websites and blogs, letters to the editor, and a rebuttal published in the alternative newsweekly the *Philadelphia City Paper*. In the latter media venue, the columnist Bruce Schimmel defended the localist campaign; in a second column he accused Cassel of "mouthing the pieties of the megacorps that succor him" (Schimmel 2005b). Although controversy is not always the most desirable form of publicity, the debate ended up publicizing the campaign, which was generally viewed as a success. Leanne Krueger-Braneky, the director of the Sustainable Business Network of Greater Philadelphia, noted:

The Cassel piece proved to create some good publicity for the campaign. My response was printed in the *Philadelphia Inquirer*, and there was a letter from Judy Wicks that was also printed in the *Inquirer*. Cassel went on to write a second column, Bruce Schimmel wrote a second column, and we ended up having eight major media hits during the campaign. We talked to consumers about how they had heard about the campaign and if it impacted their behavior in any way, and we found that the majority of people whose behavior was impacted by the campaign were following the debate closely.[27]

To what extent can the media exchange be viewed through the lens of corporate versus local ownership of the media? At the time the *Philadelphia Inquirer* was owned by the Knight-Ridder chain, and the *Philadelphia City Paper* was owned by Metroweek Corp., a privately held, Philadelphia-based publishing company that also owns other newspapers. The author of the pro-local column, Bruce Schimmel, was the founding publisher of the *Philadelphia City Paper*. He had sold the alternative weekly to the Metroweek in 1996, and one can assume that what he wrote probably reflects his own experience as an independent businessman in Philadelphia. The chairman of the parent organization Metroweek, Milton L. Rock, is the founding chair of the American Alliance of Family Businesses. Although neither of the two newspapers involved in the controversy was locally owned and independent, the *Philadelphia City Paper* was an alternative free newsweekly whose corporate owner was local and concerned with family businesses. More to the point, the author of the article was the former owner of the paper when it was locally owned and independent.[28]

There is a suggestion of a similar pattern in reporting on the organization in the region where I live, Capital District Local First. The local alternative newsweekly, *Metroland*, ran a very positive story on the organization's kickoff event, which featured an appearance by Michael Shuman. The *Daily Gazette*, another independent newspaper, ran a positive article on the organization, whereas an article in the Hearst Corporation's *Albany Times-Union* was somewhat more critical. Perhaps only in the interest of journalistic balance, the *Times-Union* article mentioned a counter-localist group in Austin called "Make Austin Weird," which was said to view localism as protectionism. Although the coverage in the large corporate newspaper was not especially negative, it provided space for an unfounded negative argument, whereas the coverage in the locally owned independent newspapers did not.[29]

In an attempt to assess the question of the extent to which local ownership of the media affects coverage of localism, I read a sample of 100 newspaper and magazine articles from an electronic database using the search phrase "buy local." The sample was mostly American newspapers, but it included some newspapers and magazines from other English-speaking countries. In general either the journalists described "buy local" events in neutral terms, or they repeated arguments and offered quotations from localist advocates. Of the 100 articles, only two could be classified as providing negative coverage of localism.[30]

One of the two negative articles was an editorial in the *Wisconsin State Journal* criticizing a plan by the mayor of Madison to encourage more government purchases from local businesses, a policy that had been supported by local first advocates in that city. The article called the measure protectionist, suggested that the mayor was pandering to the city's "liberal constituency," claimed that the program would increase red tape, and predicted that the program would lead to retaliatory measures from other cities. In turn, Madison's *Capital Times* replied with an editorial that supported the local purchasing policy and encouraged consumers to spend more of their holiday money at local businesses.[31]

The rivalry between the two newspapers dates back to when an editor resigned from the *Wisconsin State Journal* on account of its lack of support for Progressive Senator Robert LaFollette during World War I. Nearly a century later, the two newspapers retained their longstanding political rivalry, and here the liberal newspaper took up the banner of localism. Both newspapers were jointly owned by the Capital Newspapers, a Wisconsin-based chain of regional newspapers, and Lee Enterprises, an Iowa-based chain with dozens of mid-sized newspapers. However, the corporate ownership was probably a less important factor than the longstanding conservative-versus-liberal political rivalry between the newspapers and writers. In April 2008 the historical rivalry took a new turn when the liberal afternoon paper, the *Capital Times*, ceased daily print publication and migrated to the Internet.[32]

The other negative article in the sample ("Is Buying Local Always Best?") appeared in the *Christian Science Monitor*, which is known for its independent reporting. The article quoted John Clark, a World Bank development specialist and author of *Worlds Apart: The Battle for Ethical Globalization*, who expressed concern about the negative effects that anti-sweatshop boycotts have on jobs in developing countries. It also quoted Roy Jacobowitz of Acción International, a Boston-based microenterprise organization, as calling "buy local" campaigns "isolationist." The *Monitor* article also discussed the food-miles controversy and quoted Clark as claiming that growing bananas in a hothouse in a northern country would waste energy. However, it also quoted pro-local advocates, and its overall tone was one of balanced reporting of a controversy rather than slanted anti-localist message.[33]

A database search for other examples of coverage of localism in the nonlocal, national media in 2005, 2006, and the first half of 2007 ended with mixed results. Some of the coverage was positive, and some venues, such as the *New York Times*, provided consistently positive coverage of localism. The *New York Times* was still an independent media organization, although it was publicly traded and had a complex, two-tiered ownership scheme. The Public Broadcasting System carried a positive story on farm-to-cafeteria programs, National Public Radio ran a story about the value of "Eating Local, Thinking Global," and ABC discussed the strategy of buying locally in a story on reducing one's carbon footprint.[34]

Although much of the coverage in the national, corporate press was relatively positive, there was a cluster of negative articles. One example was "In Praise of Chain Stores," published in the *Atlantic Monthly* in 2006. In that article, Virginia Postrel (a libertarian) framed the "buy local" movement as a product of "bored cosmopolites" who are concerned that every place in the United States looks the same as everywhere else. In rebuttal, Postrel argued that terrain and weather, not stores, make places different; chain stores bring down prices and "spread economic discovery"; and today's children will have fond memories of meals with their families in food courts, much as an older generation now has fond memories of meals in independently owned restaurants. Postrel ignored the more serious economic claims and political rationale for localism, and it was not clear how much of the article was intended to be tongue-in-cheek.[35]

The British newsmagazine *The Economist*, read widely in the United States and known for its support of neoliberal policies, also published a negative article in late 2006. Grouping organic, fair trade, and local together, the article found problems with each one. The article raised the food-miles argument, specifically the dubious research that claimed that New Zealand lamb consumed less energy than British lamb even after shipping was taken into account. Along the same lines, the authors argued that a supermarket-based system might actually reduce total miles driven (by requiring the use of fewer large trucks on the producer end, and by not requiring consumers to make as many shopping trips as they otherwise would have to make). The article also suggested that food localism was protectionist and in conflict with fair trade.[36]

An example of localism bashing that came to my attention after completing the review discussed above was a column in *Fast Company* called "Neighborhoodlums: Exploding the Myths, Presumptions, and Pretension of the 'Buy Local' Bullies." The author mentioned a British sit-com in which the owners of a small shop ask prospective customers if they are local, and the couple ends up murdering a nonlocal customer. The author accepts the food-miles argument as the "best defense" but rejects the argument that more money recirculates in the community when a purchase is made at a local store. Apparently failing to understand the studies, she notes that the employees of chain stores live locally and spend their salaries locally. She notes the corporate appropriation of localism that is occurring, and she concludes by suggesting that the goal behind the "buy local" is "much more about shunning corporate behemoths" (Spiers 2008).

Although the portrayal of localism in *The Economist* and *Fast Company* was quite negative, the leading business magazines have not been entirely anti-local. *BusinessWeek* ran a long story about the "organic myth," but it did not discuss food localism, and in a shorter article on locally owned businesses the same magazine noted that independent grocery stores have thrived by innovating rapidly and remaining flexible. Likewise, in an article titled " 'Small-Marts' take on Wal-Mart," a senior *Fortune* writer provided mostly positive coverage of the movement in support of locally owned independent businesses, but he ended with some critical questions about the weaknesses of localism to provide major innovations in manufacturing and "its potential to morph into protectionism" (Gunther 2006b).[37]

Perhaps the paramount indication of the growing awareness of localism was a *Time* cover that featured a picture of an apple with the headline "Forget Organic. Eat Local." The article began with the consumer's dilemma of choosing between organic and local food, and it noted how the Whole Foods chain had begun to feature local food. The author also described how Google's chefs had converted to locally grown food, and he took the readers on a trip to his community-supported agriculture farm. On the choice between organic and local, the author sided in favor of local, a position that would be more grist for the mill of the agrifood researchers who argued that localism could be constructed in ways to reduce interest in sustainable agriculture.[38]

To summarize: As of 2008 the localist movement was still very new to the media, and the coverage in the national press during the preceding years does not suggest that a strongly anti-localist position had yet emerged. To be sure, there are enough degrees of freedom to leave room for journalistic coverage both for and against localism in both independent and corporate-owned media. However, there are signs of emerging anti-localist coverage, and I predict that to the extent that the localist movement becomes a threat to big-box retailers and other corporate advertisers, coverage will begin to shift. The protectionist and anti-local food-miles arguments that have already been appearing will start to become more commonplace. Likewise, to the extent that the localist movement begins to diminish the stature of nonlocal media in favor of locally owned independent media, then coverage might also become more negative.

As localism becomes more influential and more controversial, we might also begin to see the power of locally owned independent sources of news and commentary. The potential of such sources is evident in the replies to the *Economist* article, which attracted widespread criticism from bloggers and the websites of food-related organizations. In turn, their criticisms became the topic of an article in the *New York Times*, which asserted that "*The Economist* seems to be on more slippery ground when it concludes that neither organic nor locally grown food helps the environment" (D. Mitchell 2006: C5). The circulation of information from a large, mainstream, neoliberal publication through independent, Internet-based sources of news and commentary, and then back to another large, mainstream, liberal (but independent) publication provides an example of how Internet-based, independent news and commentary may play an important role in checking anti-localist sentiment that is beginning to appear in the corporate media.

Conclusion

The historical analysis presented in this chapter suggests that, among alternative national media and community media, locally owned and independent organizations that survive over the long term tend to be nonprofit organizations. Whereas localism in the retail industry occurs through small businesses, and in the energy and transportation industries largely through government organizations and publicly managed utilities, in the media industry formal nonprofit organizations appear to have a much more important place. This conclusion provides more evidence in favor of the argument that the analysis of localism should attend to its variety across industries, including variety in organizational forms. The specific organizational shape that localism takes in the media industry suggests the risks of linking an understanding of localism too closely to any particular type of organization, such as the small-business organization, the family farm, or the local government agency. Instead, organizational diversity may be an important feature in the long-term survival and success of localism.

The history of the alternative newsweeklies also suggests certain vulnerabilities for localism based on the for-profit business model, at least in the media industry. Because the alternative newsweeklies that survived the initial period of volunteer work became set up organizationally as for-profit businesses that adopted a commercial advertising revenue model, they were vulnerable to absorption by small corporate chains. It would not be surprising to see the small corporate chains eventually acquired by larger media conglomerates. In such a situation of media consolidation, transition to nonprofit status can serve as a deterrent to acquisition by outside corporations.

However, as the diverse examples indicated, nonprofit status is not a panacea. One problem is that the for-profit media conglomerates are not the only source of consolidation of small, locally owned, independent media. National Public Radio, a large nonprofit organization, has in some cases adopted positions that were detrimental to community radio and microbroadcasting. Even where external interference is kept at an arm's length, there are trends for nonlocal influence over the long term. For example, the corporate connections of large-pocket donors who fund the nonprofit organizations can lead to indirect corporate influence over community media, especially when board structures shift from staff-based representation to donor-based or expertise-based representation. Still, the importance of nonprofit organizations in community and alternative media, and in turn the importance of the media in getting the message of localism out beyond a market niche of socially and environmentally conscious consumers, suggests the overall centrality of nonprofit organizations in building at least this wing of localist pathways for change.

My analysis also suggests that by 2007 there were some signs of emerging anti-localist sentiment in the mainstream press. It would not be surprising that as the "buy local" movement grows from a situation of 100 independent business associations in the United States to hundreds, and as corporate advertisers come to see "buy local" campaigns not as quaint and reactionary oddities but as threats to retail sales growth, then anti-localist sentiment in the mainstream media would grow and solidify. In such a situation, the localist movement would find itself increasingly relying on alternative media, either in the form of national nonprofit organizations or local and independent sources of news and commentary. However, given the overall trends toward consolidation of the media, both print and electronic, and the potential loss of net neutrality, the prospects for vital independent locally controlled media remain grim.

8

Policies for an Alternative Economy

By developing public awareness of the benefits of supporting locally owned independent enterprises, advocates of localism are unlikely to bring to fruition the broader goal of building an alternative global economy. An overarching strategy is required not only to address the undercapitalization of the locally owned sector of the economy but also to provide publicly traded corporations with the incentives and opportunities to be able to solve global problems rather than to create them. In this chapter I examine fundamental transitions that could help shift the economy of the United States to life within sustainable limits that enhance fairness for all citizens. I explore policies that would enable locally owned independent organizations to flourish as well as open up the potential for publicly traded corporations to work with communities to make them more just and sustainable. Although there is certainly a need for environmental reforms such as carbon taxes, energy reduction incentives, and green technology subsidies, in this chapter I tack in a different direction by examining the policies that would be necessary to move modern capitalist societies to an economy that is adapted to our global ecology.

The "long-term" approach to policy adopted here is consistent with what Dutch social scientists call "transition theory." Their body of work is already fairly diverse, and it is worth explaining for a moment what is most useful for the present purposes. Transition theory involves an approach to policy making that adopts a time frame of decades rather than one of only a few years, considers multiple social scales of change with mutually reinforcing processes of reform, and assumes continuous adjustment as stakeholders interact with each other and learn from their policy interventions. Unlike five-year strategic plans or short-term policy fixes, the transition process is open-ended, with feedback loops to provide for the evaluation of ongoing innovations. The innovations include technologies and infrastructures, but they also involve political and regulatory systems and the development of entrepreneurial and other innovative organizations. The approach of long-term transition-oriented policy making is a valuable way of thinking about overwhelming and interlocking global problems such as climate change and poverty, and it draws attention to multiple levels of scale, such as niches (micro), regimes (meso), and landscapes (macro).[1]

The long-term and multi-scalar thinking of transition theory is a helpful way of getting a handle on complex policy issues, but I build on that approach by conceptualizing the issues in a slightly different way. Specifically, I think of the transitions as involving interlocking fields of contested policy making that themselves may cross various geographical levels of action. In this chapter I examine three policy fields in the United States that represent crucial points of intervention for building a transformation in economic organization: new ways of capitalizing localism that independent business associations could develop in partnership with mutual funds and with the support of regulatory changes; changes in local, state, and federal government policies that would support the growth of locally owned and controlled businesses; and a broader set of federal government policy reforms oriented toward changing the governance framework of the publicly traded corporation. Again, the focus of this chapter is on the United States, although a transition in the American or even the North American economy would not be meaningful unless similar changes were to occur in other countries. The policy discussion is based on the premise that outlining a series of interlocking changes in fundamental economic institutions could be the basis for enacting such changes. However, as I will suggest in the final chapter, my prognosis is that the patient is unlikely to adhere to the prescription and that collapse is a more likely outcome than transition.[2]

Financing Localism

As I demonstrated in the preceding chapters, there are many significant challenges that the localist movement faces if it is to become a part of broader social-change efforts to build an alternative global economy. One of the deepest challenges of localism is accumulating the capital required to build such an economy.

As an example, consider the following situation. For years, I patronized a locally owned independent coffee shop that was located on a busy thoroughfare that connects two cities. Meanwhile, Starbucks and Dunkin' Donuts stores continued to proliferate on that thoroughfare, and eventually the independent coffee store closed. Although I do not know the specifics of this particular store closure, it is clear from the many conversations that I have had with local owners of independent businesses in the region that they have noticed very specific effects on their revenues when new chain stores have opened up. In a way, there is nothing new in this story. However, when I look at the mutual funds that constitute my retirement portfolio, I see that corporate retailers are often well represented among the holdings of some of the funds. This is true even for funds that are screened for environmental and social governance criteria. In fact, some of the more socially and environmentally responsible companies include the very ones that are putting the independents out of business, such as Starbucks, because the screens do not include effects on locally owned businesses. In other words, as a consumer, my left hand may be buying locally, but as an investor, my right hand is supporting the very stores that are putting the locals out of business.[3]

A general problem for localism emerges: even if consumers and small businesses were to shift a significant portion of their purchases to locally owned independent enterprises (either within their region or, in a model that builds on fair trade, from similar enterprises throughout the world), they would still face the problem that much of their investments are locked up in the world of publicly traded corporations. The left hand may go local, but the right hand may not necessarily follow, because significant personal and business assets are tied up in retirement funds that may be legally restricted from investing in the small-business sector of privately held companies. As a result, even the most dedicated of localists may end up financing the very big-box stores that they wish to undermine. "Buy local" campaigns may be helping the independents to gain some steam, but well-capitalized chain stores have continued to expand and benefit from ongoing investment from individuals through their stock purchases, mutual funds, and retirement accounts. For every new independent coffee shop with fair-trade organic products and local music, there are a half-dozen new Starbucks stores. With the resources available from stock market capitalization, the large corporations have continued to colonize the remaining niches of the national and global economy, including storefronts of dense urban neighborhoods where many of the remaining independent retail businesses are located. This problem is, in my mind, a far more significant challenge for localism than any of the other challenges that I have vetted so far.

In this section I will explore various models of debt and equity financing that would help address the fundamental problem of investment. For employees who have a defined contribution retirement plan rather than a defined benefit plan, the prospect of shifting some investment out of the pension fund into retirement instruments based on the idea of import substitution, or what might be thought of as "divorcing your 401K," will also be considered. Together the elements represent the foundations of a financial infrastructure for localism, but the reader should be forewarned that at present the foundation, let alone the edifice, remains an unfinished work.

The area where debt financing and localism already work together well is the use of the local government bond authority that can back up investments in publicly owned and controlled development. A primary example, which was discussed in chapter 6, is the use of the bond authority of the city government of San Francisco to finance construction of distributed, renewable energy and energy conservation projects as part of its contract with the electricity service provider. City governments can also use their bond authority to build other types of infrastructure outside the community choice contract model, such as public transportation, so the potential use of the bond authority is quite extensive. Although revenue bonds are limited by a city's bond rating and overall financial standing, they remain an underutilized resource for supporting local public and private ownership.[4]

Debt financing may work well with localism in the case of public sector investments, but can it also work for small businesses and small investors? Often large banks are uninterested in carrying small-business loans because of their relatively high expense, but there are other sources of private debt financing, including credit unions, local banks, community loan funds, and government agencies. Independent business associations could enhance the financing of locally owned independent businesses by making such opportunities transparent to the local businesses. For example, by shifting one's savings accounts to a credit union, individuals can divert their short-term assets to local businesses, because credit unions have a higher proportion of loans to local small-businesses than large commercial banks. A similar option is to invest a portion of one's investment portfolio in a local community loan fund. There are also some national organizations, such as the Calvert Foundation's Community Investment Notes, the Reinvestment Fund Loan Fund, and Rudolf Steiner Foundation Social Finance. However, at the time of writing the rate of return on certificates of deposit in such financial instruments was generally under 4 percent per year, in contrast with the expected rate of return on equity of about 9 percent for the stock market, even 20 percent or higher for the riskier investment vehicles. As a result, locally oriented debt financing is at best a place to allocate the low-risk, low-return portion of a portfolio, but for many it is not an attractive investment option for an entire portfolio. When one takes into account inflation and taxes, the rate of return could even be negative.[5]

Another possibility for developing investment capital for locally owned independent businesses is the use of community currencies. In the United States there are a few experiments with printed local currencies, such as Ithaca Hours, BerkShares, and Burlington Bread. There are also some examples of time banking systems and many more experiments with computerized trading schemes known as "local exchange trading systems." All three types of complementary and local currencies have strengths and weaknesses, but after having read the literature and attended a multi-day conference on the topic, I concluded that the systems require substantial knowledge and commitment from a few central organizers in order to be successful. If a central player pulls out or ends up with too much currency or too many credits, the system can collapse or just slowly dwindle into disuse, and many have. The Berkshares model of local currency has so far achieved some important new innovations. One change is that the currency can be traded for American dollars at local banks, and consequently there is a way out for businesses that become concerned with accumulating too much local currency. But more relevant to the discussion here is the plan to use a portion of the local currency for local loans. If successful, the community currency will have created a new pool of investment capital for locally owned independent businesses.[6]

Another interesting innovation also comes from the Berkshires region of western Massachusetts, a situation that is not a surprise when one considers that the E. F. Schumacher Society is headquartered there. A store in Great Barrington financed a renovation by issuing "deli dollars." In effect the scrip was an in-kind bond, or coupons that were repayable with interest in purchases from the restaurant at a later date. For example, if a store were to sell $100 notes repayable in two years for purchases valued at $121, it would in effect offer bonds at a rate of 10 percent per year, which at the time of writing was a good rate in comparison with, for example, government bonds. In fact, the rate would be comparable to one that would be expected over the long term from an investment in the stock market. If a potential investor is reasonably satisfied that the store will not go out of business and that the store's products are valuable, then there is considerably less risk in comparison with the stock market. Of course, the liquidity is also lower, but a holder of the coupons could conceivably sell them, and markets might even be devised for local bonds of this sort. If the store has an average markup of 50 percent, it could take the cost of financing the bonds out of future profits without incurring a cash debt. Instead, it would lock in future sales. This type of financing could be very attractive for a small business.[7]

More generally, retail stores that are in the resale industry or that have even a portion of their stock in second-hand goods can use a similar mechanism. By paying for used goods with store credits, a store can build up an inventory without needing to cover the up-front costs of purchasing the inventory. At the same time, the goods acquired for credit can be sold for cash, and the store credits also lock in future purchases for the store. The system of self-capitalizing inventory with a lock-in of future customers makes such arrangements potentially very lucrative. Customers benefit by receiving a store credit that is worth more than the cash value of the used goods. Like the deli dollar model, self-financing through trades is highly promising, and the potential for aggregating various types of credits across businesses in a region has not been developed. They represent opportunities not only for the small retailers but also for financial companies.

When we turn to the equity (or stock) side of investing, the lack of connection between the financial needs of small businesses and those of small investors is even more evident. Whereas independent business associations are proliferating and "buy local" campaigns are becoming more prominent, there is little information available in the parallel world of local equity investing. Unfortunately, there are currently very few options available for channeling tax-deferred retirement funds into locally owned investments. A person may invest some money in an individual retirement account (IRA) held as a certificate of deposit at a credit union, but as noted above the option is only a low-risk, low-return product, and it cannot satisfy the need to have a diversified retirement portfolio. People with higher than average financial literacy may opt for a self-directed IRA and channel some of the money into small-business equity or real estate investments, but the option requires considerable knowledge and ongoing monitoring. Clearly, other investment vehicles are necessary. One possible model comes from the government of the Canadian province of Nova Scotia, which supports community economic development investment funds. The funds are designed to recapture investment revenue that is flowing out of the province and channel it back into local businesses. People who opt to put some of their savings in the funds receive a 30 percent tax credit and a partial guarantee. Because the funds are equity investments, they may earn a higher rate of return than the loan funds discussed above. If investment options such as those in Nova Scotia were to become widely available, and if they could be opened up to tax-deferred retirement savings accounts, then a significant source of capital could be unleashed to assist in the development of small businesses.[8]

At present there is little demand from consumers to have mutual fund companies offer localist financial products and to have federal and state governments facilitate their creation. In order to create political opportunities for such products to emerge, a concerted mobilization of localist and small-business umbrella organizations would have to take place. The world of state and local pension funds provides a model of how the mutual fund industry might be opened up to localist investing. The public fund managers are allowed to dedicate a portion of their portfolios to "economically targeted investments" as long as the investments have a similar risk and return profile to that of nontargeted investments. Examples of investments include affordable housing, joint public- and employee-owned corporations, commercial real estate, and small businesses. By dedicating a portion of a pension fund's investments to local economic development, the funds not only achieve a market rate of return for investors but also help to ensure a good future income stream by strengthening the local economy. With assets of more than $3 trillion in the United States, public pension funds are a potentially huge source of investment resources for localist projects, even if only a small percentage of the assets are invested locally. If the model were extended to mutual fund companies that hold defined contribution accounts, the effect would be much more significant.[9]

Real estate is another area where there is a potential for the creation of new financial products that enable retirement accounts to be invested in locally owned independent businesses. One example would be a local real estate investment trust (REIT) that invests in commercial property that is rented by a high percentage of locally owned independent businesses. Although there is now proof of concept of the community development REITs, a localist REIT that offers investment opportunities through 401K retirement plans is not yet available as an investment option. It would probably be much easier to create a localist REIT than to develop rules to allow stock fund managers to invest a portion of the portfolio in economically targeted investments.[10]

Thinking about localism and the equity investment problem may require an even deeper rethinking of retirement-oriented investing than developing new financial products. For most members of the middle class in the United States, the two greatest investments are their home and retirement accounts. The primary financial goals are to build a significant retirement account, to pay down the home mortgage, to maintain a comfortable lifestyle during the working years, and to live long enough to enjoy one's savings before dying. The personal finance and retirement industry pumps out new ideas in glossy magazines every month about how to achieve such goals, and much of the advice, like the advertisers who pay for the magazines, describes how to select the best new mutual funds and stocks for optimum, short-term gains. The industry has also developed complex algorithms that show families how much money they should have saved in order to be able to retire at a level of income that is only slightly less than the current household income. Most middle-class investors whom I know look at such algorithms and come to the grim realization that they are likely to continue working until the day they drop dead from exhaustion. Still, they may be convinced that even if they cannot "max out" various retirement options, they should put more money aside for retirement; that is, they should plough present earnings into a mutual fund that will, with luck, provide a good growth rate. The problem with this approach to retirement is that in the absence of localist financial products that are available through tax-deferred retirement savings plans, individuals end up being recruited to the growth logic of the publicly traded corporation, and the only option for socially and environmentally responsible investing is the screened fund.

As some of the more far-sighted leaders of the localist movement recognize, they need to move beyond "buy local" campaigns to solve the problem of equity investment. Can the ideas of "buy local" and "import substitution" also be extended to personal finance, and, if so, what effects would they have? Localism in general and the concept of import substitution in particular suggest a different way of thinking about one's financial future in the context of a precarious global future. One way of thinking locally in the investment field is to reconceptualize the relative weight of investment in one's home versus retirement accounts. People who are anchored in a community and are able to buy the house that they intend to retire in, or who are able to purchase their retirement property as a second home, are in a good position to adopt a different strategy of investment based on import substitution on a household level. Rather than focusing on investing as a way of achieving higher future revenue, it is possible to adopt the opposite strategy of investing to reduce future costs, an approach which has both personal financial and global environmental dividends. For example, one might relocate to a place where public transportation is readily available, or one might mobilize citizens to extend it to one's neighborhood. One could also weatherize the home, install solar panels and windmills, build a geothermal component for the heating and cooling system, buy energy-efficient appliances, build a greenhouse and backyard garden, purchase a share in a local farm, join an exercise club, change one's diet, purchase preventative health services, and invest in other options that reduce not only one's personal ecological footprint but also one's future expenses, including the risk of high medical expenses. Those changes generally substitute present expenses for future savings, but they can be analyzed financially as investments with an annualized rate of return. Furthermore, the investments operate as a personal, local, hedge fund against rising energy, transportation, health-care, and food costs. What the investments lack in liquidity, they may make up for in longevity.

A change in the federal government's policy could enable such investment transitions to take place at a much higher scale than is occurring today under the patchwork of renewable energy home investment credits. One possibility is what I term a "retirement-to-energy, no penalty early withdrawal" ("RENEW") program. Individuals could withdraw money from their defined contribution retirement accounts and invest it in energy-conservation measures for their home and possibly other properties. Although early withdrawal is already allowed for a range of difficult circumstances, such as health-care bills, the withdrawal is still taxable. Under the RENEW program, there would be no tax penalty for the withdrawal under the assumption that the investments would create increased property value and, if the owner stays in the same house, decreased retirement expenses. In other words, the program would not be conceptualized as a withdrawal of retirement investments but as a transfer of retirement investments from publicly traded corporations and government bonds to individually owned energy savings and equity. Examples of allowable investments would include installation of solar photovoltaics, solar hot water heating, wind power, geothermal, insulation, energy efficient windows and doors, and weatherization. This program would potentially scale rapidly to facilitate huge investments in energy conservation, and it would result in various transfers of wealth. First, funds would flow from general retirement investment accounts into purchases of products made by companies (mostly publicly traded) that manufacture green tech products, such as photovoltaics and insulation. One result of the RENEW program would be a shot in the arm for the green tech industry. Second, funds would flow from equity holdings in large publicly traded corporations to household ownership of the energy investments, which become part of home equity, and to local contractors, many of which are locally owned businesses.

One potential problem with the RENEW program idea is that there would likely be some opposition to a program that would make it easier for people to remove retirement savings. I have defended the idea as a transfer of retirement savings from one sector of the economy (publicly traded corporations) to another (individual home equity), but the concern with allowing a withdrawal of savings from retirement plans might trump the energy investment and future home equity return. A variant of the RENEW program that might solve the political impasse would be a "home energy savings account," something like the currently existing health savings account. The account would allow people to generate new tax-exempt savings each year, then withdraw from the account for home energy investments.

Two other models under development in the United States also have tremendous potential for localist investment. There are some cases of successful intrastate stock offerings, but the mechanism is not widely used, and the shares are much less liquid than those of publicly traded companies. Some localist leaders are working on plans for intrastate, local stock markets that are limited to residents in the state. The prospect of a local stock market could provide opportunities for the more liquid equity investment in the local economy, and it might be possible to construct tax-deferred retirement funds from local stock holdings. Another option under development builds on the private equity firm model. Although most private equity investment is oriented toward short-term investments that end in initial public offerings or sale to a large corporation, private equity firms have emerged with other missions. For example, Upstream 21 invests in small companies that have a social and environmental mission and either require help to grow or want to sell because the owner is nearing retirement. Rather than planning to buy and flip companies as most private equity companies do, it holds companies for the long term. By serving as a holding company, Upstream 21 prevents acquisition by large corporations and allows community-oriented, stakeholder forms of governance to flourish. This model probably does not hold great potential for tax-deferred retirement investments, but it is an option for accredited investors who wish to allocate a portion of their portfolio to such companies.[11]

There may also be opportunities to create a new kind of publicly traded company that benefits the local, living economy. One could imagine a holding company such as Upstream 21 that is configured as a publicly traded company, a Berkshire Hathaway of localism. There are also many services that a publicly traded company could offer to local independent businesses: directories with paid advertising of locally owned independent businesses; gift cards only valid at such businesses; searchable web-based inventories; and credit cards. Such business services are probably better offered by the for-profit sector than non-profit business associations, which have legal restrictions on providing services that directly benefit members. The business services could operate as small, start-up companies that are privately held or as member-based cooperatives, but it would also be possible to set up a publicly held company to provide such services. Although on the surface anathema to localist thinking, such publicly traded companies might be better viewed as a form of localist jiu-jitsu. In other words, they use the publicly traded stock market as a mechanism for channeling investment back into the localist sector.

In summary: The opportunities for developing greater investment capital for locally owned independent businesses and the corresponding opportunities for the locally oriented investor are largely limited to debt markets with low rates of return and relatively low risk. It is virtually impossible for individuals to take advantage of tax-deferred retirement accounts in order to invest in the local business sector. Although self-directed IRAs are a possibility for sophisticated investors, for the average investor the only currently available retirement vehicle is the IRA certificate of deposit in a local credit union. Options in real estate and equity investments with higher rates of return and risk that also would benefit locally owned independent businesses are not yet available to the non-accredited investor. In my view, addressing this problem should be the number one goal of independent business associations. This is not to say that they should abandon the consumption side of the picture and the highly visible "buy local" campaigns. However, the solution to the problem of equity investment and retirement accounts will determine whether the localist movement remains a relatively small and politically unimportant niche or whether it triggers a fundamental economic transition that fulfills the dreams of its leaders.[12]

Rethinking Small-Business Policies

Small businesses that decide to be environmentally responsible, community-oriented, and sensitive to the financial and lifestyle needs of their employees face an uphill battle. Companies that have chosen to be great instead of big (in the words of Bo Burlingham) do so without much government support. There are many policy changes, both at the local government level and at the federal government level, that would make it easier for such businesses to thrive.[13]

With respect to the local nonprofit sector, there are many points of intervention for city governments that wish to develop the portion of this sector that has an environmental and/or justice orientation. Cities can develop policies that facilitate the formation of reuse centers, community gardens, nonprofit farms, community media organizations, and credit unions. The policies can involve helping organizations to find low-cost space and legal advice, making sure that the nonprofit and small-business sectors are included in regional plans, and connecting the nonprofit sector with city government agencies and the public school system. The city's system of codes and land-use ordinances can also be a powerful tool for the development of the nonprofit sector. In addition to supporting the green spaces that can be used for community gardening, city codes can be used to support the reuse industry by requiring the full deconstruction of public buildings. Likewise, demolition permits for other buildings can be structured to require that a minimum percentage of materials be diverted from landfills into reuse. The city can also help the reuse industry to change state and federal tax codes to allow a write-off for the full value of a deconstructed house, rather than its less advantageous resale value. Many of the policies may involve developing new organizations at the niche level, but over the course of decades the growth of nonprofit organizational networks can create broader changes in a metropolitan and state government's regimes of environmental and social policy.[14]

Regarding the local public sector, there are many points of opportunity for the greening of local electricity and transportation systems. Public power, community choice, and energy-conservation utilities are three available pathways for metropolitan or urban governments to use for transitions at a significant scale toward energy conservation and renewable, distributed energy. Municipal and regional transit agencies can also link the greening of their transit fleets to energy-conservation measures and to locally supplied renewable energy, either through biofuels or electricity. Cities can also fund the greening of their fleets with revenue from a municipal electrical agency, as Seattle has done. In Chattanooga the city linked its purchase of a downtown electric bus fleet to the development of a local manufacturing plant. The city of San Francisco put parking and traffic management under the same roof as its transit agency, so that a coherent transit policy could be developed. One promising policy, for example, is to charge a toll on visitors to the central city and use the revenue to fund low-cost or free public transit within the downtown area. The policy has the double advantage of reducing the influx of privately owned cars while encouraging people to use readily available municipal buses and trolleys.

With respect to the local retail industry, there are imaginative ways in which an urban government can build partnerships with independent business associations to develop the local economy. City governments can help provide signage and other markers of independent-business districts, as has been done in Austin. They can help provide space and other resources for fledging independent business associations, and they can support "buy local" campaigns. A white paper published by the Sustainable Business Network of Greater Philadelphia suggested that cities could conduct studies of where business losses are occurring and where regional assets are located, and they could develop regional indicators to identify where public investments and purchases can be directed to help local businesses. Some cities have also developed local procurement policies that help balance the resources that tend to flow to nonlocal businesses.[15]

Tax policies and subsidies can be examined to identify opportunities to support locally owned independent businesses and to eliminate breaks for nonlocal business competitors. Many existing tax policies and subsidies favor businesses that are not locally owned or locally managed. Stacy Mitchell notes that corporate retailers often can escape paying state and federal corporate income tax, whereas small retailers suffer from disproportionately higher taxes. She also describes many cases of big-box stores that absorbed huge subsidies to assist in their construction costs; eventually, those costs were spread out over all taxpayers, including small businesses. Again, local and state governments have an opportunity to level the playing field so that the tax burden for local retailers is not disproportionately larger than for the global chains.[16]

Some cities and counties have taken the next step by passing ordinances that limit the existence of franchises and big-box stores. One approach is to use zoning laws to limit the size of retail businesses; however, the approach has some limitations, partly because the size of a category-killer store varies across industries, and partly because the superstores can relocate to a neighboring community. As Mitchell also points out, city governments can work together to set up a regional planning agency, which can reduce the ability of big-box stores to hop municipal boundaries and can also establish review processes that are anchored in goals such as strengthening local business. Another strategy is to place explicit limitations on formula businesses such as franchises. In small cities and tourist destinations, formula businesses can be detrimental to the local economy because they reduce the uniqueness and charm of the location. Some states, such as Iowa, have also enacted legislation that protects the independence of franchisees.[17]

On the topic of federal government policy, small-business associations have called for many reforms, among them universal health-care coverage, more equitable access to capital, and the elimination of taxes that unfairly disadvantage small businesses. Support for such reforms could begin with an end to the "corporate welfare" of subsidies and tax loopholes at the national level. According to the non-governmental organization Citizen Works, corporate tax loopholes are worth $76 billion in uncollected taxes. Another area of unequal treatment is research funding, which is often captured by large corporations, even in cases where small businesses are competing for the funds.[18]

In addition to changes that would benefit the small-business sector in general, locally owned independent businesses with missions of social and environmental responsibility also face significant long-term exit problems that could be addressed with government policy changes. When the original owner of a small business dies or decides to retire, public policies often restrict the available possibilities of transition. If the company is passed on to family members, estate taxes may be so large that the heirs are forced to sell the company. If a socially and environmentally responsible small company is sold to a large corporation, case studies suggest that the new corporate owner will sweep aside at least some of the social and environmental values and practices. The environmental mission may be retained, especially if the company has created a market niche based on an environmental product (for example, organic foods), but employee participation and financial benefits are likely to be aligned with broader corporate decision-making and compensation policies. Income-tax reform could assist environmentally and socially responsible small businesses by providing mechanisms to reduce the likelihood that the businesses will be sold to a large corporation and thereby lose their distinctive character.[19]

Employee ownership provides another exit strategy that avoids the often unpalatable choices among continued family ownership, when no heirs are apparent; finding a corporate buyer, who may drift from the values mission and good employee practices; and taking the company public, which entails a shift of fiduciary responsibility to anonymous shareholders. Although employee ownership does not guarantee that firms will act in more socially and environmentally responsible ways, employee-owners are more likely to live in the communities where businesses are located, and consequently they are more likely to return profits, services, and donations to the community. Employee-owners are also more likely to continue the company's traditions of environmental practices, employee participation, limited wage differentials, and community stewardship than a large corporation that purchases the firm from a retiring owner. For example, studies of worker-owned cooperatives suggest that the businesses are less growth-oriented and more resource efficient than publicly held corporations.[20]

Employee ownership programs have grown steadily in the United States, from about 1,600 in 1975 to more than 11,000 in 2003, and at present more employees are in employee stock ownership plans programs than in private-sector unions. Although most of the programs are not accompanied by meaningful worker participation in management, they nevertheless have the potential to shift corporate governance toward greater stakeholder influence. Historically both Democrats and Republicans have supported employee ownership legislation, and consequently there is some potential for ongoing bipartisan reform. Various policies could be enacted to support the development of employee plans and to assist their transition to complete employee ownership and management. For example, when an owner or group of owners decides that it is time to sell the company, a decision to sell to employees can be financially risky. The company may have to take out a loan to pay for the owner's equity share, and the debt burden can be financially harmful to the company. Federal and state government tax incentives in favor of employee ownership could help make the transition to employee ownership easier and less risky for the company.[21]

More generally, a ten-point plan developed by Jeff Gates, an attorney who worked for years with Congress to develop employee ownership legislation, includes a wide range of changes in the tax laws that would facilitate the growth of employee ownership plans. Congress has also considered legislation that would increase the amount of corporate stock owned by employees and establish the employee-owned and employee-controlled corporation as a new legal category. Opportunities for employee ownership also occur when corporations decide to sell a plant or merge significant assets.[22]

Another area in need of reform is anti-trust legislation. During the 1980s and after, court decisions and budget cuts severely limited the ability of the federal government to enforce laws designed to limit the predatory pricing policies of large corporate retailers. Although large retailers have been documented to price products below cost in the short term in order to drive out competitors, small businesses have historically been unable to find redress through the courts. Another problem area is buyer power, that is, the ability of large corporate firms to squeeze discounts and other favorable terms from suppliers. Although the Robinson-Patman Act made such action illegal, since the 1970s there has been little federal enforcement of the law. Civil lawsuits by independent booksellers during the 1990s met with only mixed success, and during the early 2000s some members of Congress were pushing to repeal the law altogether. In short, a vibrant, independent retail industry requires stronger anti-trust legislation, that is, a reversal of the trend toward ongoing weakening of existing legislation.[23]

Corporate Reform

A fundamental economic transition will also require rethinking an economy that is based on what is essentially an amoral institution: the publicly traded corporation. The publicly traded corporation's mission of maximizing shareholder returns is the product of a time when environmental problems were far less evident, societies were more concerned with exploring and maintaining control over large territories, the ecological footprint of human societies on a global scale was much smaller, and the world's population was much lower. Although the large global corporation can articulate and in some cases follow through on social and environmental responsibility goals, the goals tend to be sacrificed when profitability is at risk. The task of transforming the modern, publicly traded, industrial corporation from an engine of short-term growth that treats environmental and social degradation as an externality into a long-term steward of environmental sustainability and social fairness is daunting, but without the transition it seems likely that a significant percentage of publicly traded corporations will find that environmental, labor, and community-oriented reforms are in conflict with their fundamental mission of maximizing short-term earnings. As a result, they will find that neoliberal political ideology is the best match for their short-term, legally mandated responsibilities to shareholders, and the world's environmental and social crises will continued to be addressed in a piecemeal manner of "too little, too late" policy reforms.

There is no shortage of proposals that would inaugurate the transition of the publicly traded corporation to a civic enterprise that incorporates stakeholder participation in decision making and is guided by a broader vision of social and environmental stewardship. Seven proposals represent a good starting point, listed more or less in an order of declining likelihood of enactment and increasing political importance: public financing of political campaigns; making triple-bottom-line reporting mandatory rather than voluntary; lengthening the time horizon for corporate reporting and investing from its current focus on quarterly earnings; regulatory reform to make shareholder activism more effective; granting corporate charters on a national level and requiring stakeholder participation (rather than only shareholder ownership) in order for a company to be publicly traded; restricting the legal fiction of corporate personhood; and nationalization of some companies or industries.

Although public campaign financing is not directly related to corporate reform, it might be viewed as a precondition that would open up possibilities for other types of reform. For example, James Gustave Speth of the School of Forestry and Environmental Studies at Yale University has noted that the achievement of meaningful environmental reform is unlikely as long as anti-environmental corporations are able to influence the political process. Speth advocates public campaign financing and related policies to reduce corporate influence on policy making. There is a limited but growing track record of achievement on this reform goal. Several states have enacted voluntary public financing of campaigns, and participation rates by candidates has been high. The reforms have resulted in an increased diversity and number of candidates, but they have not yet created a complete firewall between corporate donations and political campaigns. For example, political parties may still finance candidates, and issue ads by independent organizations are still allowed. Furthermore, the related issues of restricting corporate lobbying and the revolving door between political office and lobbying position remain unresolved.[24]

In the United States there has also been considerable progress in a second area of corporate reform: transparency and reporting of social and environmental records. However, to date the reporting has been voluntary. The standard for reporting is the Global Reporting Initiative of the Coalition for Environmentally Responsible Economies (CERES), a non-governmental organization that was founded in 1989 by environmental groups and institutional investors. The voluntary reports are based on the triple bottom line of environmental, social, and economic criteria. Unfortunately, attention to social and environmental responsibility goals tends to fade when financial adversity strikes, and often the worst violators of environmental and social stewardship are the ones least likely to adopt such standards. It is also difficult for watchdog groups and government agencies to verify the claims made in voluntary reports, especially for multinational corporations that have set up shop in distant corners of the globe, where scrutiny from non-governmental organizations and independent media is absent. Ongoing campaigns by social movement organizations and socially responsible mutual funds against unsustainable forestry and fishing, sweatshops, pollution, toxic products, and union-busting tactics have, in some cases, resulted in changes in corporate policy, including pledges to source products that are certified by third-parties. However, the fact that such campaigns are still necessary suggests the persistence of deeper problems in the way that that information is diffused about the practices of modern society's fundamental economic institution.[25]

Although having mandatory reporting of social and environmental metrics may appear to be a relatively straightforward and uncontroversial proposal, the history of a recent change in mandatory reporting suggests that even such incremental policy reforms are likely to meet with stiff resistance. The Sarbanes-Oxley Act of 2002, a legislative reform that was passed in the wake of the corporate scandals surrounding Enron and other companies, created a Public Company Accounting Oversight Board, tightened regulations for the accounting profession, and increased the fiduciary responsibilities of boards of directors. The main function of the law was to restore investor confidence in the reliability of financial reports rather than to enhance corporate responsibility in the general terms that I have been outlining. However, even the rather meager effort to enhance corporate responsibility has met with a rising chorus of calls from the business press to repeal the legislation. Some observers worry that American start-ups are launching initial public offerings in foreign stock markets as a way to avoid the cost of financial compliance reports, which can be burdensome for small publicly traded companies. The history of Sarbanes-Oxley suggests that direct, legislative approaches to mandating increased reporting of social and environmental responsibility will likely meet with stiff resistance by publicly traded corporations. Furthermore, the history suggests that it is difficult for one country to enact legislative changes when others do not.[26]

A third group of legislative reforms, mostly having to do with reporting standards as well, would complement the triple-bottom-line approach by shifting the short-term orientation of the publicly traded corporation. Giving the publicly traded corporation and institutional investors some breathing room might free them to integrate longer-term thinking based on social and environmental principles into their corporate strategies. Among the proposed reforms related to time horizons are the following:

• Lengthen financial reporting periods.

• Count research and development as long-term rather than short-term expenses.

• Enact a tax on short-term trades on a sliding scale from less than 24 hours to a month.

• Limit the degree to which fund manager compensation is tied to short-term performance.

• Change the period of stockholder elections of boards from every year to once every five years.[27]

Reforms that combine mandated reporting on environmental and social responsibility performance with an increase in the financial time horizon would help open up some room for large corporations to blend the hard-headed, single bottom-line concerns of business with the broader long-term interests of our planet and global society. Enhanced reporting of social and environmental data would enable corporations to demonstrate successful performance in comparison with their competitors, just as it would allow financial analysts and non-governmental organizations to identify worst cases and motivate the laggards to improve performance. To the extent that poor performance on social and environmental metrics becomes the focus of stock market analysts, social movement mobilization, and media attention, investor perceptions of risk for the worst offenders would increase, and as a result poor performance on goals of environmental and social responsibility could affect stock performance. There are many "ifs" in the scenario, but with the continuing adjustments to policies and incentive schemes that a transition theory approach suggests, the spotlighting of poor performance could be a powerful mechanism to motivate corporations to escape from the straightjacket of short-term growth in earnings and lip service to social and environmental responsibility.

Another approach comes from grassroots activism directed at corporate policies rather than government policies. The term "shareholder activism" refers to two kinds of grassroots action. Environmental, labor, and human rights organizations have proposed shareholder resolutions as one tactic among many in broader campaigns to encourage corporate responsibility. However, civil-society organizations generally do not control significant voting blocks, and their resolutions are rarely embraced by the majority of shareholders. In contrast, institutional investors such as pension funds, banks, investment companies, and insurance companies are more able to influence corporate policy and engage in a different type of shareholder activism. Since the 1970s institutional investors have steadily increased their percentage of ownership of publicly traded corporations, and by 2000 they held more than half the traded shares for most large companies. In addition, during those decades institutional ownership of stock also became more concentrated.

On the surface, the increasing concentration of ownership by large institutional investors holds out great potential for creating a countervailing power that could lead to a shift in mission of the publicly traded corporation. However, as corporate legal scholar Lawrence Mitchell has noted, to date large institutional investors have tended to define "shareholder activism" in very narrow terms that are quite distinct from the varieties of shareholder activism characteristic of groups concerned with labor, the environment, and human rights. For institutional investors, shareholder activism has generally meant encouraging boards to dismiss underperforming managers or lobbying the Securities and Exchange Commission to make it easier for shareholders to change board members. Even TIAA-CREF (the pension fund for educators and people in related professions), CalPERS (the California Public Employees Retirement System), and the AFL-CIO pension fund have channeled their shareholder activism mostly into efforts to enhance shareholder value rather than to advance more ambitious goals of social and environmental responsibility. As a result, shareholder "activism" has meant little more than increasing the ability of shareholders to make companies more profitable and to shore up short-term stock prices. The potential of shareholders to generate more profound reforms remains unrealized.[28]

Nevertheless, there are some promising signs of institutional shareholder activism that exhibit a broader vision of social and environmental stewardship. The exceptions to the narrow vision of improved accountability tend to occur among the socially responsible mutual funds. Some of them have a record of attending annual shareholder meetings and presenting resolutions on environmental and social responsibility goals that are consistent with the resolutions of environmental, human rights, and other social-change organizations, which also hold some stock in the companies. Although the resolutions are often voted down, they generate publicity and can be combined with other campaigns that counter corporate greenwashing, and in some cases the measures affect corporate policy. As investment in socially responsible mutual funds increases, and as investors in pension funds demand a broader vision of shareholder activism from the funds, we would expect to see growth in a more politically and ethically oriented form of shareholder activism. Legislative action that would create incentives for investors to shift to socially responsible investment vehicles might spur a transition toward greater use of such funds and the kinds of pressures that they exert via shareholder resolutions and reforms in corporate governance.[29]

Although the four categories of reform discussed so far would create some opportunities for a shift toward greater social and environmental responsibility, they do not address directly the fundamental mission of the publicly traded corporation as existing only to provide a return on equity to shareholders. A much more profound legislative approach to corporate reform—and therefore a proposal that would likely encounter even greater resistance—involves rethinking the basis of corporate charters. In the United States the right to define, issue, and revoke charters is held by state governments. In a few cases there have been campaigns to de-charter companies. For example, in California there was a campaign to de-charter the Union Oil Company of California (Unocal) because of alleged human rights abuses associated with the construction of a pipeline in Myanmar and other foreign operations. However, few expected that the state of California would revoke the charter of a large, well-established corporation, and the state's attorney general rejected the petition. Even if the campaign had succeeded, the corporation would have been able to move to another state. Because interstate competition creates a race to the bottom in corporate charter requirements, some reformers have suggested that corporations should be chartered at the national level, where stronger standards of social and environmental responsibility could be required.[30]

Although the chartering of corporations at the national level could shift the problem of a race to the bottom to the international level, there is some evidence that other countries have taken a broader approach to corporate governance. In continental Europe and Japan corporate charters have historically emphasized governance based on a broad range of stakeholders, including employees and customers, in contrast with the focus on shareholders in the Anglophone countries. Suggestions of stakeholder governance can also be found in the United States, where automobile manufacturers have included labor union representation on the board of directors in exchange for labor concessions, and stakeholders often have a seat on the boards of nonprofit organizations. To an increasing degree, the stakeholder model is also seen in some corners of the socially responsible investment community. For example, the "B corporation" model requires a change in a corporation's by-laws to reflect stakeholder accountability. A legislative reform that would mandate that corporations above a certain size shift to a "B corporation" model would be another fundamental building block toward transitioning the publicly traded corporation to an organization that is more able to contribute solutions to global problems.[31]

Other than public financing of political campaigns, the reform proposals discussed above have not received much legislative attention. Given the lack of political opportunities for direct legislative intervention in corporate governance structures, other avenues of reform also should be explored. One alternative field for corporate reform is the judicial system. An end to the legal fiction of corporate personhood would represent a reform even more profound than the legislative and shareholder approaches discussed above. In the United States the concept of corporate personhood dates back to the nineteenth century, when state legislatures exerted much more control over corporations. During that period state governments placed strict limitations on the terms of corporate charters, the rights of the corporations to property ownership, and ability of corporations to make donations to political campaigns. In *Santa Clara County v. Southern*

Pacific Railroad Company, the US Supreme Court granted corporations the legal status of "personhood," which entitled them to equal protection under the law as outlined in the Fourteenth Amendment. A series of other Supreme Court decisions extended the rights of corporations to other rights granted to individual citizens, including rights associated with the first ten amendments. One might argue that the legal status of corporate personhood benefits small businesses and farms, and consequently a restriction on corporate personhood could have negative repercussions for small corporations as well. However, the ability to use corporate personhood in, for example, lawsuits and the funding of political campaigns is much greater among large corporations, and consequently the reform movement directed at corporate personhood is generally concerned with large corporations whose "rights" have run into conflict with those of small communities or the press. Although not all "rights" granted to corporations would have to be revoked, there have been growing calls to rescind the rights that most facilitate the negative effects of corporate power on elections, free speech, and the ordinances and regulations of local and state governments.[32]

The political opportunities for a legislative overhaul of the concept of corporate personhood are limited at the moment, but there are some cases in the courts. The Community Environmental Legal Defense Fund is exploring litigation based on a challenge to the concept as part of its work with local-level community resistance to factory farms in Pennsylvania. State legislation passed in 1997 allowed farmers to contract with sewerage haulers to dump the waste on their fields. Testing was so lax that, in effect, farms became toxic waste dumps. As a way to stop the poisoning of local land and watersheds, local governments began passing ordinances against the corporate ownership of farms and the spreading of sewerage sludge. In 2002 the factory farm industry responded by convincing the state legislature to pass a law that explicitly forbade a local governmental body from regulating agriculture in its district. Although a mobilization of community and environmental groups prevented the law from passing, corporations began to sue the local governments, alleging that their constitutional rights, which stem from the doctrine of corporate personhood, had been violated. Some local governments have passed ordinances that specifically state that corporations shall not be considered "persons" within their districts. Similar bills have been introduced in state legislatures across the country, and some of the Midwestern states have outlawed corporate ownership of farms. Eventually the litigation against corporate personhood may reach the United States Supreme Court and trigger a national debate on the question "Are large, geographically dispersed business firms entitled to the same rights as human individuals, and do such rights trump the rights of local governments to self-determination?"[33]

A final political reform worth reconsidering is public ownership of high-carbon consuming, energy-related companies or industries. Examples include the major coal, natural gas, oil, electricity, airline, rail, and automotive companies. Clearly, the topic has almost no political mileage in the political culture of the United States today, but it is worth noting that most of the world's oil supply is in the hands of nationalized corporations, and most passenger rail transportation is also publicly owned. The crucial role of the energy and transportation industries in making a transition toward a global society that operates within ecologically sustainable limits makes them a prime candidate for nationalization. More effectively, the threat of public ownership might be raised to shift corporate strategy of specific companies that have especially poor environmental and social records. Although the transition to energy use within ecological limits could be accomplished within the framework of publicly regulated private ownership, the resistance that private owners of fossil-fuel capital have mounted to environmental reform proposals suggests that the transition would be much more difficult to achieve in a timely way. As the scenarios of peak oil, peak natural gas, and climate change unfold in future decades, the proposals of Barry Commoner's Citizens Party may yet find a second life. In other countries, including those of Latin America and Europe, the publicly owned sector was never as diminished as in the United States, and sentiment in favor of national government ownership of some industries has grown. However, in the United States it is likely that only a profound economic and ecological crisis would reopen political debate on the topic of nationalization. Acute economic crises may trigger the nationalization of financial services firms, but the more chronic quality of ecological problems suggests that nationalization in the energy and transportation industries may be less likely.[34]

Conclusion

In this chapter I have discussed reform proposals that involve independent business associations, local governments, and the federal government in the United States. The analysis does not exhaust the possibilities for reform. For example, addressing the democracy deficit of international governmental organizations would also help open up political opportunities at the national and local level. I have not discussed the international level of reforms here partly because my focus has been on the United States and partly because others have already provided a good synthesis of proposals. For example, the policy analysts Thad Williamson, David Imbroscio, and Gar Alperovitz have summarized a range of international reforms that could enable "local democracy in a global era," including a world financial authority to regulate global markets, a public international investment fund, restructuring of the mission and organization of the International Monetary Fund and World Bank, and protection of "good nontariff barriers" to trade such as labor, environmental, and health standards.[35]

The proposals for starting points for a fundamental economic transition may seem unrealistic to many readers, and certainly there is little likelihood that some of the more profound proposals for reform of the publicly traded corporation will be enacted in the absence of overwhelming systemic crises. Reforms that challenge the fundamental role of the publicly traded corporation will meet with stiff resistance by a powerful institution that dominates the media and the government not only in the United States but in many other countries. However, in the long run it will be impossible to avoid a fundamental conflict between a global ecology that limits resource consumption and a global economy that is based on ongoing growth of revenue and profits without constraints on the social and environmental effects of concentrated accumulation. Although it is possible to have some economic growth alongside dematerialization of resource consumption, the goal will be impossible to achieve without a thorough economic transition of the scope outlined in this chapter.

Solving the pressing global problems of energy consumption, climate change, pollution, resource depletion, and inequality requires more creativity than returning to the invisible hand of eighteenth-century liberalism or the visible hand of nineteenth- and twentieth-century socialism. Although market-based policies such as emissions trading schemes and public ownership approaches such as the renationalization of some firms will continue to have a place in the policy experiments of the twenty-first century, such approaches should not exhaust the imagination of economic reform. Instead, the legal basis of the publicly traded corporation should be reformed to shift it toward stakeholder participation, long-term planning, and social and environmental responsibility. At the same time, the legal playing field should be leveled so that other types of economic organizations that are locally owned and concerned with the quality of life of their host communities have a better chance to flourish.

During the early 2000s most political opportunities for reform at the federal government level were closed with the exception of the regulation of financial reporting requirements and the financial services industry, but as I have suggested there has been continual experimentation with policy reforms at the local level. Likewise, broad and fundamental economic changes favorable to both environmental sustainability and social justice are occurring in other countries and world regions, especially in Europe and Latin America. To the extent that the United States becomes increasingly isolated as the outlier defending a crumbling edifice of neoliberalism, then a crisis of legitimacy at the international level may open up political opportunities for the more profound changes in corporate governance such as federal chartering, stakeholder representation, and restrictions on the doctrine of corporate personhood. Meanwhile, the opportunities for initiating a transition process may be greater for more incremental changes, such as the creation of localist financial products, policies that support the development of the small-business sector, an increased emphasis on social and environmental reporting, and a broader scope for shareholder resolutions from institutional investors.

Conclusion

The globalization of societies has not meant the end of the local but instead its reconstitution. Among the many types of localization in the United States are the high-tech manufacturing clusters located in global cities, the hyperlocalism of large retail and information corporations, grassroots movements to relocalize society to adjust to a resource-constrained and post-carbon world, and the devolution of federal responsibilities to state and local governments. A fifth type of localization, which has been termed here "localism," is a reform movement based largely on the sense that place-based communities have lost political and economic sovereignty to multinational corporations. Put more positively, localists are concerned with achieving greater local ownership and more democratic steering of regional economies.

Understanding the localist movement in the United States requires attention to its internal diversity. As I have shown, localist political thought draws on various strands of political ideology, including liberalism, neoliberalism, communalism, and socialism. In many ways the strongest parallel with existing political ideologies is early-twentieth-century Progressivism. Localist politics in the twenty-first century offer considerable potential for the small-business sector to rebuild political coalitions that were characteristic of the Progressive Era. Another type of internal diversity is organizational. Small businesses are the primary driver of the "buy local" movement, but other types of organizations play a significant role in the broader localist movement, and the range and frequency of organizational forms varies by industry. In view of the diversity of localism in the United States, it can be misleading to base generalizations about the movement on one industry or a segment of the

industry. To some degree the analyses of localism in the agrifood literature, which were based primarily on the study of sustainable agricultural
networks, were not generalizable across other fields of localist action.
Nevertheless, the literature posed important questions that can inform
an inquiry into the politics of localism. Foremost among the questions
has been the extent to which localist politics can contribute to resolving
environmental and social problems.

Situating Localism

Localism as a movement for a transition in economic and political organization emerged partially because of democracy deficits that have weakened public participation in national and international policy making.
Without stronger democratic institutions, the United States and other
countries have been unable to provide comprehensive solutions to fundamental problems of sustainability and justice. However, even with the
closure of political opportunities at the national and international levels,
alternative economic institutions have proliferated and grown alongside
broader movements for reform of the global economy. Locally owned
small businesses, employee-owned firms, community-oriented nonprofit
organizations, local government agencies, local public-private partnerships, fair-trade cooperatives, and credit unions are all elements of an
alternative global economy that is not necessarily based on the assumptions of endless growth and maximization of profits regardless of costs
to the environment and society. To the extent that localists engage in the
work of building an alternative global economy, the localist movement
can be viewed as a sibling of the anti-globalization movements. Of
course, with a class address in the small-business sector rather than in
the working class, the peasantry, or the green middle class, localists tend
to adopt a reformist, market-oriented, and policy-oriented repertoire of
action instead of street protest. With those limitations in mind, I suggest
that localism has a place to play alongside other anti-globalization movements for the transformation of the world's economy.

As a political phenomenon, localism cannot be classified easily within
the traditional left-right polarities of the political field. With its anti-
corporate but not anti-capitalist politics, the movement has accumulated

naysayers on both the traditional political right and left. One often-heard verdict on localism, generally coming from neoliberal quarters and the big-business sector, is that its economics are protectionist. Even worse, localism represents the dying gasp of small businesses that are being swept away by the efficiencies of the global economy. For example, the critics argue, when cities enact zoning restrictions that limit the number of franchise stores or the size of retail stores, or when they enact procurement policies in favor of local businesses, they are creating marketplace inefficiencies akin to trade barriers. The policies lessen the advantages to all that are accrued through free trade across regions and countries. I have examined a variety of such inefficiency criticisms and the responses that one can find in the localist literature. Perhaps the most fundamental response is the argument made by the localist leader Michael Shuman: any policies that might appear to be protectionist in favor of locally owned independent businesses still fall far short of the many government subsidies in favor of global corporations, such as tax reductions, zoning changes, infrastructure support, and other transfers to the nonlocal sector. From this perspective, localists are not advocating protectionism for small businesses as much as they are seeking to level a playing field that is heavily tilted away from locally owned businesses, which generally do pay their full tax burden and often end up footing the bill for the economic development projects that favor nonlocal capital.[1]

Another possible verdict on localism, coming especially from the radical and liberal positions in the political field, is that it is a failure on environmental and justice grounds. Those critics of localism argue that the small-business sector of the economy has done little to address fundamental problems of ecological sustainability, and likewise the sector does not adequately address problems of inequality. Localism can be reduced to a fashion of Saturday mornings spent meeting and greeting friends at the local farmers' market and Saturday afternoons spent on green home-improvement projects or shopping at local stores. In such instances individuals may find the good life, but they may be turning their backs on the world's environmental and social problems. Moreover, the emphasis on the marketplace through "buy local" and fairtrade campaigns plays into the anti-statist and devolutionary politics of neoliberalism and repeats the failed political strategy of withdrawal found in communalism. Even where the green and local converge, critics such as the sociologist James O'Connor note that most ecological problems cannot be solved at the local level. From the liberal and radical perspective, localism is not only a failure but a dangerous diversion of political energy from the proper target of action in an era of global capitalism: protest-based social movements directed at the nation-state, international governmental organizations, and multinational corporations.[2]

By drawing attention to the diversity of localist politics, I have suggested that the potentially pernicious streak identified by critics of the left can be separated from more globally oriented, sustainable, and just forms. As a movement localism can also open out to coalitions with other social movements, such as the anti-globalization, environmental, and fair-trade movements. Such approaches can be identified with regularity in some localist organizations, especially those affiliated with the Business Alliance for Local Living Economies. I have also identified a range of organizations where local ownership concerns have come together with justice and/or sustainability goals, including reuse centers, community gardens, nonprofit urban farms, some types of locally owned electricity and public transportation, and some forms of independent media. Where localist organizations exhibit a self-conscious understanding of the position of geographically localized communities in a global economy and a concern with issues of sustainability and justice, they can develop deeper and, to use the phrase of Melanie DuPuis and David Goodman again, more "reflexive politics." In this book I have gone beyond the recognition of a need for reflexive politics to draw out and analyze instances that already exist. Localism can offer a vision of what kind of local *and* global society we want to live in rather than a defensive and uncaring posture with respect to the rest of world. It is possible for individuals, families, and communities to engage in a form of localism that is rooted in a broader analysis of the fundamental contradiction between an economy governed by amoral publicly traded corporations and the need to have an economy that solves global problems of sustainability, justice, and democracy.[3]

Nevertheless, it will be necessary to continue to inspect carefully locally owned and controlled enterprises at a variety of points of action: missions, products, production processes, labor and organizational practices, and political positions. To be successful, independent business associations should be concerned with more than getting consumers to "buy local" in order to preserve small businesses and local flavor. Local businesses should also function in socially and environmentally responsible ways, connect the politics of community sovereignty with those of justice and sustainability, and link the improvement of local communities with national and international programs of economic reform. "Buy local" campaigns can be a helpful tactic in a broader strategy of economic reform, but in a global economy consumers could also be educated about the value of buying from independently owned values-oriented companies regardless of their location. New zoning regulations that favor locally owned independent businesses can be a helpful tactic, but citizens and politicians could also embrace the broader challenge of corporate reform as outlined in the previous chapter. Mobilizations to stop the incursions of global corporations that are willing to place the quality of life of a region at risk may be necessary, but as environmental justice activists have long noted, such "not in my backyard" struggles could be linked to global environmental justice campaigns in order to avoid shifting a polluter from one site to another.[4]

The Significance of Localism

One might agree with my conclusion that the localist movement is variable and that there are wings of the movement that contribute to the goal of building a more sustainable and just society, but one might still wonder whether localism is a politically significant phenomenon or whether it is merely a small diversion in the flood tides of globalization. Is localism historically trivial, or is it significant? It will be impossible to answer the question for decades, but it *is* possible to look at some underlying conditions and trends that affect the prognosis of localism. For example, as a reform movement localism offers several advantages that suggest some potential for widespread political significance. First, people care about their communities and can sometimes be mobilized to political action over local political issues when similar issues at a broader geographical scale do not attract the same degree of passion. There is mobilization potential in this movement. Second, the banner of local ownership provides a broad political frame under which cross-class and cross-ethnic coalitions can be built. The mobilization potential is broad. Third, the movement has an economic base in the small-business sector, local nonprofit organizations, and locally controlled public enterprises, where organizational and economic resources can be made available for supporting reform action. The mobilization potential has access to economic resources. Fourth, the repertoire of action, which involves a mixture of political reform and consumption politics rather than street protest, is appealing to those who may be reluctant to assume the risks of violent repression that accompanies extra-institutional political action such as street protest. There is limited potential for heavy repression.

Given those conditions, one might expect to find favorable growth trends. One measure is the growth of the two alliance organizations in the United States, AMIBA and BALLE. In less than a decade, independent business associations in Boulder and Philadelphia grew into national umbrella organizations with dozens of affiliated organizations. By 2008 localism was a vibrant grassroots movement with a strong economic base in the small-business and community-oriented-nonprofit sectors. The growth trends suggest that interest in and support for locally owned and controlled enterprises will continue to increase in future decades.

However, the history of localist efforts from the 1920s and the 1930s, when an anti-chain-store movement achieved significant legislative victories before fizzling out, should serve as a cautionary tale. A similar fate befell the appropriate-technology movement of the 1970s. Although localism in the early 2000s has adopted a different strategy from the anti-chain-store movement and is considerably more pragmatic than the "small is beautiful" economics of the 1970s, might it also be overwhelmed by the floodtides of corporate consolidation? One outcome is that localism as a political reform movement could evolve into a specialty niche market that provides local flavor and locally oriented goods and services with a social and environmental responsibility message. Meanwhile, one might further argue, the bulk of consumption increasingly will be channeled into the big-box stores, Internet-based corporate retail, and globalized systems of production and distribution with very weak certification systems. A drive to the edge of any city in the United States, not to mention increasingly cities in many other parts of the world, suggests that the era of superstores is only just beginning, and an inspection of their products reveals increasing awareness of the marketplace potential of labeling and certification schemes.

Furthermore, when one looks more closely at growth statistics, the argument that localist organizations are relatively insignificant becomes more credible. On the one hand, there is evidence for dramatic growth in a wide range of localist organizations and projects, not just independent business associations but also community-supported agriculture farms, farmers' markets, community gardens, distributed and off-grid energy production, locally owned biofuel companies, community-controlled electricity, energy conservation, car-sharing programs, public transportation, ecovillages, cohousing, the reuse industry, credit unions, community health programs, free clinics, and community media. On the other hand, when placed against the broader backdrop of market share, the exemplars of localism remain relatively small and economically insignificant, at least in the United States.[5]

Consider two examples to show how growth figures can be deceptive. Farmers' markets represent one dramatic success story for localism, because they grew from about 300 across the United States in 1970 to more than 4,000 in 2006, when they had surpassed $2 billion in sales. However, the absolute market share pales in comparison with the $1 trillion that Americans spend on food each year. Likewise, community-supported agriculture (CSA), in which consumers pay a seasonal subscription fee for a weekly bag of groceries from a local farm, has also undergone dramatic growth since its importation to the United States in the 1980s. In 20 years, the number of CSA farms went from zero to as many as 1,700. However, a study of the average revenue of such farms in 2002 indicated that it was only approximately $10,000, so the overall revenue from CSA farms was again minuscule relative to farm revenue.[6]

Skeptics could argue that the high growth rates but small overall market shares are suggestive of a mixture of social movement and niche industry that, like the organic food movement before it, has yet to become a target of appropriation by large corporations. In many mature industries, the general trend has been toward consolidation into larger and larger enterprises. This is the problem of scale for localism: how can locally owned businesses and other organizations grow to become the dominant part of industries for which the trend is toward corporate consolidation and franchises?

To answer the question, it is first worth remembering that a large part of the American economy still rests in the hands of small and medium-size businesses, many of which are locally owned and privately held. Although there is a trend toward consolidation, it can be explained as a result of public policies that favor larger corporations rather than "natural" efficiencies of marketplace dynamics. Arguments that assume that larger enterprises are always more efficient are increasingly discredited, and much of the contemporary wisdom within the private sector points to the value of agility that can accompany small, entrepreneurial organizations that work together in cooperative networks. As Michael Shuman showed in *The Small-Mart Revolution*, some industries are consolidating, but others show signs of decentralization. But if the outcome of the conflicting trends of ongoing consolidation and decentralization is historically contingent, what factors will determine which direction becomes dominant? I suggest that there are three main factors that will determine the eventual historical significance of localism.[7]

First, the fate of localism will depend largely on innovations in financial products and markets and regulatory reforms that support locally owned independent businesses. Although "buy local" campaigns are a helpful starting point for consumer education, they will be ineffective unless they are accompanied by "bank local" and "invest local" campaigns. Otherwise, investment will continue to flow into global corporations. Solving the investment problem will require developing innovative financial products and government programs, as well as changing regulatory barriers that make it difficult for individuals to allocate a greater portion of retirement savings to the local economy.

In addition to favorable government policies and innovation in financial products, a second factor that will affect the relative success of localism is the capacity of the movement to provide leadership in the transformation of the private sector toward triple bottom line practices. Once small businesses take the step from self-definition as locally owned independent enterprises to socially and environmentally responsible enterprises, they are able to project a coherent message that their form of business responsibility is structurally superior to that of publicly traded corporations. Although large corporations may claim to embrace social and environmental responsibility missions, they are often unable or unwilling to carry through on such promises because they have a fiduciary responsibility to anonymous shareholders who demand ongoing growth of profitability and revenue as the single or paramount goal. Large corporations may embrace the rhetoric of triple bottom line thinking and stakeholder governance, but they are legally responsible to perform based on the single bottom line of profitability. In contrast, privately held small businesses provide a more credible vehicle for reconfiguring the business world as a source of solutions to environmental and social problems. To the extent that this structural condition can become a platform for leadership, the localist movement is likely to gain both credibility and consumer support. That credibility will be enhanced when we find large publicly traded corporations deciding to repurchase stock and "go private" in order to have the freedom to pursue social and environmental reform.

The third factor that will affect the fate of localism is the ability to reposition it as part of the broader project of building an alternative global economy of "global localism." Many small, independent producers who are strongly committed to their communities want to sell their products in both local and nonlocal markets, and locally made products are not always available to consumers. In order for localism to work in a global economy, there must be a way of connecting consumers in one location with nonlocal products made by distant, independent, small businesses that share social and environmental responsibility values. The strategy of "global localism" would involve transforming the localist retail industry from hybrid localism—locally owned and independent but selling nonlocal products often made by publicly traded corporations—to a retail industry that sells products with a significantly different provenance from that of the chain stores. As BALLE's co-founder Judy Wicks says, localism would involve supporting efforts everywhere to build a local living economy by purchasing both from locally owned independent businesses in one's region and from similar businesses throughout the world.[8]

To date fair-trade and fair-made products are the closest approximation to a solution that would connect consumers with values-oriented, locally owned, independent producers outside their home locale. An emerging body of scholarship indicates that the world of alternative trade organizations has attained significant achievements but, like localism, also faces significant challenges. The challenges include gender equity in farmers' cooperatives, lack of understanding of fair trade by farmers in developing countries, and cooptation of "fair trade" labels by large corporations that have developed their own certification schemes. Furthermore, the prospect of integrating alternative trade networks with localism also raises the question of how "fair trade" schemes of alternative trade organizations can be brought together with the "fair bought" politics of localism. In the early stages of the fair-trade movement, small farmers, cooperatives, and craftspeople in low-income countries sold to consumers in wealthy countries through nonprofit stores operated by religious organizations, such as Ten Thousand Villages. Fair-trade organizations decided to scale up by selling the products through corporate retail outlets. The decision to sell through corporate retail chains granted producers access to more consumers, but in the process the fair-trade movement has become less integrated with retail localism. The change has also facilitated the development of misleading certification schemes by retail and food processing companies.[9]

The early fair-trade model suggests the possibility of a different type of product label that more consistently embodies the idea of local ownership throughout the commodity chain, from small manufacturers and farmers' cooperatives to locally owned independent stores. A "global localism" label or some other way of bringing about fair-made and "buy local" convergence in the marketplace would allow consumers to participate in an economy that is parallel to that of the publicly traded corporation. The Internet may provide a great resource for connecting such businesses. To the extent that "global localism" emerges, localism may end up being defined as based less on place than on the principles of independent ownership, environmental stewardship, fair working conditions, and concern for place-based communities that improve social conditions for both production and consumption. A second-generation iteration on both fair trade and localism could bring the two together under the mantle of "fair-made and fair-bought" products.[10]

Will Localism Be Co-opted?

To the extent that localism is successful, it will face a new risk of cooptation, because large corporations will come to see localist rhetoric as a new market opportunity. For example, retail corporations will begin to feature and test local products much in the way that they tested organic products and brought them into conventional commodity chains. The process of incorporation or absorption into the mainstream generally also entails transformation of the more movement-based alternative, as I have explored in some detail for several industries in *Alternative Pathways in Science and Industry*. Will localism transform the world of large publicly traded corporations or simply be absorbed by them?

One example of appropriation is the confusing status of foods that are grown with a local designation (e.g., "Vermont maple syrup") for sales mostly in nonlocal markets. The foods utilize place-based branding for differentiation in a crowded global marketplace, and as a result they are less an example of localism than of how the local can become branded for sale in global commodity chains. Here the concept of the "local" does not necessarily have any linkages with social and environmental responsibility goals, and companies that produce "local" products may not even be locally owned or privately held. The development of place-based (sometimes called "terroir") brands will create confusion in the consumer marketplace over what exactly is being valued when the phrase "buy local" is invoked. Here, advocates of localism will benefit from drawing attention to the distinction between products produced and sold by locally owned and independent businesses and those that have a place-based designation but are produced and sold by multinational corporations. Creating and maintaining that distinction in a marketplace of increased product labeling diversity will be a fundamental but significant challenge.[11]

Another example of the potential incorporation and transformation of localism involves the inclusion of locally made or grown products within the offerings of corporate retailers. For example, in one supermarket that I visited, a display of produce proudly labeled "locally grown" was the first item that I encountered upon entry. It was, alas, just one display in a very large store. In this example, the supermarket was a large but privately held metropolitan chain with a deep civic commitment to its area and surrounding foodshed, but if it had been a nonlocal publicly traded corporation, then the locally grown food would have been sold locally but severed from locally owned independent retail stores.

"Corporate localism" may sound like an oxymoron, but Wal-Mart, always attuned to future consumer trends, has already begun testing a "buy local" program that advertises products made within the state of Ohio and sold at an Ohio-based branch of the store. Likewise, craft breweries that are subsidiaries of large corporations are avoiding use of the name of the corporate parent when developing and marketing their beer. Another opportunity for cooptation comes from franchises. For example, one local franchise in my region has a sign hanging by the cash register: "locally owned and independent." Of course, it is not "independent" in the sense used by the independent business associations. They generally exclude franchises from their memberships, because franchise rules restrict local purchasing preferences and many other policies that could enable import substitution. However, it will take a vibrant localist movement to discredit such framings as local wash.[12]

Through strategies of absorption, large corporations may decide to sell a percentage of locally made products as loss leaders in order to siphon off consumers from locally owned retail stores. At that point localism will have achieved a partial victory alongside partial cooptation. To some degree, the histories of the 1970s appropriate-technology movement and the early organic farming movement will be repeated: there will be incorporation into mainstream industry but also transformation and dilution. Unless independent business associations adopt a strategy of global localism, one can easily imagine a situation in which the locally oriented consumer is faced with the choice of buying a nonlocal product from a locally owned retail outlet, such as nonlocal fruit sold in the local food cooperative, or a local product from a nonlocal chain store.

A similar choice involves shopping at a locally owned independent retail store or buying socially and environmentally responsible products in a nonlocal retail store. Some large retail companies have embraced environmental public-relations campaigns and reframed their products and retail stores as green, and they have also started to offer fair-made and fair-trade products. If such products were to become more widely available in the corporate retail stores than in the small independent retailers, then consumers would be put in a bind between choosing between one type of product preference (socially and environmentally responsible products) and another (locally owned independent stores). The distinction between fair made and fair bought could be set up as a consumer choice rather than a marketplace convergence. Large corporate retailers would be able to divide consumers and get some to shift the goal of buying locally to a position in their consumer preferences below buying from socially and/or environmental responsible producers. Furthermore, keeping track of all the various designations of products (such as local, organic, and fair-trade) could produce "label fatigue" and confusion in the marketplace. Some consumers may simply give up on the idea of consumption as a political practice and revert back to consumerist visions of shopping.[13]

Because of the complex patterns of appropriation that are emerging, the locally owned independent store can only win by paying attention to the provenance of its products and by joining in a vigorous independent business association that promotes a strong message, storefront branding, and other techniques of consumer education. If it shifts toward what I call the "global localist" paradigm and sells products that are from other locally owned, independent, and socially and environmentally responsible enterprises located throughout the world, then it will offer something that the big-box store cannot, because the retail end of the commodity chain is also locally owned. However, the locally owned independent store will also have leveraged a transformation of corporate retail by pushing it to include locally owned, socially and environmentally responsible, independent enterprises in its product mix. Furthermore, as retail shifts increasingly to the Internet, localism will have a coherent message for consumers. Similar to the idea of a "triple bottom line," localism will exhort web-based consumers to pay attention to the double provenance of fair-made and fair-bought products: made by locally owned and independent producers in accordance with the best environmental and social standards, and sold through a locally owned and independent Internet retailer that also meets the best standards of social and environmental responsibility. Organizational certifications such as B corporation status might be brought in to provide transparency and credibility for claims of social and environmental responsibility.

As was suggested in chapter 7, the Internet raises a complex set of issues for localism. Independent booksellers cringe when a customer asks for an item that is out of stock, the seller offers to order it, and the customer says, "No, thanks. I'll get it on Amazon." But independent booksellers have also developed websites that make it possible for consumers to identify locally owned independent stores. Small retailers can also sell books and other products on the Internet, either on their own websites or in aggregations. The next phase of Internet use is to define commodity chains that use locally owned socially and environmentally responsible organizations, from the producer to the retailer. There is tremendous potential for moving the retail product side of localism online, because the Internet offers the opportunity for shopping convenience that is generally missing in the small, mom-and-pop shops, which have limited hours and inventories.

The problems that I have outlined in this section apply most to the retail industry, especially stores that sell manufactured products and processed food. Fresh food is somewhat different from other retail products because of the quality of the food and the comfort associated with purchasing from local farmers. The service industries are also more resistant to corporate cooptation, because local reputations allow the better service-oriented firms to survive at a small scale. In fact, the combination of service with retail and resale, such as a bicycle store that specializes in new high-quality products, low-price used bicycles, and repairs, is one way for small retail stores to survive the intense competitive pressures from larger retailers and etailers.

To some extent the problems of corporate competition that retail faces also apply to the media industry, where large corporations are utilizing the Internet in their hyperlocalization strategies to build online social networks of place-based communities. The hyperlocalized online communities can then become sources of advertising revenue that are returned as profits to distant media and communications companies. As in the retail field, the community media field will have to draw attention to the value of local ownership and the "be the media" potential of media localism. Here, the nonprofit status of locally owned media and the educational programs that enable those organizations to train members of the local community will enable differentiation from the hyperlocalization projects of corporate media.

The situation is less parallel with retail in the cases of public electricity power and public transportation, because public ownership weakens the potential for the pattern of incorporation and transformation of localism that is more evident in the retail industry. Furthermore, there is greater potential for energy production to become localized through the development of distributed, renewable energy systems and hydrogen fuel cells for storage. In summary: It is again necessary to pay attention to the varieties of localism before making generalizations, because the risk of incorporation and transformation described for the retail industry will not necessarily appear in the same form in other industries, such as media, energy, and public transportation.

Localism, Collapse, and Resilience

In addition to the potential that localism offers as one countervailing force to corporate-led globalization, the movement may also play a role in reducing the fragility of society when confronted with disaster. No one knows what the world will look like in 2050, but the trends suggest scenarios that would better be described as thorny rather than rosy: accelerating climate change, pervasive chemical pollution in the biosphere, post-peak oil and natural gas, higher amounts of coal consumption, heavy strains on water supplies, infrastructures unequipped to handle flooding and drought, a world population of 9 billion people with at least one-fifth living in slums, increased terrorism and crime, heightened surveillance, greater civil liberties abuses, intensified struggle for global resources between China and the West, and privatized armies and police forces prone to ruthless violence. Given such systemic strains, it seems likely that disasters of all sorts—natural, human, and hybrid—will occur with increasing frequency.

As the journalist Naomi Klein has argued, disasters have become political opportunities for elites to push forward a neoliberal agenda at moments when resistance movements and local governments are crippled. Rather than use disasters to rebuild sociotechnical systems so that future catastrophes can be prevented, elites have seized the opportunities to put in place programs that enable them to increase their accumulation of wealth via the growth of large publicly traded corporations and the dismantling of public agencies and small-businesses. Corporate leaders may respond to disasters with public displays of emergency humanitarian assistance, which after all has good public-relations value and enhances the brand in the marketplace, but at the same time they often support political efforts to increase the scope of neoliberal governance, including the privatization of disaster relief and reconstruction. A perverse feedback loop operates in which neoliberalism generates the lack of investment in infrastructure and prevention that would mitigate disasters, but when the disasters occur, opportunities are opened for further neoliberal reforms. If neoliberalism remains an enduring feature of the political landscape of the twenty-first century, and if one agrees with the criticisms of liberals, radicals, and localists alike that neoliberalism is not likely to solve the world's social and environmental crises, then one is left with an uncomfortable prognosis for the twenty-first century: collapse in the form of an increasing frequency and variety of disaster.[14]

In the 30-year update of the influential book *The Limits to Growth*, the authors claimed that the world's human population had exceeded its carrying capacity on a number of dimensions, and they showed that their scenarios of overshoot and collapse were becoming realized. They suggested that collapse will ensue over a time scale of decades reaching into the middle of the twenty-first century. The poor countries and even some of the poor within the wealthy countries will face increasing episodes of starvation, epidemics, droughts, floods, deforestation, crime waves, riots, and warfare. The prospect of a grim twenty-first century is a far cry from the vision of a coordinated, planned, multilateral response to world poverty and environmental destruction articulated in the United Nations' documents of the 1980s and the 1990s, let alone the optimism that still pervades the proclamations of green corporations and mainstream political leaders. Although the transition scenario and policies outlined in the previous chapter are a hopeful prescription, I am convinced that, as the twenty-first century unfolds, most of the proposed reforms will not be enacted. Well into twenty-first century, when the history of disasters and political instability becomes more poignant, elites may begin to accept significant reforms, much as occurred in the United States during the Great Depression. Until that point is reached, we may see the ongoing promulgation of policies that increasingly isolate the wealthy countries from the poor ones and the wealthy within countries from their poorer neighbors. With isolation will come increasing levels of surveillance and authoritarianism.[15]

The responses to civilizational collapse in the past are a sobering warning for the prospects of today's global economy. The anthropological record suggests that when small-scale, non-industrial societies have exceeded their local carrying capacity, they have developed a few basic types of innovations with some regularity: warfare and trade, to gain access to resources controlled by neighboring societies; stockpiling and social reorganization, to make more efficient use of existing resources and to smooth out periods of resource shortages; and technological change, to make more efficient use of resources. The solutions give a fairly good picture of our world today: resource wars, decline of trade barriers, stockpiling of energy resources, privatization and deregulation, and technological innovation. Resource wars, free trade, privatization, deregulation, and other policies sanctioned by neoliberal political ideologies legitimate a global economic system that allows the world's more powerful countries to continue to have access to the resources of the less powerful. Only technological innovation and social reorganization hold out any hope of a long-term, equitable, and harmonious solution to the world's pressing problems of finding a way to live within ecological limits that does not jettison most of the world's poor into a pit of misery and genocide. However, even if the modern global economy is technically capable of providing the needed innovation in time to avoid the more horrific scenarios of global collapse, the growth logic of the publicly traded corporation and the financial markets that guide it will, in my view, make it impossible to achieve the change before human suffering on an unprecedented scale occurs.[16]

In the anthropological literature on collapse, a hopeful finding is that similar catastrophes, even the same environmental events such as a global cooling episode, can have very different effects in different societies. The explanation has hinged on the concept of "resilience," that is, the flexibility and adaptability of the society's institutions to dramatic changes such as disaster. It seems likely that climate change and other ecological changes will increase the frequency and severity of disaster, as will warfare over increasingly valued and strained natural resources. The worst effects will probably be shouldered by the poor in the coastal regions of Africa, Latin America, and South and Southeast Asia. Collapse could also be more pervasive, but whatever its scope, it will likely take different forms in different places. A world based on free-market neoliberalism is hardly in a good position to develop the resilience needed to confront collapse in a responsible way. In contrast, a democratic world in which the political priorities of nation-states and international governmental organizations enable regional communities to have greater control over their economic and political destinies would be in a better position to put in place the structures—from the mundane, such as public sewerage and water control systems to the intangible, such as networks of trust and self-help—that are required to build societal resilience. Clearly, the construction of resilient societies will require reforms up and down the geographical scale, from global financial institutions through national governments to the local level. In my mind, localism can be part of the solution, not part of the problem, especially if it continues to develop in the ways that I have outlined in this book. As the collapse scenarios of the twenty-first century unfold, the world will need all the partial solutions and all the resilience it can muster.[17]

Notes

Introduction

1. For a lengthier discussion of globalization, with references, see Hess 2007a: 8–15. (N.B.: Page numbers are given for books only.)

2. On "remaking of the relationship," see Martello et al. 2004. On the glocal, see Robertson 1995. On global cities, see Sassen 2000: 59–116.

3. Castells and Hall 1994: 1–39; Sassen 2000: 59–116.

4. Covert 2006; Howe 2007; Kooser 2007; Manly 2006; McGregor 2008; Saporito 2007.

5. Greene 2004; Jacob 1997: 3–53; Jackson 2004; Relocalization Network 2008. British Green Party leaders have also linked localization to environmental politics (Woodin and Lucas 2004: 145–214). Curtis (2003) presents a rationale from an ecological economics perspective.

6. Holland et al. 2007: 107–129, 233–234. On the effects of devolution on advocacy in five industries, see Hess 2007a: 171–233. On the "New Localism," see Coaffee 2005; Stoker 2004.

7. On bowling alone, see Putnam 2000: 15–29.

8. For a more detailed discussion of types of social change action and alternative pathways, see Hess 2007a: 3–8. For a similar perspective on pathways for change, see Gottlieb 2001: xiv–xvi.

9. On coalitions, globalization, and anti-globalization movements, two essays that have influenced me are Buttel and Gould 2004 and Konefal and Mascarenhas 2005.

10. My definition builds on Shuman's (2006: 112) but is oriented toward a slightly larger geographical scale.

11. The term "global localism" is not original here; a similar use can be found in Woodin and Lucas 2004, and Medley and Kalibo (2007) use the term in a discussion of conservation and local knowledge.

12. On the history of Ben and Jerry's and the alternative of companies with a social and environmental mission that have attempted to remain in private hands with local owners, see Bamburg 2006: 1–14; Hammel and Denhart 2007: 1–27; Hollender and Fenichel 2004: 211–247. A 2008 search on the website CorpWatch.org found 149 pages on the parent company, most of them pertaining to questionable practices.

13. DuPuis and Goodman 2005; DuPuis et al. 2006. For a similar approach to place-based alternative economies, see Gibson-Graham 2006: 79–99. For a related approach that draws out the rich internal diversity of a movement, see Gottlieb 1993.

14. Daly 1990; Daly 1996: 9.

15. On localism in Germany, see Brand 2005: 55–65.

Chapter 1

1. Harvey 2005: 39–63, 183–206.

2. On globalization and inequality in the United States, see Schmitt 2000; Williamson et al. 2002: 34–50; Wilterdink 2000. According to a report by the International Monetary Fund (2007: 135–169), increases in within-nation inequality were due to foreign direct investment, whereas trade liberalization reduced inequality. Foreign direct investment increases inequality by raising the demand for skilled workers, but conversely in the United States it also decreases demand for highly paid, less skilled workers. Schmitt criticizes the trade-technology framework and instead focuses on the effects of globalization on the bargaining power of workers.

3. On the failed transition in energy policies, see Brown et al. 2006.

4. Hawken et al. 1999: 159–169, 260–284. On the connection between sustainability and justice in subsequent work, see Hawken 2007: 89–138. On eco-efficiency approaches more generally, see DeSimone et al. 1997: 23–46; Porter and Van der Linde 1995.

5. Gelbspan 2004: 182–205; World Commission on Environment and Development 1987: entire volume.

6. Bourdieu 1977: 164–171.

7. Marx and Engels 1978.

8. On dematerialization, see Daly 1996: 34–35; for a more policy-oriented approach, see Brown 2001. For examples of other critics of mainstream environmental politics and economics, see O'Connor 1998: 135–178; Schnaiberg 1980: 205–273. On ecological modernization, see Mol 1995: 29–59.

9. Thomas Friedman (2007), a journalist who has defended corporate-led globalization, also defends corporate greening as a general strategy for the United States to regain moral leadership in the world. For examples of the reporting of

the problematic aspects of corporate greening in the business press, see Elgin 2007; Gunther 2006a. Sklair (2001: 198–254) provides a more detailed and analytical account of the limitations of corporate greening. On the tendency of corporations to sacrifice greening to profits, see Weinberg 1998.

10. The argument that increased technological efficiency can coincide with overall increases in consumption is known as the Jevons paradox. William Stanley Jevons, a nineteenth-century economist, observed the growth in coal consumption that followed the introduction of a more efficient steam engine. The insight also underlies the work of critics such as York and Rosa (2003).

11. On think tanks, public relations, and corporate-sponsored anti-environmentalism, see Beder 1997: 75–139. On the resignation of the climate scientist and the influence of corporations on energy policy, see Gelbspan 2004: 36–61. On the George W. Bush administration and the censorship of scientists such as James Hansen, see Bowen 2008: 98–142. On business influence on climate change policy more generally, see Layzer 2007.

12. The comment extends Beck 1994 by looking at the second-order risks and side effects that are generated by ameliorative technologies.

13. Meadows et al. 2004: xxi. Again, I am drawing on the argument among radical sociologists (see, e.g., York and Rosa 2003) that the crucial metric is global levels of environmental sinks and withdrawals. Some countries may be paragons of ecological modernization, but they may also be able to do so by exporting pollution, environmental degradation, and the worst effects of collapse to developing countries.

14. Gunther 2006a.

15. On disaster capitalism, see Klein 2007: 406–442.

16. Micklethwait and Wooldridge 2003: 15–78.

17. Schnaiberg 1980: 207–247; York and Rosa 2003; Daly 1996: 35.

18. On de-industrialization and Commoner, see Mol 1995: 11; York and Rosa 2003. On the used of mixed policies to achieve the greening of industry, see Commoner 1971: 284. On Commoner's thought and on his election bid, see Egan 2007: 139–170.

19. On the environmental record of Eastern Bloc countries, see Feshbach and Friendly 1992: 1–25. Gille (2007: 203–212) notes that reuse practices were actually very strong in Hungary, and probably other Eastern Bloc countries, during the 1950s and the 1960s, but that in many ways the environmental situation deteriorated after that period.

20. Wilson and Purushothaman 2003.

21. Engels 1978; Miller 1999: xiii–xiv; Pitzer 1997: 3–13.

22. Bookchin 1971: 85–139, 1990: 179–204. See also Sale 1980: 419–519; O'Conner 1998: 283–284; Light 1998: 1–25, 343–383. Late in life, Bookchin (2002) expressed preference for the term "communalism" over "anarchism" and

described himself as a "libertarian socialist." Although I am drawing out some of the differences between communalism and socialism, they could also coexist as complementary political strategies for social change.

23. Miller 1999: 225–242.

24. Wood 1984: 243–274, 317–325; Schumacher 1973: 254–292.

25. On the localism and its relationship with the devolution and privatization of welfare and other policies, see Hess 2007a: 171–234. On the convergences of localism with neoliberalism in the context of rural regions, see DuPuis and Goodman 2005. On the ordinances against franchises and zoning for big-box superstores, see Mitchell 2000: 37–53, 2006: 192–218. On the politicization of the consumerism in the United States, see Cohen 2003: 345–397.

26. For example, Eaton (2008) argues that in Niagara, Ontario, the political strands shifted in response to changes in the provincial government.

27. The research of Hinrichs and Allen (2007), who analyzed documents from "buy local" food organizations and found substantial evidence in favor of the community and local economics theme but little evidence for concern with equity in the sense used here, is consistent with the argument that localism has more to do with the sovereignty of communities than with justice for the poor or other historically marginalized groups.

28. Ferguson 2005; Ong 2006: 17–18.

29. Johnston 2003: 3–17, 266–277.

30. The criticisms made by Wicks and other localist leaders might be compared with that of environmental sociologists who suggest that the mandate for continued corporate profit-seeking makes it difficult for large publicly traded corporations to maintain stable and long-term commitments to social and environmental responsibility goals. Treadmill-of-production theorists such as Pellow et al. (2000) note that large corporations tend to sacrifice their social and environmental responsibility goals when they run into conflicts with profitability. They note that the "emancipation" of ecological and social values from profitability concerns that ecological-modernization theorists such as Arthur Mol (1995, 2000) hoped to find in the corporate world is short-lived, contingent, and subject to reversal. A localist perspective on the debate suggests that the potential for the "emancipation" of social and environmental responsibility concerns from profitability goals may be easier to find on a more consistent basis in the world of the locally owned independent economy, where autonomous and stable enterprises can pursue a form of business that is driven by a mix of economic and non-economic values. On this well-known debate in environmental sociology, see also Buttel 2004; York and Rosa 2003; Mol and Spaargaren 2000, 2005; Scheinberg 2003. On my localist perspective on the debate, it is worth adding that there is also a potential convergence with the management literature on family business, where some studies have found that family firms have higher levels of stewardship and community involvement than non-family firms (Craig and Dibrell 2006; Dyer and Whetten 2006; Litz and Stewart 2000). Note,

however, that the category of "family business" can include publicly traded firms with high levels of family ownership.

31. Hollender and Fenichel 2004: 1–3.

32. The point is suggested but not developed by Schnaiberg and Gould (1994: 51). Again, this issue is complex and needs to be thought through as a question of statistical probabilities. The boards of privately held corporations have a fiduciary responsibility to all shareholders, so a minority of shareholders could sue the majority if the majority were to decide to invest a large percentage of profits in higher wages or community benefit projects. However, closely held private corporations have greater freedom to define their corporate purpose around social and environmental responsibility values. Most if not all "B corporations," or public benefit stakeholder corporations, are privately held.

Chapter 2

1. Although I do not engage directly with the literature of Science and Technology Studies (STS) in this book, this is the most STS-oriented of the chapters, and it is a continuation of my longstanding interest in social movements, science, and innovation. The important and growing body of work of my colleagues Scott Frickel, Kelly Moore, and Daniel Kleinman in the "new political sociology of science," which also draws attention to knowledge, publics, social movements, and industrial innovation, has influenced this chapter. See Frickel and Moore 2005: 185–323; Kleinman 1991: 102–122.

2. Blakely and Bradshaw 2002: 43–47.

3. On the technopole, the triple helix, and the global city, see respectively Castells and Hall 1994: 1–39; Etzkowitz et al. 1998: 1–20; Sassen 2000: 59–116.

4. On the Danish wind cluster, see Jørgensen and Karnøe 1996; Jørgensen and Strunge 2002. On the Freiburg solar cluster, see Solar Region Freiburg 2008.

5. Sassen 2000: 135–137.

6. Shuman (2006: 24–34) provides a critique of the high-tech strategy in South Carolina, where significant resources went into attracting an automobile plant to the region. Even if one were to conclude in favor of the long-term success of the strategy, the region might have been more successful had it chosen a diversified strategy that also supported locally owned small businesses.

7. Shuman 2006: 24–34. See also Persky et al. 1993.

8. Silva 2007.

9. Bruton 1998; Love 2005.

10. Massey and Capoferro 2006; Portes 1994; Portes and Roberts 2005; Silva 2007.

11. Bruton 1998. Productivity growth rates were below 1 percent, versus 3 percent in Taiwan (ibid.). One explanation for the lower productivity is that

import-substitution policies tended to develop manufacturing broadly rather than focus on industries where the greatest productivity was possible.

12. Bruton 1998.

13. For an example of the moderate approach to reforming import-substitution policies, see Baer 1972. On the role of dictatorships in dismantling import-substitution developmentalism, see Klein 2007: 49–168.

14. On the history, see Bruton 1998 and Silva 2007. On import substitution in the Asian high-tech sector, see Amsden 2004. On mixed strategies, see McKay and Milner 2002.

15. On problems with the replication of export-oriented development, see Bruton 1998. On the effects of export-oriented policies in low-income countries, see Singer 1988. On the end of the import-substitution era and the negative effects of trade liberalization on the quality of life in cities, see Davis 2006: 151–173; Portes and Roberts 2005.

16. Davis 2006: 70–94, 151–173.

17. On chapter 11 of NAFTA, which weakens environmental regulations at both a state and national level, see Moyers 2002. On dissatisfaction with globalization among blue-collar voters and the 2008 presidential campaign, see Solomon and Hitt 2007.

18. Hines 2000: 68–69, 110, 132.

19. Greider 2007; Hindery 2007.

20. Jacobs 1969: 156–164. See also Jacobs 1984: 35–47, 142–143. The term "import replacing" (meaning replacing with goods that the city can make for itself) can be distinguished from "import substituting" (replacing with goods that the city already produces), but I have not found the distinction important for the present purposes. See also Persky et al. 1993.

21. Institute for Local Self Reliance 1991; Morris and Hess 1975: 46–68; Morris 1982: 109–177.

22. On the Homegrown Project, see Imbroscio 1997: 49–95. On the other projects, see Lerner 1998: 231–242; Persky et al. 1993; Sandro 1994.

23. Perksy et al. 1993; Power 1996: 7–56; Markusen 2007; Rutland and O'Hagan 2007.

24. Shuman 2000: 51–58; Shuman 2006: 50–55.

25. For an entry into the literature on the organic food and back-to-the-land movements, see Hess 2004, 2007a: 126–135, 194–195. On import substitution, see Bellows and Hamm 2001. On agricultural localism and economies of scope, see Marsden et al. 2002 and Renting et al. 2003. For a review of alternative food networks, see Winter 2004. For a critique and explanation of post-productivism, see Evans et al. 2002. For a response from the post-productivist theorist Brian Ilbery and his colleagues (who, like Marsden, suggest the value of short food-supply chains in the formation of "stronger" alternative food networks), see Watts et al. 2005.

26. According to DuPuis and Block (2008), the federal courts restricted localization regulations for dairy markets.

27. S. Mitchell 2006: 164–177; Shuman 2006: 174.

28. On different products, see Shuman 2006: 3–6. On prices at supermarkets versus those at farmers' markets, see Breach 2007; Halweil 2004: 211; La Trobe 2001; Oakley and Appel 2005. On price flexing, see S. Mitchell 2006: 127–137.

29. Ajilore 2004; Civic Economics 2002, 2004, 2007; Institute for Local Self-Reliance 2003.

30. Civic Economics 2002; Shuman 2006: 30; Tolbert 2005; Tolbert et al. 2002.

31. See also Swenson 2004.

32. Goldschmidt 1978: 394–395, 455–487.

33. Stated more in the language of economics, to the extent that the negative and positive externalities of nonlocal and local ownership can be quantified, they could be internalized through differential local tax rates. On the tax issue, see S. Mitchell 2006: 163–191; Shuman 2006: 30. On the factors that correlate with a vibrant small-business sector, see Tolbert et al. 2002; Tolbert 2005. On the effects of Wal-Mart stores both generally and specifically for indicators of community health, see Artz and Stone 2006; Basker 2007; Fishman 2006: 137–166; Goetz and Swaminathan 2006; Goetz and Rapasingha 2006; Greenwald 2005; Norman 2004; Stone 1995. Similar concerns have been raised for other large chains, such as Tesco (Shaffer et al. 2007).

34. Ricardo 1929: 108–122.

35. Furtado 1968: 87–92; Felipe and Vernengo 2002. Even the simple example of the banana and apple involves very complex politics (Koeppel 2007: 1–8, 51–93).

Chapter 3

1. Hahnel (2007) points to the weaknesses in the small-business sector on justice grounds. For one example of injustice and local elites, see Logan and Molatch 2007: 50–98.

2. On the firm-size wage effect, see Bayard and Troske 1999; Belfield and Wei 2004; Brown et al. 1990: 29–51; Edmiston 2007; Groothuis 1994; Heyman 2007; Idson and Oi 1999; Paez 2003; Troske 1999.

3. On boutiques, see Spiers 2008. On whiteness, see Slocum 2007.

4. Reich 1991: 301–315; Monbiot 2003. See also the criticism by John Clark, the former World Bank manager, that localism represents an "unhealthy provincialism" (MacDonald 2006), discussions in urban studies on enclavism (e.g., Davis 1992: 221–263), and the discussion in the rural sociology literature on "defensive localism" (Winter 2003).

5. Winner 1986: 61–84; Szasz 2007: 4.

6. Cohen 2003: 227–240; DuPuis et al. 2006; Harrison 2004; Hinrichs and Allen 2008.

7. Reynolds et al. 2002: 8. I am indebted to my colleague Rob Chernow for pointing out this study to me.

8. On the negative side effects of large retail chains, see Goetz and Swaminathan 2006; Goetz and Rapasingha 2006; S. Mitchell 2006: 3–127.

9. On the wage effect in the retail sector, see Edmiston 2007. On the effect of the opening of a Wal-Mart on overall retail wages in a local economy, see Neumark et al. 2007.

10. Tolbert 2005; Tolbert et al. 2002. On local ownership of third places, see Oldenburg 2002: 1–8. The term "third places" is used in contrast with the home and the workplace, which are referred to as the first and second places.

11. Miles 2007; Saunders et al. 2006; Watkiss 2005. Research that questions the food-miles assumption adopts a life-cycle assessment methodology that takes into account total energy used in food production and distribution rather than simply the energy used in transporting food to market. Where food production is more sustainable owing to lower heating costs, lower petrochemical inputs, and other factors, the total energy consumed may be lower. Furthermore, corporate food systems and supermarkets aggregate food shipments, and consumers can purchase many items on one shopping trip to a supermarket. Consequently, in at least some cases the larger scale of the retail outlets of the nonlocal corporate system may be more energy efficient. Comparisons between the two systems suggest that there is considerable variation across food products (Wallgren 2006).

12. Miles 2007; Saunders et al. 2006; Watkiss 2005.

13. Shuman 2007.

14. Maniates 2002; Princen 2005.

15. Hollender and Fenichel 2004: 253–260; Weinberg 1998.

16. Mol 1995: 36.

17. On the tendency for publicly traded corporations to underinvest in environmental technologies and products when stock values are at risk, see Sklair 2001: 198–254; Weinberg 1998. On the chemical plants and local ownership, see Grant et al. 2004. On the correlation with nonprofit organizations, see Tolbert et al. 2002; Tolbert 2005.

18. On just sustainabilities, see Agyeman 2005: 79–106; Bullard 2007. The table is adapted from Hess 2007a: 239.

Chapter 4

1. Schragger 2005.

2. Schragger (2005) provides a detailed legal history of the legislation and court cases. See also Ingram and Rao 2004; S. Mitchell 2006: 3–9, 205–210.

3. Hanchett 1996, S. Mitchell 2006: 3–32.

4. On opposition to infrastructure, including big-box stores, see Hess 2007a: 109–113. On technology-oriented and product-oriented movements, see Hess 2007a: 123–170. For a comparison of "buy local" campaigns with other historically similar "buycotts" (such as "buy black"), see Hinrichs and Allen 2008.

5. Lifestyles of Health and Sustainability 2008.

6. American Independent Business Alliance 2008. Co-op America (2008) is a very different type of organization; more national in scope, it explicitly supports sustainability and social justice goals, but membership is not restricted to cooperatives or even locally owned independent businesses. Although Co-op America is not directly oriented toward the needs of locally owned independent businesses, it is developing local "green pages" listings and regional green festivals, and it also supports campaigns in favor of community-oriented investing and fair trade.

7. Case study of the Sustainable Business Network of Greater Philadelphia in Hess et al. 2007.

8. Business Alliance for Local Living Economies 2008.

9. Case study of Austin Independent Business Alliance in Hess et al. 2007.

10. Case study of the Austin Independent Business Alliance in Hess et al. 2007 (based on an interview will Melissa Miller). Also see Gregor 2006, 2007. For background information on Austin and the place of Barton Springs in its political culture, see Moore 2007: 29–72.

11. Case study of Local Exchange in Hess et al. 2007. Also see Sustainable Connections 2008.

12. Case study of the Sustainable Business Network of Greater Philadelphia in Hess et al. 2007.

13. Guthman et al. 2006.

14. I conducted the case studies of the reuse centers in Austin, Berkeley, Oakland, and Portland. Graduate students conducted the case studies of Baltimore (Govind Gopakumar), Burlington (Richard Arias Hernández), and Pittsburgh (Rachel Dowty). All the studies are published in Hess et al. 2007. Although some research on the broader resale industry has been published (e.g., Horne and Maddrell 2002: 118–135), little has been published on reuse centers (Andrews and Maurer 2001).

15. Case studies in Hess et al. 2007.

16. Case study of Austin's Re-Store in Hess et al. 2007.

17. Case study of the Rebuilding Center in Hess et al. 2007.

18. Case studies of the Austin Re-Store, the Loading Dock, and The Reuse People in Hess et al. 2007.

19. Case studies of the Austin Re-Store, Rebuilding Center, and Recycle North in Hess et al. 2007. Also see Green Worker Cooperative 2007.

20. Case studies of the Austin Re-Store, Construction Junction, Rebuilding Center, and Urban Ore in Hess et al. 2007.

21. Case studies of ReCycle North and the Loading Dock in Hess et al. 2007.

Chapter 5

1. On the 100-mile challenge, see Smith and MacKinnon 2007. See also Kingsolver 2007: 1–23; McKibben 2007: 46–94.

2. On the local trap, see Born and Purcell 2006. On defensive localism, see Winter 2003. On parochialism and localism, see Hinrichs 2003.

3. On the Cascadian Farms case, see Pollan 2006b: 144–145, 151–158. On the bifurcation thesis, see Campbell and Liepens 2001; Guthman 2002, 2004: 14–41; Lockie and Halpin 2005.

4. Hinrichs and Allen 2007; Goodman and Goodman 2007; DuPuis and Goodman 2005. See also Allen et al. 2003; DuPuis et al. 2006; Guthman et al. 2006; Harrison 2004; Hinrichs and Allen 2008; Trauger 2007. On the tradeoff between direct sales and small storeowners, see Morris and Bueller 2003. On localism and food security issues, see Ferris et al. 2001; Gottlieb 2001: 181–272; Gottlieb and Fisher 1996; Guthman et al. 2006; Hinrichs 2003. On saving small farms as itself a kind of justice issue, see Bell 2004: 56–58.

5. Lawson 2005: 23–117; von Hassell 2002: 27–58.

6. Ferris et al. 2001. On nutrition education, see Flanigan and Varma 2006; Hess et al. 2007. On the British study, see Holland 2004. On the upstate New York study, see Armstrong 2000.

7. On the upstate New York study, see Armstrong 2000. On the Philadelphia study, see Hanna and Oh 2000. On the New York City gardens, see Schmelzkopf 1996, 2002; Saldivar-Tanaka and Krasny 2004.

8. I conducted site visits and interviews in Philadelphia, Portland, Sacramento, San Francisco, and Seattle. Graduate students studied Boston (Rachel Dowty), Cleveland (Colin Beech), Denver (Richard Arias Hernández), and Detroit (Govind Gopakumar).

9. On the two concepts of rights, see Staeheli et al. 2002.

10. Case studies of the Cleveland, Denver, and Seattle community gardens in Hess et al. 2007.

11. City of Sacramento 2004; City of Portland 2008; case studies of the Portland and Sacramento community gardens in Hess et al. 2007.

12. Case studies of San Francisco and Philadelphia community gardens in Hess et al. 2007.

13. On the issue of scale and neoliberalism, see also Peck and Tickell 2002.

14. On the changes in food security politics, see Eisinger 1998: 91–122; Poppendieck 1998: 4–19; Tarasuk and Eakin 2003.

15. On the neoliberal policies and New York, see Harvey 2005: 44–48. On Operation Green Thumb, see Smith and Kurtz 2003.

16. Smith and Kurtz 2003; Staeheli et al. 2002.

17. Smith and Kurtz 2003; DuPuis et al. 2006.

18. City of Boston 2002; case study of Boston community gardens in Hess et al. 2007.

19. City of Sacramento 2008; case study of Sacramento community gardens in; Hess et al. 2007.

20. Case study of Seattle community gardens in Hess et al. 2007.

21. Case study of Portland Community Gardens in Hess et al. 2007.

22. On the new zoning law, see Brady 2007. On community gardening in Cleveland more generally, see Kious 2004; EcoCity Cleveland 2007; Hess et al. 2007.

23. On the Detroit community gardens see Hess et al. 2007. On Los Angeles see South Central Farms 2008.

24. Staeheli et al. 2002.

25. Case study of Boston community gardens in Hess et al. 2007. See also City of Boston 2002.

26. Case study of Seattle community gardens in Hess et al. 2007.

27. Case study of Philadelphia community gardens in Hess et al. 2007; Pennsylvania Horticultural Society 2007.

28. Friends of Portland Community Gardens 2007; Growing Gardens 2007.

29. Case study of San Francisco community gardens in Hess et al. 2007.

30. Detroit's "Farm a Lot" program of community assistance begin in the Office of Neighborhoods in the mayor's office, was transferred to the Recreation Department, and appears to have been discontinued in 2006 (Kavanaugh 2006).

31. Case studies of Sacramento and Seattle community gardens in Hess et al. 2007

32. American Community Gardening Association 2008a, b.

33. On rooftop gardens and condominium development, see the case study of Seattle community gardens in Hess et al. 2007. For an overview of the

entrepreneurial urban farm, including for-profit farms, see Kaufman and Bailkey 2000: 10–54.

34. Soil Born Urban Agriculture Project 2008; Zenger Urban Agricultural Park 2008; case studies of Sacramento and Portland community gardens in Hess et al. 2007.

35. Case study of San Francisco community gardens in Hess et al. 2007; City of San Francisco 2007.

36. ReVision House 2008; Food Project 2008; Denver Urban Gardens 2008; Earth Works 2008; case studies of Boston, Denver, and Detroit in Hess et al. 2007.

37. One might also argue that the nonprofit farm is an example of post-productivism in agriculture. But, as I discussed in chapter 2, there are several critiques of the value of the concept, which in any case was developed more for rural agriculture (e.g., Evans et al. 2002).

Chapter 6

1. This chapter builds on and extends Hess 2007a: 192–200, which includes a discussion of home power and reform efforts in support of green buildings.

2. On concern with visual impacts, see Pasqualetti 2002. On various negative effects, see Firestone and Kempton 2007.

3. On the gap between general and local acceptance and the pattern of decline, see Wolsink 2006. On cross-national comparisons, see Toke et al. 2008.

4. On local investment, see Breukers and Wolsink 2007; Gross 2007; Jobert et al. 2007. On the Denmark case, see Hvelpund 2006; Ladenburg 2008. For general background on the local wind ownership in the country, see Jørgensen and Karnøe 1996; Jørgensen and Strunge 2002; Sovacool et al. 2008. On wind in Wales, see Devine-Wright 2005; Hinshelwood 2001; Woods 2003. On Japan, see Maruyama et al. 2007. On community wind power in the US, see Bolinger 2005. For more on financing and political support, see Gubbins 2007; Heiman and Solomon 2004; Palm 2006; Reilly 2007.

5. For background literature on localism and energy in the United States, see Curtis and Anshuman 2004; Pickford 2001; Public Power 2003, 2006. In the United Kingdom, "community-based localism" in renewable energy policy appears to be gaining support (Walker et al. 2007). In the case of Vermont, my research is based on attending a conference session, bibliographic materials from the session, and reports on the organization's website.

6. Hampton and Reno 2003: 88–93, 232. On the peak in public power utilities, see Schneiberg 2007.

7. Hampton and Reno 2003: 171–184. For more on the history of restructuring up to 1996, see Hirsh 1999: 207–271, 292–293.

8. Paterson 2003: 14. A study by the American Public Power Association showed that in the aggregate public power providers compared favorably with investor owned utilities on a variety of emissions and renewable energy metrics (Pickford 2001). On local energy more generally, see Morris 2001.

9. Case studies of Austin, Sacramento, and Seattle electric power in Hess et al. 2007.

10. Ibid.

11. Ibid. On Seattle and the Kyoto Protocol, see Langston 2007.

12. Case study of Seattle City Light in Hess et al. 2007.

13. Ibid.

14. Ibid.

15. Ibid.

16. Case study of San Francisco Electric Power in Hess et al. 2007. See also Fenn 2004; Roberts 1999. On some problems that have emerged with the northern Ohio aggregation, see Littlechild 2007.

17. Ibid.

18. Ibid. The original case study has a long quote from Fenn on the point.

19. Efficiency Vermont 2008a, 2008b; Sacks 2004.

20. Efficiency Vermont 2008b, 2008c; Sacks 2004.

21. Efficiency Vermont 2008b, 2008c.

22. On transit racism in the United States, see Bullard et al. 2004. On the Los Angeles mobilizations, see Bus Riders Union 2000, 2002, 2005, 2008. On Boston, see Alternatives for Community and Environment 2008; Duffy 2000; Saleos 2003.

23. Hess 2007b.

24. For more details, see Hess 2007b. There have been a handful of social science studies on sustainable transportation (e.g., Rosen 2001) and the transition to fuel-cell vehicles (e.g., Cohen 2006 and Hekkert and van de Hoed 2004), but my research and that of a companion essay (Valderrama and Beltrán 2007) are the first to analyze controversies over clean fuel and bus technology from a social science perspective.

25. On carcinogens, see Weinhold 2002; International Agency for Research on Cancer 1989. On the World Health Organization, see International Programme on Chemical Safety 1996. On the 70 percent figure, see South Coast Air Quality Management District 2000. On the 41 contaminants, see California Air Resources Board 1998.

26. On non-attainment cities and the report in general, see Natural Resources Defense Council 1998.

27. For more details, see Hess 2007b; Prakesh 2007.

28. On the federal standards, see Environmental Protection Agency 2006; Washington State University Extension Program 2004. On the California standards, see California Air Resources Board 2005b; Peckham 2003. On the 48 versus 28 agencies, see California Air Resources Board 2005b.

29. I review the test data and fleet decisions in more detail in Hess 2007b. On the test data, see California Air Resources Board 2002a, 2002b, 2004, 2005a; Cohen 2005; Melendez et al. 2005. On the Cleveland Study, see Heywood et al. 2002. On the National Renewable Energy Laboratory study, see Eudy 2002. On Los Angeles, see Jager and Littman 2005. On the natural gas industry study, see Watt 2000.

30. Case study of Metro Transit in Hess et al. 2007.

31. Ibid.

32. Case study of Chattanooga Area Regional Transit Authority in Hess et al. 2007.

33. Metro Transit of King County 2008.

34. Case study of Metro Transit in Hess et al. 2007; Morris 2006.

35. Bullard et al. 2004; Hess 2007b; case study of Alameda-Contra Costa County Transit in Hess et al. 2007.

36. Case study of Metro Transit in Hess et al. 2007.

Chapter 7

1. On the statistics, see Bagdikian 2000: preface. Barsamian (2001: 2) reviews the consolidation statistics as they increased in various editions of Bagdikian's influential book. Alger (1988: 33) has come up with similar but somewhat longer lists that also included Microsoft, Gannett (newspapers), and the French conglomerate Matra-Hachette Filipacchi, but there is consensus on the issue that the mass media have become heavily dominated by a small number of firms. On consolidation in the American broadcast and radio media, see also Compaine and Gomery 2000: 1–26, 193–358. On the 1990s legislation, see Alger 1998: 97–114.

2. For a review of the differing perspectives on consolidation, see Horwitz 2007. The size of the Gannet chain in 1998, in terms of both percentage of total circulation and gross circulation, was about equivalent to that of the Hearst chain in 1946. On the newspaper chains, see Compaine and Gomery 2000: 12–13. On radio consolidation, see Hilliard and Keith 2005: 106–137.

3. On the reversal of ownership from World War II to 1989, see Bagdikian 2000: 4. On the loss of participation and the demise of the fairness doctrine, see Hilliard and Keith 2005: 61–105, 140–147, 200–213; Napoli 2001.

4. Media localism from 1920 through 1934 may have reflected the modernizing project of the national middle class rather than true concern with protecting local

media content, but the policies shifted after 1934 (Kirkpatrick 2006). On the history of the doctrine of media localism and policies, see Hilliard and Keith 2005: 2, 31–49, 65; Horwitz 2007; Napoli 2007. On the "rule of sevens" and provisions of the 1996 act, see Nieto and Schmitt 2004: 169.

5. McChesney 2004: 58–63. On the government report, see Federal Communications Commission 2004.

6. On the commercialization of radio in the early twentieth century, see McChesney 1993: 12–37. On the failure of educational radio before the 1950s, see Leach 1999. On the relationship between policies of the period and media localism, see Hilliard and Keith 2005: 30–54.

7. On the events surrounding government support of public broadcasting, see Current.Org 2008. On concerns with media diversity and the civil rights movement, see Horwitz 2007.

8. On the Nixon veto and history of the 1960s and the 1970s, see Barsamian 2001: 10–61. On the European cases and the effects of quasi-advertising on public broadcasting in the United States, see Alger 1998: 207–227. On the direct censorship by conservatives, see Starr 2003. See also Citizens for Independent Public Broadcasting 1999. Even in Europe the position of public broadcasting eroded after 1980 due to satellite television and the rise of commercial stations. Venerable public broadcasting networks, such as the British Broadcasting Corporation, lost audience for general shows (although not news), and it was under increasing pressure from its national government to adopt a more commercial posture.

9. Free Press 2008. The media watchdog organizations, which analyzed and criticized coverage, were themselves subject to attack from conservative organizations. For example, see Hearst 1996 on the progressive Fairness and Accuracy in Media Reporting organization and the conservative Media Research Center.

10. I make this claim based on several years of working on the circulation and finances of liberal and left publications that included some of the magazines mentioned above.

11. On the Ford Pinto story, see Dowie 1977. On the smoking story, see Blair 1979. The discussion of the boycott is based on memory from when I worked there and at an affiliated organization, but it is also mentioned on various websites. As with the commercial print media, nonprofit progressive media can also seek the benefits of integrated print and electronic publishing. One example is Z-net, an off-shoot of *Z Magazine* that provides a free listserv and offers additional information services for contributors (Barsamian 2001: 63). I am not including in this discussion the more lifestyle-oriented magazines or home magazines, many of which provide coverage of environmental and occasionally localist issues (e.g., *Mother Earth News*, *Natural Home Magazine*, and *Utne Reader*).

12. On the shift toward nonprofit ownership in the newspaper industry, see Blitstein 2008.

13. Again, the observations are based on working with various progressive nonprofit non-governmental organizations and alternative press organizations during the 1970s and the early 1980s.

14. There is already a substantial literature on Pacifica and the conflicts of the late 1990s and the early 2000s. This paragraph draws mostly on Land 1999: 6, 27–38, 74–78, 127–132 and on Lasar 1999: 1–26, 190–213, but see also Barsamian 2001: 75–82; McChesney 2001; Pierce 2002: 82–90; Walker 2002. On backfire and the media, see Martin 2007: 169–218. As of the time of writing, Goodman's program had returned to Pacifica and was also being broadcast to hundreds of community radio and public access television stations (Ratner 2005).

15. See Free Speech 2008; Link TV 2008; OneWorld 2008.

16. See Embardo 2001. *The Village Voice* dates back to reform efforts in the city's politics during the 1950s.

17. The statistics on the alternative weekly association are from the Association of Alternative Newsweeklies 2008. Total revenue for the association's newspapers was about $345 million in 1999 (Ardito 1999). The association required newspapers to be independent publishers, so the category is distinguished from the larger field of 3000 community newspapers, represented by the Association of Free Community Papers. About 80 percent of the community newspapers were owned by dailies (Gilyard 2002). On the general effects of consolidation and comparison of the chains, see McAuliffe 1999; *Utne Reader* 1997. On the purchase of Alternative Media, Inc., and the sale of other chains, see Hazen 2000. On the *LA Weekly*, see Wiener 2007.

18. On the specific case of the effects of acquisition on the *East Bay Express*, see Kingston 2001. On the related issue of dilution of labor politics in consolidated weeklies, see Harris 2005a, 2005b.

19. On Gannett's task force, see Gilyard 2002. On upward age drift, see Moses 2002.

20. On the relocalization of radio during the 1950s, see Hilliard and Keith 2005: 55–61. Statistics on the growth of community radio in the United States can be found in the Archives of the National Federation of Community Broadcasters (University of Maryland Libraries; http://www.lib.umd.edu). On the history in general, see Durlin and Melio 2000. On the Healthy Station Project, see Fairchild 2001: 106. On the stations that were targeted for defunding and the impact on the stations oriented toward ethnic minority groups, see Dunaway 2002. On pressure to increase syndicated content, see Dunaway 2002; Nieckarz 2002; Starr 2003.

21. On the role of public broadcasting and community broadcasting in limiting microbroadcasting, see Barlow 1988; Brand 2004; Fairchild 1998, 2001: 106–107. On the FCC ruling in 2000 and the subsequent politics, see Dunbar-Hester 2008; Karr 2005; Sakolsky 2001; Smith 2003.

22. On diversity and media content, see Horwitz 2007. On the Federal Communications Commission rulings and minority radio and television networks, see Browne 2005: 83–87. On growth of ethnic media in general and acquisitions, see Hsu 2002. On advertisers and discrimination, see Ofori 1999. On the effects of the loss of minority ownership on programming, see National Telecommunications and Information Administration 1997, 2000. On the negative effects of the post-1985 policies of the Federal Communications Commission, see Unity: Journalists of Color 2008; Wilson 2001. On minority representation in the national media, see American Society of Newspaper Editors 2007; Fears 2004; Unity: Journalists of Color 2004. On the claim of loss of African-American local news due to Clear Channel and Black Radio, see Black Commentator 2003. Since the 1970s, when African-Americans began moving to the suburbs, African-American newspapers also faced financial hardship, increasing dependence on white advertisers, and problems of redefinition. In contrast, the television networks Black Entertainment Network, Telemundo, and Univision grew during the 1990s, largely through satellite links to cable television stations, and as they grew, they were able to improve news coverage. However, two of them were acquired by larger telecommunications firms, so they can no longer be counted as minority-owned media.

23. King and Mele 1999; Pierce 2002: 139–158. The Alliance for Community Media (2008), founded in 1976, represents 3000 PEG and community media organizations.

24. On the Bay area project, see Howley 2005: 73–74; Kubicek and Wagner 2002. On the history of community networks, see Beamish 1999; Kubicek and Wagner 2002; Gurstein 2000: 12–13; Silver 2004. Castells (2001: 146–155) describes the history of the Amsterdam Digital City, Europe's largest community network, and the conflicts that emerged between the foundation board and the activists who originated the network.

25. Barsamian 2001: 68–69; Pierce 2002: 167–169; Morris 2004; Platon and Deuze 2003; Sarver 2005.

26. On the statistic for blogs, see Kline and Burstein 2005: 3–24.

27. Case study of the Sustainable Business Network of Greater Philadelphia in Hess et al. 2007; Buy Local Philly 2008; Cassel 2005a, 2005b; Schimmel 2005a, 2005b.

28. Nelton 1995, Schimmel 2006. In 2006 Knight-Ridder was sold to the McClatchy Group, another national chain, which subsequently sold the newspaper to a group of local owners.

29. Churchill 2007; Hardin 2006; Schlett 2007.

30. The sample was taken from LexisNexus for the two-year period before April 2007. Similar searches on the same database and another database revealed a huge overlap in articles. I read the first 100 articles on the search.

31. *Capital Times* 2006; *Wisconsin State Journal* 2006.

32. Capital Newspapers 2008.

33. MacDonald 2006.

34. On the coverage in the *New York Times*, see Burros 2006; McWilliams 2007; D. Mitchell 2006; Rifkin 2006; Severson 2006. On the whole, the food columnist Michael Pollan is sympathetic to localism in food; see especially Pollan 2006a. By 2008, some of the *New York Times*'s coverage was negative (Dubner 2008; Tierney 2008). The discussion of national press coverage is based on extensive searches in multiple databases. On the television and radio coverage, see Hayes 2006; National Public Radio 2006; Sandell 2006. The television networks also picked up other reports, such as the *Christian Science Monitor* article, on their websites.

35. Postrel 2006.

36. "Good Food?" *The Economist*, December 9, 2006: 12. See also D. Mitchell 2006.

37. Brady 2006; Perman 2006.

38. Cloud 2007. On the agrifood research, see Winter 2003.

Chapter 8

1. On transition theory, see Cohen 2006; Geels 2002, 2007; Rotmans et al. 2001; van der Brugge 2005.

2. My approach is also consistent with a discussion in the urban studies and geography literature that advocates linking localist efforts with reform efforts at a broader scale. See, e.g., DeFilippis 1999; Lake 2002; Pendras 2002.

3. At the time of writing, Dunkin' Donuts was held by a group of private equity firms, so it is not a particularly good example for this argument. However, it seemed likely that the private equity firms would eventually sell the company or take it public.

4. Williamson et al. 2002: 146–164.

5. See also Henderson 2006: 75–90.

6. For introductions to the topic, see Greco 2001: 86–124; Hess 2007a: 223. The notes on Berkshares are based on a guest lecture by Susan Witt (2008).

7. On Deli Dollars and other scripts used to capitalize businesses, see Swann and Witt 1995.

8. Province of Nova Scotia 2008.

9. Hebb et al. 2004; Williamson et al. 2002: 165–190.

10. Levy and Purnell 2006.

11. Upstream 21 2008. On intrastate stock markets, see Shuman 2006: 129. The term "stakeholder" refers to persons who have an interest in the company

but are not necessarily shareholders, such as employees, community members, environmentalists, and consumers.

12. I am developing a perspective suggested by Shuman in his visit to the New York Capital District in 2007, when he noted that the debt portion of localist financing has been largely solved, and equity financing remains the problem.

13. Burlingham 2005: 1.

14. For more details on the policy suggestions that emerged for the specific sectors, see Hess and Winner 2007.

15. Day 2005; Sustainable Business Network of Greater Philadelphia 2003.

16. S. Mitchell 2006: 163–191.

17. Ibid.: 192–258.

18. On small-business associations and their proposed reforms, see National Federation of Independent Businesses 2008; National Small Business Association 2008. On uncollected taxes, see Citizen Works 2008. On the failure to provide solar energy funding for entrepreneurial ventures, see Reece 1979: 2–3, 135–138, 177–187.

19. On succession and exit problems, see Burlingham 2005: 154–190. On the risk of loss of mission after acquisition, see Hollender and Fenichell 2004: 211–247.

20. On cooperatives and growth, see Booth 1998: 179–187.

21. On the employee ownership statistics, see Williamson et al. 2002: 189–210. On the debt burden, see Burlingham 2005: 166.

22. On the employee-owned and controlled corporation as a new legal category, see Williamson et al. 2002: 209.

23. Lynn 2006; S. Mitchell 2006: 163–191.

24. Levin 2006; Speth 2008: 179; Thompson 2006.

25. Coalition for Environmentally Responsible Economies 2008. Greider (2003: 118) also discusses the investment-risk ratings of the firm Innovest, and he argues that the stocks of firms with better social and environmental scores also perform better. On the social movement campaigns, see O'Rourke 2005. Many of the proposals for corporate reform can also be found in the works of advocates of localism, such as Korten 1999: 163–182.

26. By making top management responsible for financial statements, and by backing up the responsibility with the threat of prison terms, the law also provided an incentive for corporate managers and boards to improve financial reporting. Another result of the reform was to separate research analysis and investment banking within investment banks, a change that was intended to help restore credibility to analyst reports that had been subject to increasing pressure from the investment banking side of the banks (Auger 2005: 206–207).

27. Lipton and Rosenblum 1991; Mitchell 2001: 129–134, 162, 182–184.

28. Mitchell 2001: 165–166, 174–182.

29. One example is the Canadian labor-sponsored investment funds, which select only businesses that meet labor, environmental, and local ownership standards. See Cavanagh and Mander 2004: 153.

30. Moshkiber 1998.

31. On the continental European and Japanese stakeholder model of capitalism, see Albert 1993: 127–163. The trend in global capitalism may be toward dominance of the Anglophone model of shareholder capitalism (Albert 1993: 169–190; Mitchell 2001: 270–275), but within that model various alternative legal definitions and ownership arrangements are also emerging (Albert 2002; B Corporation 2008; Upstream 21 2008).

32. ReclaimDemocracy.org and POCLAD (Program on Corporations, Law, and Democracy) are two examples of current thinking and activism around corporate personhood.

33. Some communities may also use the mechanism of legal appeals over local ordinances to draw attention to the loss of sovereignty under the corporate-dominated, undemocratic rule-making bodies of the World Trade Organization and regional free trade agreements (Kaplan 2003).

34. Commoner 1971: 281–284. On Latin America and anti-privatization sentiment, see Klein 2007: 450–458. Freudenberg (2005) provides quantitative evidence that in each industry much of the environmental degradation is the product of one or two companies that have the worst record. If a policy of limited nationalization or even just the threat of it were pursued, those companies might be the ones targeted for public ownership.

35. Williamson et al. 2002: 267–309.

Conclusion

1. Shuman 2006: 174.

2. O'Connor 1998: 273.

3. DuPuis and Goodman 2005.

4. On the cautionary note of environmental justice scholars, see Bullard et al. 2004; Pellow and Brulle 2005.

5. Many of the statistics that document growth since the 1960s are discussed in Hess 2007a: 171–235.

6. On farmers' markets, see A. Brown 2001, 2002; Bullock 2000; US Department of Agriculture 2000, 2007. On the size of the food industry in the United States, see Plunkett Research 2008. On CSA farms and income, see Stevenson et al. 2004.

7. Shuman 2006: 42–46, 225–234.

8. Wicks 2004: 5.

9. On gender inequality and other aspects of inequality in fair-trade cooperatives, see Lyon 2007a,b. On the lack of understanding of fair trade among growers, see Doane 2007; Dolan 2007. On some problems that have occurred with large corporations that have displaced "fair trade" labels with their own producer preference systems, see Daviron and Ponte 2005: 193–198; Smith 2007. On the cooptation of certification schemes in general, see Conroy 2007: 241–254.

10. I would include the Business Alliance for Local Living Economies 2008 and organic food cooperatives such as Organic Valley Family of Farms 2008 as examples of "global localism," that is, organizations that link diverse and geographically disperse networks of consumers and producers around the goal of building the independent locally owned sector of the economy.

11. On the production of local food for nonlocal markets, see Bérard and Marchenay 2006; Sonnino and Marsden 2006. Fonte (2006) suggests that the shift from localism to local branding inevitably includes the use of certification, a general feature of what Callon et al. (2002) call the "economy of qualities."

12. On Wal-Mart, see Sheban 2007. On craft beers, see Kesmodel 2007. On corporate appropriation of localism in the food sector, see Jackson et al. 2007.

13. On label fatigue, see Goodman 2004.

14. Klein 2007: 385–405.

15. On overshoot and collapse, see Meadows et al. 2004: xxi. On the prognosis of surveillance and authoritarianism, see Klein 2007: 423–442.

16. On small-scale societies and the adaptive strategies, see Johnson and Earle 1987: 16–18.

17. On resilience, see Redman et al. 2007. On collapse from a comparative and an anthropological perspective, see Chew 2001: 1–13; Costanza et al. 2007: 379–470; Diamond 2005: 419–485; Tainter 1998: 1–21, 29–52.

Bibliography

Agyeman, Julian. 2005. *Sustainable Communities and the Challenge of Environmental Justice*. New York University Press.

Ajilore, Gbenga. 2004. Toledo-Lucas County Merchant Study. Urban Affairs Center, University of Toledo.

Albert, Michel. 1993. *Capitalism vs. Capitalism: How America's Obsession with Individual Achievement and Short-Term Profit Has Led It to the Brink of Collapse*. Four Walls Eight Windows.

Albert, Michel. 2002. Quels modèles d'enterprise pour un développement durable? Académie des Sciences Morales et Politiques. http://www.asmp.fr.

Alger, Dean. 1998. *Megamedia: How Giant Corporations Dominate Mass Media, Distort Competition, and Endanger Democracy*. Rowman and Littlefield.

Allen, Patricia, Margaret Fitzsimmons, Michael Goodman, and Keith Warner. 2003. "Shifting Plates in the Agrifood Landscape: The Techtonics of Alternative Food Initiatives in California." *Journal of Rural Studies* 19 (1): 61–75.

Alliance for Community Media. 2008. About the ACM. http://www.ourchannels.org.

Alternatives for Community and Environment. 2008. About ACE. http://www.ace-ej.org.

American Community Gardening Association. 2008a. Advocacy. www.communitygarden.org.

American Community Gardening Association. 2008b. Current Campaigns. http://www.communitygarden.org.

American Independent Business Alliance. 2008. About AMIBA: AMIBA History. http://amiba.net.

American Society of Newspaper Editors. 2007. Diversity Slips in U.S. Newsrooms. http://www.asne.org.

Amsden, Alice. 2004. "La Sustitución de importaciones en las industrias de alta tecnología: Prebisch renace en Asia." *Revista de la CEPAL* 82: 75–90.

Andrews, Clinton, and Maurer, Jamie. 2001. "Materials Exchanges: An Exploratory U.S. Survey." *Local Environment* 6 (2): 149–168.

Ardito, Stephanie. 1999. "The Alternative Press: Newsweeklies and Zines." *Database* 22 (3): 14–18.

Armstrong, Donna. 2000. "A Survey of Community Gardens in Upstate New York: Implications for Health Promotion and Community Development." *Health and Place* 6: 319–327.

Artz, Georgeanne, and Kenneth Stone. 2006. "Analyzing the Impact of Wal-Mart Supercenters on Local Food Store Sales." *American Journal of Agricultural Economics* 88 (5): 1296–1303.

Association of Alternative Newsweeklies. 2008. About AAN. http://aan.org.

Auger, Philip. 2005. *The Greed Merchants: How the Investment Banks Played the Free Market Game*. Penguin.

Baer, Werner. 1972. "Import Substitution and Industrialization in Latin America: Experiences and Interpretations." *Latin American Research Review* 7 (1): 95–122.

Bagdikian, Ben. 2000. *The Media Monopoly*. Beacon.

Bamburg, Jill. 2006. *Getting to Scale: Growing Your Business without Selling Out*. Berrett-Koehler.

Barlow, William. 1988. "Community Radio in the U.S.: The Struggle for a Democratic Medium." *Media, Culture, and Society* 10 (1): 81–105.

Barsamian, David. 2001. *The Decline and Fall of Public Broadcasting*. South End.

Basker, Emek. 2007. "The Causes and Consequences of Wal-Mart's Growth." *Journal of Economic Perspectives* 21 (3): 177–198.

Bayard, Kimberly, and Kenneth Troske. 1999. "Examining the Employer-Size Wage Premium in the Manufacturing, Retail Trade, and Service Industries Using Employer-Employee Matched Data." *American Economic Review* 89 (2): 99–103.

B Corporation. 2008. About B Corp. http://www.bcorporation.net.

Beamish, Anne. 1999. "Approaches to Community Computing: Bringing Technology to Low-Income Groups." In *High Technology and Low-Income Communities*, ed. D. Schön, B. Sanyal, and W. Mitchell. MIT Press.

Beck, Ulrich. 1994. "The Reinvention of Politics: Towards a Theory of Reflexive Modernization." In *Reflexive Modernization: Politics, Tradition, and Aesthetics in the Modern Social Order*, ed. U. Beck, A. Giddens, and S. Lash. Stanford University Press.

Beder, Sharon. 1997. *Global Spin: The Corporate Assault on Environmentalism*. Chelsea Green.

Belfield, Clive, and Xiangdong Wei. 2004. "Employer Size-Wage Effects: Evidence from Matched Employer-Employee Survey Data in the UK." *Applied Economics* 36: 185–193.

Bell, Michael. 2004. *Farming for Us All: Practical Agriculture and the Cultivation of Sustainability*. Pennsylvania State University Press.

Bellows, Anne, and Michael Hamm. 2001. "Local Autonomy and Sustainable Development: Testing Import Substitution in Localizing Food Systems." *Agriculture and Human Values* 18: 271–284.

Bérard, Laurence, and Philippe Marchenay. 2006. "Local Products and Geographical Indications: Taking Account of Local Knowledge and Biodiversity." *International Social Science Journal* 58 (187): 109–116.

Black Commentator. 2003. "Who Killed Black Radio News?" *Black Commentator* No. 44, May 29. http://www.blackcommentator.com.

Blair, Gwenda. 1979. "Why Dick Can't Stop Smoking." *Mother Jones*, January: 31–42.

Blakely, Edward, and Ted Bradshaw. 2002. *Planning Economic Development: Theory and Practice*. Sage.

Blitstein, Ryan. 2008. "The Bottom Line for Nonprofit News." *Miller-McCune*, April–May: 60–69.

Bolinger, Mark. 2005. "Making European-Style Community Wind Power Development Work in the U.S." *Renewable and Sustainable Energy Review* 9 (6): 556–575.

Bookchin, Murray, 1971. *Post-Scarcity Anarchism*. Ramparts.

Bookchin, Murray. 1990. *Remaking Society: Pathways to a Green Future*. South End.

Bookchin, Murray. 2002. "Communalist Project." *Harbinger* 3 (1): 20–35.

Booth, Douglas. 1998. *The Environmental Consequences of Growth: Steady-State Economics as an Alternative to Ecological Decline*. Routledge.

Born, Brandon, and Mark Purcell. 2006. "Avoiding the Local Trap." *Journal of Planning and Research* 26 (2): 195–207.

Bourdieu, Pierre. 1977. *Outline of a Theory of Practice*. Cambridge University Press.

Bowen, Mark. 2008. *Censoring Science: Inside the Political Attack on Dr. James Hansen and the Truth of Global Warming*. Dutton.

Brady, Diane. 2006. "The Organic Myth: Pastoral Ideals Are Getting Trampled as Organic Food Goes Mass Market." *Business Week*, October 16: 51–56.

Brady, Dustin. 2007. "Councilman Introduces First Zoning Designation for Community Gardens." *Plain Press*, September. http://www.nhlink.net/plainpress.

Brand, Keith. 2004. "The Rebirth of Low-Power FM Broadcasting in the U.S." *Journal of Radio Studies* 11 (2): 153–168.

Brand, Ralf. 2005. *Synchronizing Science and Technology with Human Behavior*. Earthscan.

Breach, Sam. 2007. "The Farmers' Market versus Safeway: Something to Ponder." *Beck and Posh*, May 20. http://beckposhnosh.blogspot.com.

Breukers, Sylvia, and Maarten Wolsink. 2007. "Wind Power Implementation in Changing Institutional Landscapes: An International Comparison." *Energy Policy* 35 (5): 2737–2750.

Brown, Allison. 2001. "Counting Farmers' Markets." *Geographical Review* 91 (4): 655–674.

Brown, Allison. 2002. "Farmers' Market Research 1940–2000: An Inventory and Review." *American Journal of Alternative Agriculture* 17 (4): 167–176.

Brown, Charles, James Hamilton, and James Medoff. 1990. *Employers Large and Small*. Harvard University Press.

Brown, Lester. 2001. *Eco-economy: Building an Economy for the Earth*. Norton.

Brown, Marilyn, Benjamin Sovacool, and Richard Hirsh. 2006. "Assessing U.S. Energy Policy." *Daedalus* 135 (3): 5–11.

Browne, Donald. 2005. *Ethnic Minorities, Electronic Media and the Public Sphere: A Comparative Approach*. Hampton.

Bruton, Henry. 1998. "A Reconsideration of Import Substitution." *Journal of Economic Literature* 36 (2): 903–936.

Bullard, Robert. 2007. "Smart Growth Meets Environmental Justice." In *Growing Smarter: Achieving Livable Communities, Environmental Justice, and Regional Equity*, ed. R. Bullard. MIT Press.

Bullard, Robert, Glenn Johnson, and Angel Torres. 2004. "Dismantling Transit Racism in Metro Atlanta." In *Highway Robbery: Transportation Racism and New Routes to Equity*, ed. R. Bullard, G. Johnson, and A. Torres. South End.

Bullock, Simon. 2000. "The Economic Benefits of Farmers' Markets." *Real Food News*. http://www.foe.co.uk.

Burlingham, Bo. 2005. *Small Giants: Companies That Choose to Be Great Instead of Big*. Penguin.

Burros, Marian. 2006. "In Oregon, Thinking Local." *New York Times*, January 4.

Business Alliance for Local Living Economies. 2008. Mission, Vision, and Principles. http://www.livingeconomies.org.

Bus Riders Union. 2000. "Bus Riders Union Coalition Pressures MTA to Reverse Diesel Policy and Buy 370 Clean Fuel Buses." *Bus Riders Union News Analysis*, June 4. http://www.busridersunion.org.

Bus Riders Union. 2002. Bus Riders Union Stops MTA in Its Tracks: U.S. Supreme Court Rejects MTA Appeal. http://www.busridersunion.org.

Bus Riders Union. 2005. Bus Riders Union Wins Federal Court Order to Expand MTA's Metro Rapid Bus Fleet and Service. http://www.busridersunion.org.

Bus Riders Union. 2008. Overview and History. http://www.busridersunion.org.

Buttel, Frederick. 2004. "The Treadmill of Production: An Appreciation, Assessment, and Agenda for Research." *Organization and Environment* 17 (3): 323–336.

Buttel, Frederick, and Kenneth Gould. 2004. "Global Social Movement (s) at the Crossroads: Some Observations on the Trajectory of the Anti-Corporate Globalization Movement." *Journal of World Systems Research* X (I): 37–66.

Buy Local Philly. 2008. About the Campaign. http://www.buylocalphilly.com.

California Air Resources Board. 1998. Findings of the Scientific Review Panel on the Report on Diesel Exhaust. http://www.arb.ca.gov.

California Air Resources Board. 2002a. Briefing Paper on Interim Results and Tentative Conclusions for ARB's Study of Emissions from "Late-Model" Diesel and CNG Heavy-Duty Transit Buses. http://www.arb.ca.gov.

California Air Resources Board. 2002b. Report of Partial Results: Emissions from Two Oxidation Catalyst-Equipped CNG Buses. http://www.arb.ca.gov.

California Air Resources Board. 2004. Study of CNG and Diesel Transit Bus Emissions. ftp://ftp.arb.ca.gov.

California Air Resources Board. 2005a. CARB's Study of Emissions from In-Use CNG and Diesel Buses. http://www.arb.ca.gov.

California Air Resources Board. 2005b. Proposed Amendments to the Exhaust Emissions Standards for 2007–2009 Model-Year Heavy Duty Urban Transit Bus Engines and the Fleet Rule for Transit Agencies. http://www.arb.ca.gov.

Callon, Michel, Cécile Méadel, and Vololona Rabeharisoa. 2002. "The Economy of Qualities." *Economy and Society* 31 (2): 194–217.

Campbell, Hugh, and Ruth Liepins. 2001. "Naming Organics: Understanding Organic Standards in New Zealand as a Discursive Field." *Sociologia Ruralis* 41 (1): 21–39.

Capital Newspapers. 2008. About Us. www.capitalnewspapers.com.

Capital Times. 2006. "Holiday Hint: Buy Local" [editorial], November 24.

Cassel, Andrew. 2005a. "Sure—Act Locally, but Buy Globally." *Philadelphia Inquirer*, May 1: E1.

Cassel, Andrew. 2005b. "Still Not Buying a 'Buy Local' Push." *Philadelphia Inquirer*, May 15: E1.

Castells, Manuel. 2001. *The Internet Galaxy: Reflections on Business, the Internet, and Society.* Oxford University Press.

Castells, Manuel, and Peter Hall. 1994. *Technopoles of the World: The Making of Twenty-First Century Industrial Complexes.* Routledge.

Cavanagh, John, and Jerry Mander, eds. 2004. *Alternatives to Economic Globalization: A Better World Is Possible.* Berrett-Koehler.

Chew, Sing. 2001. *World Ecological Degradation: Accumulation, Urbanization, and Deforestation 3000 B.C.–A.D. 2000.* AltaMira.

Churchill, Chris. 2007. "Small Merchants United to Thrive." *Albany Times Union*, October 5.

Citizens for Independent Public Broadcasting. 1999. About Our Launch. http://www.cipbonline.org.

Citizen Works. 2008. Democracy: Corporate Welfare. http://www.citizenworks.org.

City of Boston. 2002. Open Space Plan 2002–2008. http://www.cityofboston.gov.

City of Portland. 2008. Portland Multnomah Food Policy Council. http://www.portlandonline.com.

City of Sacramento. 2004. Food Charter for the City of Sacramento. http://sacgardens.org.

City of Sacramento. 2008. Community Gardens. http://www.cityofsacramento.org.

City of San Francisco. 2007. Final Minutes: Park, Recreation, and Open Space Advisory Committee, February 6. http://www.ci.sf.ca.us.

Civic Economics. 2002. Economic Impact Analysis: A Case Study.

Civic Economics. 2004. The Andersonville Study of Retail Economics.

Civic Economics. 2007. The San Francisco Retail Diversity Study.

Clark, John. 2003. *Worlds Apart: The Battle for Ethical Globalization.* Kumarian.

Cloud, John. 2007. "My Search for the Perfect Apple." *Time*, March 12: 42–50.

Coaffee, Jon. 2005. "Guest Editorial: New Localism and the Management of Regeneration." *International Journal of Public Sector Management* 18 (2): 108–113.

Coalition for Environmentally Responsible Economies. 2008. About Us. http://www.ceres.org.

Cohen, Joshua. 2005. "Diesel vs. Compressed Natural Gas for School Buses: A Cost-Effectiveness Evaluation of Alternative Fuels." *Energy Policy* 33 (13): 1709–1722.

Cohen, Lizabeth. 2003. *A Consumer's Republic: The Politics of Mass Consumption in Postwar America.* Knopf.

Cohen, Maurie. 2006. "A Social Problems Framework for the Critical Appraisal of Automobility and Sustainable Systems Innovation." *Mobilities* 1 (1): 23–38.

Commoner, Barry. 1971. *The Closing Circle: Nature, Man, and Technology.* Alfred A. Knopf.

Compaine, Benjamin, and Douglas Gomery. 2000. *Who Owns the Media? Competition and Concentration in the Mass Media Industry*. Erlbaum.

Conroy, Michael. 2007. *Branded! How the 'Certification Revolution' Is Transforming Global Corporations*. New Society.

Co-op America. 2008. National Green Pages. http://www.coopamerica.org.

Costanza, Robert, Lisa Graumlich, and Will Steffen. eds. 2007. *Sustainability or Collapse? An Integrated History and Future of People on Earth*. MIT Press.

Covert, James. 2006. "Search Engines Help Shoppers to Buy Locally." *Wall Street Journal*, December 21.

Craig, Justin, and Clay Dibrell. 2006. "The Natural Environment, Innovation, and Firm Performance: A Comparative Study." *Family Business Review* 19 (4): 275–289.

Current.Org. 2008. History of Public Broadcasting in the United States. http://www.current.org/history.

Curtis, Fred. 2003. "Eco-localism and Sustainability." *Ecological Economics* 46 (1): 83–102.

Curtis, Monica, and Khare Anshuman. 2004. "Energy Conservation in Electric Utilities: An Opportunity for Restorative Economics at SaskPower." *Technovation* 24 (5): 395–402.

Daly, Herman. 1990. "Toward Some Operational Principles of Sustainable Development." *Ecological Economics* 2 (1): 1–6.

Daly, Herman. 1996. *Beyond Growth: The Economics of Sustainable Development*. Beacon.

Daviron, Benoit, and Stefano Ponte. 2005. *The Coffee Paradox: Global Markets, Commodity Trade and the Elusive Promise of Development*. Zed Books.

Davis, Mike. 1992. *City of Quartz: Excavating the Future in Los Angeles*. Vintage Books.

Davis, Mike. 2006. *Planet of Slums*. Verso.

Day, Catherine. 2005. "Buying Green: The Crucial Role of Public Authorities." *Local Environment* 10 (2): 201–209.

DeFilippis, James. 1999. "Alternatives to the 'New Urban Politics': Finding Locality and Autonomy in Local Economic Development." *Political Geography* 18 (8): 973–990.

Denver Urban Gardens. 2008. Delaney Farm. http://www.dug.org.

DeSimone, Livio, Frank Popoff, with the World Business Council for Sustainable Development. 1997. *Eco-Efficiency: The Business Link to Sustainable Development*. MIT Press.

Devine-Wright, Patrick. 2005. "Local Aspects of U.K. Rural Energy Development: Exploring Public Beliefs and Policy Implications." *Local Environment* 10 (1): 57–69.

Diamond, Jared. 2005. *Collapse: How Societies Choose to Fail or Succeed.* Viking.

Doane, Molly. 2007. "Relationship Coffees and Producer Relations: Shifting Significations within the Fair Trade System." Presented at annual meeting of American Anthropological Association.

Dolan, Catherine. 2007. "Arbitrating Moral Equivalency in Global Commodity Chains." Presented at annual meeting of American Anthropological Association.

Dowie, Mark. 1977. "Pinto Madness." *Mother Jones*, September–October: 18–32.

Dubner, Stephen. 2008. "Do We Really Need a Few Billion Locavores?" *New York Times*, June 9.

Duffy, Jim. 2000. "Silver Lining in Boston." *Mass Transit*, November–December: 10–26.

Dunaway, David. 2002. "Community Radio at the Beginning of the 21st Century: Commercialism vs. Community Power." In *Community Media in the Information Age: Perspectives and Prospects*, ed. N. Jankowski and O. Prehn. Hampton.

Dunbar-Hestor, Christina. 2008. "Geeks, Meta-Geeks, and Gender Trouble: Activism, Identity, and Low-Power FM Radio." *Social Studies of Science* 38 (2): 201–232.

DuPuis, Melanie, and Daniel Block. 2008. "Sustainability and Scale: U.S. Milk Market Orders as Relocalization Policy." *Environment and Planning A* 40 (8): 1987–2005.

DuPuis, Melanie, and David Goodman. 2005. "Should We Go Home to Eat? Toward a Reflexive Politics of Localism." *Journal of Rural Studies* 21: 359–371.

DuPuis, Melanie, David Goodman, and Jill Harrison. 2006. "Just Values or Just Value? Remaking the Local in Agro-Food Studies." *Research in Rural Sociology and Development* 12: 241–268.

Durlin, Marty, and Cathy Melio. 2000. The Grassroots Radio Movement in the U.S. http://grradio.org.

Dyer, Gibb, and David Whetten. 2006. "Family Firms and Social Responsibility: Preliminary Evidence for the S&P 500." *Entrepreneurship Theory and Practice* 30 (6): 785–802.

Earth Works. 2008. Our Earth Works Projects. http://www.earth-works.org.

Eaton, Emily. 2008. "From Feeding the Locals to Selling the Locale: Adapting Local Sustainable Food Projects in Niagara to Neocommunitarianism and Neoliberalism." *Geoforum* 39 (2): 994–1006.

EcoCity Cleveland. 2007. Our Big Merger. http://www.ecocitycleveland.org.

Edmiston, Kelly. 2007. The Role of Small and Large Business in Economic Development. Federal Reserve Bank of Kansas City.

Efficiency Vermont. 2008a. About Us. http://www.efficiencyvermont.com.

Efficiency Vermont. 2008b. Efficiency Vermont 2007: Preliminary Executive Summary. http://www.efficiencyvermont.com.

Efficiency Vermont. 2008c. Year 2007 Preliminary Results and Savings Estimate Report. http://www.efficiencyvermont.com.

Egan, Michael. 2007. *Barry Commoner and the Science of Survival: The Remaking of American Environmentalism.* MIT Press.

Eisinger, Peter. 1998. *Toward an End to Hunger in America.* Brookings Institution.

Elgin, Ben. 2007. "Little Green Lies." *Business Week*, October 29: O45–O52.

Embardo, Ellen. 2001. Voices from the Underground. Radical Protest and the Underground Press in the 'Sixties': An Exhibition. University of Connecticut Libraries. http://www.lib.uconn.edu.

Engels, Friedrich. 1978. "Socialism: Utopian and Scientific." In *The Marx-Engels Reader*, ed. R. Tucker. Norton.

Environmental Protection Agency (EPA). 2006. Heavy-Duty Highway Diesel Program. http://www.epa.gov.

Etzkowitz, Henry, Andrew Webster, and Peter Healy. 1998. *Capitalizing Knowledge: New Intersections of Industry and Academia.* State University of New York Press.

Eudy, Leslie. 2002. "Natural Gas in Transit Fleets: A Review of the Transit Experience." Presented at Bus and Paratransit Conference, American Public Transportation Association, Minneapolis. http://www.apta.com.

Evans, Nick, Carol Morris, and Michael Winters. 2002. "Conceptualizing Agriculture: A Critique of Postproductivism as the New Orthodoxy." *Progress in Human Geography* 26 (3): 313–332.

Fairchild, William. 1998. "The Canadian Alternative: A Brief History of Unlicensed and Low-Power Radio." In *Seizing the Airwaves*, ed. R. Sakolsky and S. Dunifer. AK Press.

Federal Communications Commission. 2004. Do Local Owners Deliver More Localism? Some Evidence from Broadcast News. http://www.freepress.net.

Fairchild, William. 2001. *Community Radio and Public Culture.* Hampton.

Fears, Darrell. 2004. "Minority Voices Join Forces at Unity Convention." *Washington Post*, August 4.

Felipe, Jesus, and Vernengo, Matías. 2002. "Demystifying the Principle of Comparative Advantage: Implications for Developing Countries." *International Journal of Political Economy* 32 (4): 49–75.

Fenn, Paul. 2004. San Francisco Declares "Energy Independence." http://www.local.org/independ.html.

Ferguson, James. 2005. "Seeing Like an Oil Company: Space, Security, and Global Capital in Neoliberal Africa." *American Anthropologist* 107 (3): 377–382.

Ferris, John, Carol Norman, and Joe Sempik. 2001. "People, Land, and Sustainability: Community Gardens and the Social Development of Sustainable Development." *Social Policy and Administration* 35 (5): 559–568.

Feshbach, Murray, and Alfred Friendly Jr. 1992. *Ecocide in the USSR: Health and Nature Under Siege*. Basic Books.

Firestone, Jeremy, and Willett Kempton. 2007. "Public Opinion about Large Offshore Wind Power: Underlying Factors." *Energy Policy* 35 (3): 1584–1598.

Fishman, Charles. 2006. *The Wal-Mart Effect: How the World's Most Profitable Company Really Works—and How It's Transforming the American Economy*. Penguin.

Flanigan, Shawn, and Roli Varma. 2006. "Promoting Community Gardening to Low-Income Participants in the Women, Infants, and Children Programme (WIC) in New Mexico." *Community, Work, and Family* 9 (1): 69–74.

Fonte, Maria. 2006. "Slow Food's Presidia: What Do Small Producers Do with Big Retailers?" *Research in Rural Sociology and Development* 12: 203–240.

Food Project. 2008. About Us. http://www.thefoodproject.org.

Free Press. 2008. Free Press and the Free Press Action Fund. http://www.freepress.net.

Free Speech TV. 2008. About Free Speech TV. http://www.freespeech.org.

Freudenburg, William. 2005. "Privileged Access, Privileged Accounts: Toward a Socially Structured Theory of Resources and Discourses." *Social Forces* 84 (1): 89–114.

Frickel, Scott, and Kelly Moore, eds. 2005. *The New Political Sociology of Science: Institutions, Networks, and Power*. University of Wisconsin Press.

Friedman, Thomas. 2007. "The Greening of Geopolitics." *New York Times Magazine*, April 15.

Friends of Portland Community Gardens. 2007. About Us. http://www.friendspdxgardens.org.

Furtado, Celso. 1968. *The Economic Growth of Brazil: Survey from Colonial to Modern Times*. University of California Press.

Geels, Frank. 2002. "Technological Transitions as Evolutionary Reconfiguration Processes: A Multi-Level Perspective and a Case Study." *Research Policy* 31 (8–9): 1257–1274.

Geels, Frank. 2007. "Transformations of Large Technical Systems: A Multilevel Analysis of the Dutch Highway System (1950–2000)." *Science, Technology, and Human Values* 32 (2): 123–149.

Gelbspan, Ross. 2004. *Boiling Point: How Politicians, Big Oil and Coal, Journalists, and Activists Are Fueling the Climate Crisis—and What We Can Do to Avert Disaster.* Basic Books.

Gibson-Graham, J.-K. 2006. *A Post-Capitalist Politics.* University of Minnesota Press.

Gille, Zsuzsa. 2007. *From the Cult of Waste to the Trash Heap of History: The Politics of Waste in Socialist and Postsocialist Hungary.* Indiana University Press.

Gilyard, Burl. 2002. "McPaper Co. Wants Smallfries with That." *American Journalism Review* 24 (8): 14–15.

Goetz, Stephen, and Anil Rapasingha. 2006. "Wal-Mart and Social Capital." *American Journal of Agricultural Economics* 88 (5): 1304–1310.

Goetz, Stephen, and Hema Swaminathan. 2006. "Wal-Mart and County-Wide Poverty." *Social Science Quarterly* 87 (2): 211–226.

Goldschmidt, Walter. 1978. *As You Sow: Three Studies in the Social Consequences of Agribusiness.* Allanheld, Osmun.

Gomory, Ralph, and William Baumol. 2001. *Global Trade and Conflicting National Interests.* MIT Press.

Goodman, David. 2004. "Rural Europe Redux? Reflections on Alternative Agro-Food Networks and paradigm Change." *Sociologia Ruralis* 44 (1): 3–16.

Goodman, David, and Michael Goodman. 2007. "Localism, Livelihoods, and the 'Post-Organic': Changing Perspectives on Alternative Food Networks in the United States." In *Alternative Food Geographies: Representation and Practice*, ed. D. Maye, L. Holloway, and M. Kneafsey. Elsevier.

Gottlieb, Robert. 1993. *Forcing the Spring: The Transformation of the American Environmental Movement.* Island.

Gottlieb, Robert. 2001. *Environmentalism Unbound: Exploring New Pathways for Change.* MIT Press.

Gottlieb, Robert, and Andrew Fisher. 1996. "Community Food Security and Environmental Justice: Searching for a Common Discourse." *Agriculture and Human Values* 3 (3): 23–32.

Grant, Don, Andrew Jones, and May Trautner. 2004. "Do Facilities with Distant Headquarters Pollute More? How Civic Engagement Conditions the Environmental Performance of Absentee Managed Plants." *Social Forces* 83 (1): 189–204.

Greco, Thomas. 2001. *Money: Understanding and Creating Alternatives to Legal Tender.* Chelsea Green.

Greene, Gregory. 2004. The End of Suburbia: Oil Depletion and the Collapse of the American Dream. Electric Wallpaper Co.

Greenwald, Robert. 2005. *Wal-Mart: The High Cost of Low Prices* (DVD). Disinformation Co.

Green Worker Cooperative. 2007. "Coming Soon: ReBuilders Source." *Green Worker News*, summer.

Gregor, Katherine. 2006. "Choose Austin First." *Austin Chronicle*, December 8.

Gregor, Katherine. 2007. "Another Northcross Lawsuit: Allendale Neighborhood Association." *Austin Chronicle*, July 6.

Greider, William. 2003. *The Soul of Capitalism: Opening Paths to a Moral Economy*. Simon and Schuster.

Greider, William. 2007. "The Establishment Rethinks Globalization." *The Nation*, April 30: 11–14.

Groothuis, Peter. 1994. "Turnover: The Implication of Establishment Size and Unionization." *Quarterly Journal of Business and Economics* 33 (2): 41–53.

Gross, Catherine. 2007. "Community Perspectives of Wind Energy in Australia: The Application of a Justice and Community Fairness Framework to Increase Social Acceptance." *Energy Policy* 35 (5): 2727–2736.

Growing Gardens. 2007. About Us. http://www.growing-gardens.org.

Gubbins, Nicholas. 2007. "Community Energy in Practice." *Local Economy* 22 (1): 80–84.

Gunther, Marc. 2006a. "The Green Machine." *Fortune*, August 7: 42–57.

Gunther, Marc. 2006b. " 'Small-Marts' Take on Wal-Mart." *Fortune*, August 30.

Gurstein, Michael, ed. 2000. *Community Informatics: Enabling Communities with Information and Communications Technologies*. Idea Publishing Group.

Guthman, Julie. 2002. "Commodified Meanings, Meaningful Commodities: Rethinking Production-consumption Links through the Organic System of Provision." *Sociologia Ruralis* 42 (4): 295–311.

Guthman, Julie. 2004. *Agrarian Dreams: The Paradox of Organic Farming in California*. University of California Press.

Guthman, Julie, Amy Morris, and Patricia Allen. 2006. "Squaring Farm Security and Food Security in Two Types of Alternative Food Institutions." *Rural Sociology* 71 (4): 662–685.

Hahnel, Robin. 2007. "Eco-localism: A Constructive Critique." *Capitalism Nature Socialism* 18 (2): 62–78.

Halweil, Brian. 2004. *Eat Here: Reclaiming Homegrown Pleasures in a Global Supermarket*. Norton.

Hammel, Laury, and Gun Denhart. 2007. *Growing Local Value: How to Build Business Partnerships That Strengthen Your Community*. Berrett-Koehler.

Hampton, Howard, and Bill Reno. 2003. *Public Power: The Fight for Publicly Owned Electricity*. Insomniac.

Hanchett, Thomas. 1996. "U.S. Tax Policy and the Shopping Center Boom of the 1950s and 1960s." *American Historical Review* 101 (4): 1082–1110.

Hanna, Autumn, and Pikai Oh. 2000. "Rethinking Urban Poverty: A Look at Community Gardens." *Bulletin of Science, Technology, and Society* 20 (3): 207–216.

Hardin, Chet. 2006. "Think Local, Act Local." *Metroland* Nov. 30.

Harris, Mark. 2005a. 'Alternative' Media Quietly Sells Out to Whole Foods Market. http://www.wholeworkersunite.org.

Harris, Mark. 2005b. What Exactly Does it Mean to be "Pro-Labor"? More on "Alternative" Media Quietly Selling out to Whole Foods Market. http://baltimore.indymedia.org.

Harrison, Julie. 2004. "Invisible People, Invisible Places: Connecting Air Pollution and Pesticide Drift in California." In *Smoke and Mirrors: The Politics and Culture of Air Pollution*, ed. E. M. DuPuis. New York University Press.

Harvey, David. 2005. *A Brief History of Neoliberalism*. Oxford University Press.

Hawken, Paul. 2007. *Blessed Unrest: How the Largest Movement in the World Came into Being and Why No One Saw It Coming*. Viking.

Hawken, Paul, Amory Lovins, and L. Hunter Lovins. 1999. *Natural Capitalism: Creating the Next Industrial Revolution*. Little, Brown.

Hayes, Bryan. 2006. "Schools Go Local for Better Food." *NewsHour*, Public Broadcasting Corporation, May 30.

Hazen, Don. 2000. "Are We Running Out of Alternatives?" *AlterNet*, April 26. http://www.alternet.org.

Hearst, Andrew. 1996. "Watchdog Watch: FAIR vs. MRC." *Columbia Journalism Review* 35 (4): 16.

Hebb, Tessa, Gordon Clark, and Lisa Hagerman. 2004. U.S. Public Sector Pension Funds and Urban Revitalization: An Overview of Policy and Programs. http://urban.ouce.ox.ac.uk.

Heiman, Michael, and Barry Solomon. 2004. "Power to the People: Electric Utility Restructuring and the Commitment to Renewable Energy." *Annals of the Association of American Geographers* 94 (1): 94–116.

Hekkert, Marko, and Robert van den Hoed. 2004. "Competing Technologies and the Struggle Towards a New Dominant Design: The Emergence of the Hybrid Vehicle at the Expense of the Fuel Cell Vehicle?" *Greener Management International* 47: 29–44.

Henderson, Hazel. 2006. *Ethical Markets: Growing the Green Economy*. Chelsea Green.

Hess, David. 2004. "Organic Food and Agriculture in the U.S.: Object Conflicts in a Health-Environmental Movement." *Science as Culture* 13 (4): 493–513.

Hess, David. 2007a. *Alternative Pathways in Science and Industry: Activism, Innovation, and the Environment in the United States.* MIT Press.

Hess, David. 2007b. "What Is a Clean Bus? Object Conflicts in the Greening of Urban Transit." *Sustainability: Science, Practice, and Policy* 3 (1): 1–14.

Hess, David. 2008. "Localism and the Environment." *Sociology Compass* 2 (2): 625–638.

Hess, David, and Langdon Winner. 2007. "Enhancing Justice and Sustainability at the Local Level: Affordable Policies for Local Government." *Local Environment* 12 (4): 1–17.

Hess, David, Colin Beech, Rachel Dowty, Govind Gopakumar, Richard Arias Hernandez, and Langdon Winner. 2007. Case Studies of Sustainability, the Politics of Design, and Localism. http://www.davidjhess.org.

Heyman, Fredrik. 2007. "Firm Size or Firm Age? The Effect on Wages Using Matched Employer-Employee Data." *Labour* 21 (2): 237–263.

Heywood, J., Borak, J., Parsley, B., Pickett, T., and Widener, M. 2002. FY 2003 Two Hundred Bus Procurement. Expert Panel Report to Massachusetts Bay Transportation Authority.

Hilliard, Robert, and Michael Keith. 2005. *The Quieted Voice: The Rise and Demise of Localism in American Radio.* Southern Illinois University Press.

Hindery, Leo. 2007. "Are Free Trade Policies Working?" Testimony before the U.S. Senate Commerce Subcommittee on Interstate Commerce and Tourism, April 18. http://commerce.senate.gov.

Hines, Colin. 2000. *Localization: A Global Manifesto.* Earthscan.

Hinrichs, C. Clare. 2003. "The Practice and Politics of Food System Localization." *Journal of Rural Studies* 19 (1): 33–45.

Hinrichs, C. Clare, and Patricia Allen. 2007. "Buying into 'Buy Local': Engagements of United States Local Food Initiatives." In *Alternative Food Geographies: Representation and Practice*, ed. D. Maye, L. Holloway, and M. Kneafsey. Elsevier.

Hinrichs, C. Clare, and Patricia Allen. 2008. "Selective Patronage and Social Justice: Local Food Consumer Campaigns in Historical Context." *Journal of Agricultural and Environmental Ethics* 21 (4): 329–352.

Hinshelwood, Emily. 2001 "Power to the People: Community-led Wind Energy—Obstacles and Opportunities in a South Wales Valley." *Community Development Journal* 36 (2): 96–110.

Hirsh, Richard. 1999. *Power Loss: The Origins of Deregulation and Restructuring in the American Electric Utility System.* MIT Press.

Holland, Dorothy, Donald Nonini, Catherine Lutz, Lesley Bartlett, Marla Frederick-McGlathery, Thaddeus Guldbrandsen, and Enrique Murillo Jr. 2007. *Local Democracy Under Siege: Activism, Public Interests, and Private Politics.* New York University Press.

Holland, Leigh. 2004. "Diversity and Connections in Community Gardens: A Contribution to Local Sustainability." *Local Environment* 9 (3): 285–305.

Hollender, Jeffrey, and Stephen Fenichell. 2004. *What Matters Most: How a Small Group of Pioneers Is Teaching Social Responsibility to Big Business, and Why Big Business Is Listening.* Basic Books.

Horne, Suzanne, and Avril Maddrell. 2002. *Charity Shops: Retailing, Consumption, and Society.* Routledge.

Horwitz, Robert. 2007. "On Media Concentration and the Diversity Question." In *Media Diversity and Localism: Meaning and Metrics*, ed. P. Napoli. Erlbaum.

Howe, Jeff. 2007. "Breaking the News." *Wired*, August: 86–90.

Howley, Keven. 2005. *Community Media: People, Places, and Communication Technologies.* Cambridge University Press.

Hsu, Hua. 2002. "Ethnic Media Grows Up: Will Increasing Mainstream Attention Alter the Ethnic Media Landscape?" *Colorlines* 5 (3): 7–9. http://www.arc.org.

Hvelplund, Freda. 2006. "Renewable Energy and the Need for Local Energy Markets." *Energy : Technologies, Resources, Reserves, Demands, Impact, Conservation, Management, Policy* 31 (13): 2293–2302.

Idson, Todd, and Walter Oi. 1999. "Workers Are More Productive in Large Firms." *American Economic Review* 89 (2): 104–108.

Imbroscio, David. 1997. *Reconstructing City Politics: Alternative Economic Development and Urban Regimes.* Sage.

Ingram, Paul, and Hayagreeva Rao. 2004. "Store Wars: The Enactment and Repeal of Anti-Chain-Store Legislation in America." *American Journal of Sociology* 110 (2): 446–487.

Institute for Local Self-Reliance. 1991. ILSR: A 20-Year Track Record Promoting Sustainable Communities. http://www.ilsr.org.

Institute for Local Self-Reliance. 2003. The Impact of Locally Owned Businesses v. Chains: A Case Study in Midcoast Maine.

International Agency for Research on Cancer. 1989. *Diesel and Gasoline Exhausts.* IARC Monographs on the Evaluation of Carcinogenic Risks to Humans 46: 41. International Programme on Chemical Safety (IPCS). http://www.inchem.org.

International Monetary Fund. 2007. *World Economic Outlook: Globalization and Inequality.*

International Programme on Chemical Safety. 1996. *Diesel Fuel and Exhaust Emissions.* Environmental Health Criteria 171. World Health Organization.

Jackson, Peter, Polly Russell, and Neil Ward. 2007. "The Appropriation of 'Alternative' Discourses by 'Mainstream' Food Retailers." In *Alternative Food*

Geographies: Representation and Practice, ed. D. Maye, L. Holloway, and M. Kneafsey. Elsevier.

Jackson, Ross. 2004. "The Ecovillage Movement." *Permaculture Magazine* 40: 25–30.

Jacob, Jeffrey. 1997. *New Pioneers: The Back-to-the-Land Movement and the Search for a Sustainable Future*. Pennsylvania State University Press.

Jacobs, Jane. 1961. *The Death and Life of Great American Cities*. Vintage Books.

Jacobs, Jane. 1969. *The Economy of Cities*. Vintage Books.

Jacobs, Jane. 1984. *Cities and the Wealth of Nations*. Random House.

Jager, Rick, and Marc Littman. 2005. Metro Marks Earth Day Milestone by Taking Delivery of 2,000th Clean Air Transit Bus. Los Angeles County Metropolitan Transit Authority, April 15. http://www.metro.net.

Jobert, Arthur, Pia Laborgne, and Solveig Mimler. 2007. "Local Acceptance of Wind Energy: Factors of Success Identified in French and German Case Studies." *Energy Policy* 35 (5): 2751–2760.

Johnson, Allen, and Timothy Earle. 1987. *The Evolution of Human Societies: From Foraging Group to Agrarian State*. Stanford University Press.

Johnston, Robert. 2003. *The Radical Middle Class: Populist Democracy and the Question of Capitalism in Progressive Era Portland, Oregon*. Princeton University Press.

Jørgensen, Ulrik, and Peter Karnøe. 1996. "The Danish Wind-Turbine Story: Technical Solutions to Political Visions?" In *Managing Technology in Society*, ed. A. Rip, T. Misa, and J. Schot. Pinter.

Jørgensen, Ulrik, and Lars Strunge. 2002. "Restructuring the Power Arena in Denmark: Shaping Markets, Technology, and Environmental Priorities." In *Shaping Technology, Guiding Policy*, ed. K. Sørensen and R. Williams. Edward Elgar.

Kaplan, Jeffrey. 2003. "Consent of the Governed: The Reign of Corporations and the Fight for Democracy." *Orion Magazine*, November–December: np.

Karr, Rick. 2005. "Prometheus Unbound." *The Nation*, May 23: 22–27.

Kaufman, Jerry, and Martin Bailkey. 2000. Farming Inside Cities: Entrepreneurial Urban Agriculture in the United States. Working Paper WP00JK1, Land Institute.

Kavanaugh, Kelli. 2006. How Detroit's Gardens Grow. http://www.modelmedia.com.

Kesmodel, David. 2007. "To Trump Small Brewers, Beer Makers Get Crafty." *Wall Street Journal*, October 26.

King, Donna, and Christopher Mele. 1999. "Making Public Access Television: Community Participation, Media Literacy, and the Public Sphere." *Journal of Broadcasting and Electronic Media* 43 (4): 603–623.

Kingsolver, Barbara, with Camille Kingsolver and Steven Hopp. 2007. *Animal, Vegetable, Miracle: A Year of Food Life*. HarperCollins.

Kingston, Tim. 2001. "Ownership." *Columbia Journalism Review* 40 (3): 44–45.

Kious, Adele. 2004. Preserving Community Gardens in Cleveland: Sustaining Long-Term Financial, Social, and Environmental Value. http://www .ecocitycleveland.org.

Kirkpatrick, Bill. 2006. "Localism in American Media Policy, 1920–1934: Reconsidering a 'Bedrock Concept.'" *Radio Journal* 4 (1–3): 87–110.

Klein, Noami. 2007. *The Shock Doctrine: The Rise of Disaster Capitalism*. Metropolitan Books.

Kleinman, Daniel. 1991. *Science and Technology in Society: From Biotechnology to the Internet*. Wiley.

Kline, David, and Dan Burstein. 2005. *Blog! How the Newest Media Revolution Is Changing Politics, Business, and Culture*. CDS Books.

Koeppel, Dan. 2007. *Banana: The Fate of the Fruit That Changed the World*. Hudson Street.

Konefal, Jason, and Michael Mascarenhas. 2005. "The Shifting Political Economy of the Global Agrifood System: Consumption and the Treadmill of Production." *Berkeley Journal of Sociology* 49: 76–96.

Kooser, Amanda. 2007. "Go Local." *Entrepreneur*, March: 72–75.

Korten, David. 1999. *The Post-Corporate World: Life After Capitalism*. Kumarian.

Kubicek, Herbert, and Rose Wagner. 2002. "Community Networks in Generational Perspective: The Change of an Electronic Medium within Three Decades." *Information, Communication, and Society* 5 (3): 291–319.

Ladenburg, Jacob. 2008. "Attitudes toward On-Land and Offshore Wind Power Development in Denmark: Choice of Development Strategy." *Renewable Energy* 33 (1): 111–118.

Lake, Robert. 2002. "Bring Back Big Government." *International Journal of Urban and Regional Research* 26 (4): 815–822.

Land, Jeff. 1999. *Active Radio: Pacifica's Brash Experiment*. University of Minnesota Press.

Langston, Jennifer. 2007. "City Beats Its Goal, but Auto Emissions Still Are Growing." *Seattle Post-Intelligencer*, October 30.

Lasar, Matthew. 1999. *Pacifica Radio: The Rise of an Alternative Network*. Temple University Press.

La Trobe, Helen. 2001. "Farmers' Markets: Consuming Local Produce." *International Journal of Consumer Studies and Home Economics* 25 (3): 181–192.

Lawson, Laura. 2005. *City Bountiful: A Century of Community Gardening in the United States*. University of California Press.

Layzer, Judith. 2007. "Deep Freeze: How Business Has Shaped the Global Warming Debate in Congress." In *Business and Environmental Policy: Corporate Interests in the American Political System*, ed. M. Kraft and S. Kamieniecki. MIT Press.

Leach, Eugene. 1999. Turning out Education: The Cooperation Doctrine in Radio, 1922–1938. http://www.current.org.

Lerner, Steve. 1998. *Eco-Pioneers: Practical Visionaries Solving Today's Environmental Problems*. MIT Press.

Levin, Steven. 2006. "Keeping It Clean: Public Financing in American Elections." *National Civic Review* 95 (4): 8–17.

Levy, Judd, and Kenya Purnell. 2006. "Case Study: The Community Development Trust Taps Wall Street Investors." *Community Development Investment Review* 2 (1): 57–63.

Lifestyles of Health and Sustainability. 2008. LOHAS Background. www.lohas.com.

Light, Andrew, ed. 1998. *Social Ecology after Bookchin*. Guilford.

Link TV. 2008. History. http://www.linktv.org.

Lipton, Martin, and Steven Rosenblum. 1991. "A Proposal for a New System of Corporate Governance: The Quinquennial Election of Directors." *University of Chicago Law Review* 38: 187.

Littlechild, Stephen. 2007. Municipal Aggregation and Retail Competition in the Ohio Energy Sector. http://www.electricitypolicy.ok.uk.

Litz, Reginald, and Alice Stewart. 2000. "Charity Begins at Home: Family Firms and Patterns of Community Involvement." *Nonprofit and Voluntary Sector Quarterly* 29 (1): 131–148.

Lockie, Stewart, and Darren Halpin. 2005. "The 'Conventionalisation Thesis' Reconsidered: Structural and Ideological Transformation of Australian Organic Agriculture." *Sociologia Ruralis* 45 (4): 284–307.

Logan, John, and Harvey Molotch. 2007. *Urban Fortunes: The Political Economy of Place*. University of California Press.

Love, Joseph. 2005. "The Rise and Decline of Economic Structuralism in Latin America." *Latin American Research Review* 40 (3): 100–125.

Lynn, Barry. 2006. "Breaking the Chain: The Antitrust Case Against Wal-Mart." *Harper's*, July: 29–36.

Lyon, Sarah. 2007a. "Fair for Whom? Assessing Fair Trade's Impact on Latin American Women in the Development Process." Presented at annual meeting of American Anthropological Association.

Lyon, Sarah. 2007b. "May Coffee Farmers and Fair Trade: Assessing the Benefits and Limitations of Alternative Markets." *Culture and Agriculture* 29 (2): 100–112.

MacDonald, G. Jeffrey. 2006. "Is Buying Local Always Best?" *Christian Science Monitor*, July 24.

Maniates, Michael. 2002. "Individualization: Plant a Tree, Buy a Bike, Save the World?" In *Confronting Consumption*, ed. T. Princen, M. Maniates, and K. Conca. MIT Press.

Manly, Lorne. 2006. "Seeking to Cash In on the 'Hyperlocal.'" *New York Times*, December 31.

Markusen, Ann. 2007. "A Consumption Base Theory of Development: An Application to the Rural Cultural Economy." *Agricultural and Resource Economics* 36 (1): 9–23.

Marsden, Terry, Jo Banks, and Gillian Bristow. 2002. "The Social Management of Rural Nature: Understanding Agrarian-Based Rural Development." *Environment and Planning A* 34: 809–825.

Martello, Marybeth Long, and Sheila Jasanoff. 2004. "Globalization and Environmental Governance." In *Earthly Politics: Local and Global in Environmental Governance*, ed. S. Jasanoff and M. L. Martello. MIT Press.

Martin, Brian. 2007. *Justice Ignited: The Dynamics of Backfire*. Rowman and Littlefield.

Maruyama, Yasushi, Makoto Nishikido, and Tesunari Iida. 2007. "The Rise of Community Wind Power in Japan: Enhanced Acceptance through Social Innovation." *Energy Policy* 35 (5): 2761–2769.

Marx, Karl, and Frederich Engels. 1978. "Manifesto of the Communist Party." In *The Marx-Engels Reader*, ed. R. Tucker. Norton.

Massey, Douglas, and Chiara Capoferro. 2006. "Savese Quien Pueda: Structural Adjustment and Emigration from Lima." *Annals of the American Academy of Political and Social Science* 606 (July): 116–127.

McAuliffe, Kevin. 1999. "No Longer Just Sex, Drugs, and Rock 'n' Roll." *Columbia Journalism Review* 37 (6): 40–44.

McChesney, Robert. 1993. *Telecommunications, Mass Media, and Democracy: The Battle for Control of U.S. Broadcasting, 1928–1935*. Oxford University Press.

McChesney, Robert. 2001. "Pacifica—A Way Out." *The Nation*, January 25: 5–6.

McChesney, Robert. 2004. *The Problem of the Media: U.S. Communication Politics in the Twenty-First Century*. Monthly Review Press.

McGregor, Jena. 2008. "At Best Buy, Marketing Goes Micro." *Businessweek*, May 26: 052–054.

McKay, Andrew, and Chris Milner. 2002. "On Mixed Strategies for Development." *Review of Development Economics* 6 (3): 303–338.

McKibben, Bill. 2007. *Deep Economy: The Wealth of Communities and the Durable Future*. Times Books.

McWilliams, James. 2007. "Food That Travels Well." *New York Times*, August 6.

Meadows, Donella, Jørgen Randers, and Dennis Meadows. 2004. *Limits to Growth: The Thirty-Year Update*. Chelsea Green.

Medley, Kimberly, and Humphrey Kalibo. 2007. "Global Localism: Recentering the Research Agenda for Biodiversity conservation." *Natural Resources Forum* 31 (2): 151–161.

Melendez, M., J. Taylor, J. Zuboy, W. Wayne, and D. Smith. 2005. Emissions Testing of Washington Metropolitan Area Transportation Authority (WMATA) Natural Gas and Diesel Buses. Technical Report NARL/TP 540–36355, Office of Scientific and Technical Information, U.S. Department of Energy. http://www.eere.energy.gov.

Metro Transit of King County. 2008. Pilot Program for Use of Biodiesel Fuel. http://transit.metrokc.gov.

Micklethwait, John, and Adrian Wooldridge. 2003. *The Company: A Short History of a Revolutionary Idea*. Weidenfeld and Nicholson.

Miles, Tracey. 2007. Food Miles Issue Heats Up. http://www.organicpathways.co.nz.

Miller, Timothy. 1999. *The 60s Communes: Hippies and Beyond*. Syracuse University Press.

Mitchell, Dan. 2006. "*The Economist* on 'Fair Trade.'" *New York Times*, December 16.

Mitchell, Lawrence. 2001. *Corporate Irresponsibility: America's Newest Export*. Yale University Press.

Mitchell, Stacy. 2000. *The Home Town Advantage: How to Defend Your Main Street against Chain Stores—and Why It Matters*. Institute for Local Self-Reliance.

Mitchell, Stacy. 2006. *Big-Box Swindle: The True Cost of Mega-Retailers and the Fight for America's Independent Businesses*. Beacon.

Mol, Arthur. 1995. *The Refinement of Production: Ecological Modernization Theory and the Chemical Industry*. International Books.

Mol, Arthur, and Gert Spaargaren. 2000. "Ecological Modernisation Theory in Debate: A Review." *Environmental Politics* 9 (1): 17–49.

Mol, Arthur, and Gert Spaargaren. 2005. "From Additions and Withdrawals to Environmental Flows: Reframing Debates in the Environmental Social Sciences." *Organization and the Environment* 18 (1): 91–108.

Monbiot, George. 2003. "The Myth of Localism." *Guardian*, September 9.

Moore, Steven. 2007. *Alternative Routes to the Sustainable City: Austin, Curitiba, and Frankfurt*. Rowman and Littlefield.

Morris, Carol, and Henry Bueller. 2003. "The Local Food Sector: A Preliminary Assessment of its Form and Impact in Gloucestershire." *British Food Journal* 105 (8): 559–566.

Morris, David. 1982. *Self-Reliant Cities: Energy and the Transformation of Urban America.* Sierra Club.

Morris, David. 2001. *Seeing the Light: Regaining Control of Our Electricity System.* Institute for Local Self Reliance.

Morris, David. 2006. Ownership Matters: Three Steps to Ensure a Biofuels Industry That Truly Benefits Rural America. http://www.newrules.org.

Morris, David, and Karl Hess. 1975. *Neighborhood Power: The New Localism.* Beacon.

Morris, Douglas. 2004. "Globalization and Media Democracy: The Case of Indymedia." In *Shaping the Network Society,* ed. D. Schuler and P. Day. MIT Press.

Moses, Lucia. 2002. "Alternative Approaches." *Editor and Publisher,* December 2: 14–20.

Moshkiber, Russell. 1998. The Death Penalty for Corporations Comes of Age. http://www.corpwatch.org.

Moyers, Bill. 2002. "Trading Democracy." *Now,* Public Broadcasting Corporation.

Napoli, Philip. 2001. "The Localism Principle in Communications Policymaking and Policy Analysis: Ambiguity, Inconsistency, and Empirical Neglect." *Policy Studies Journal* 29 (3): 372–387.

Napoli, Philip. 2007. "Introduction: Media Diversity and Localism—Meaning, Metrics, and Policy." In *Media Diversity and Localism: Meaning and Metrics,* ed. P. Napoli. Erlbaum.

National Federation of Independent Businesses. 2008. Issues. http://www.nfib .com.

National Public Radio. 2006. Eating Local, Thinking Global. http://www.npr .org.

National Small Business Association. 2008. Priority Issues. http://www.nsba .biz.

National Telecommunications and Information Administration. 1997. Minority Commercial Broadcast Ownership Overview. http://www.ntia.doc.gov.

National Telecommunications and Information Administration. 2000. Changes, Challenges, and Charting New Courses: Minority Commercial Broadcast Ownership in the United States. http://search.ntia.doc.gov.

Natural Resources Defense Council. 1998. Exhausted by Diesel: How America's Dependence on Diesel Emissions Threatens Our Health. http://www.nrdc.org.

Nelton, Sharon. 1995. "Creating a Constituency for Family Businesses: American Alliance of Family Businesses." *Nation's Business*, March: 50.

Neumark, David, Junfu Zhang, and Stephen Ciccarella. 2007. Effects of Wal-Mart on Local Labor Markets. Discussion Paper 2545, Institute for the Study of Labor (IZA), Bonn. http://www.newrules.org.

Nieckarz, Peter, Jr. 2002. "The Business of Public Radio: The Growing Commercial Presence Within Local National Public Radio." *Journal of Radio Studies* 9 (2): 209–226.

Nieto, Amber, and John Schmitt. 2004. *A Student's Guide to Media Law.* Rowman and Littlefield.

Norman, Al. 2004. *The Case Against Wal-Mart.* Raphel Marketing.

Oakley, Emily, and Mike Appel. 2005. "Are Supermarkets Cheaper Than Farmers' Markets?" *Southern Tier Produce News*, November: 5–7.

O'Connor, James. 1998. *Natural Causes? Essays in Ecological Marxism.* Guilford.

Ofori, Kofi. 1999. When Being No. 1 Is Not Enough. Office of Communications Business Opportunities, Federal Communications Commission. http://www.fcc .gov.

Oldeburg, Ray. 2002. *Celebrating the Third Place: Inspiring Stories about the "Great Good Place" at the Heart of Our Communities.* Marlowe.

OneWorld. 2008. A Brief History. http://us.oneworld.net.

Ong, Aihwa. 2006. *Neoliberalism as Exception: Mutations in Citizenship and Sovereignty.* Duke University Press.

Organic Valley Family of Farms. 2008. Our History: Born in a Barn! http://www .organicvalley.coop.

O'Rourke, Dara. 2005. "Market Movements: Nongovernmental Organization Strategies and Consumption." *Journal of Industrial Ecology* 9 (1–2): 115–128.

Paez, Paul. 2003. "The Effect of Firm Size on Wages in Colorado: A Case Study." *Monthly Labor Review* 2003: 11–17.

Palm, Jenny. 2006. "Development of Sustainable Energy Systems in Swedish Municipalities: A Matter of Path Dependency and Power Relations." *Local Environment* 11 (4): 445–457.

Pasqualetti, Martin. 2002. "Living with Wind Power in a Hostile Landscape." In *Wind Power in View: Energy Landscapes in a Crowded World*, ed. M. Pasqualetti, P. Gipe, and R. Righter. Academic.

Paterson, Jim. 2003. "The Energy Grows Greener." *Public Power* 61 (July–August): 12–17.

Peck, Jamie, and Adam Tickell. 2002. "Neoliberalizing Space." *Antipode* 34 (3): 380–404.

Peckham, Jack. 2003. "World-Wide Diesel Fuels, Emissions Harmonization Gets New Push from Engine, Vehicle Maker CEO's." *Diesel Fuel News* 7 (2): 1–3.

Pellow, David, and Robert Brulle. 2005. "Power, Justice, and the Environment: Toward Critical Environmental Justice Studies." In *Power, Justice, and the Environment: A Critical Appraisal of the Environmental Justice Movement*, ed. D. Pellow and R. Brulle. MIT Press.

Pellow, David, Allan Schnaiberg, and Adam Weinberg. 2000. "Putting the Ecological Modernization Theory to the Test: The Promises and Performances of Urban Recycling." *Environmental Politics* 9: 109–137.

Pendras, Mark. 2002. "From Local Consciousness to Global Change: Asserting Power at the Local Scale." *International Journal of Urban and Regional Research* 26 (4): 823–833.

Pennsylvania Horticultural Society. 2007. PHS Makes Philadelphia Green. http://www.pennsylvaniahorticulturalsociety.org.

Perman, Stacy. 2006. "Indie Grocery Stores Beat Back the Bigs." *BusinessWeek*, November 8: 13.

Persky, Joseph, David Ranney, and Wim Wiewel. 1993. "Import Substitution and Local Economic Development." *Economic Development Quarterly* 7 (1): 18–29.

Pickford, Evan. 2001. *Shades of Green: Public Power's Environmental Profile*. American Public Power Association.

Pierce, Steve. 2002. The Community Teleport: Participatory Media as a Path to Participatory Democracy. Ph.D. dissertation, Science and Technology Studies Department, Rensselaer Polytechnic Institute.

Pitzer, Donald, ed. 1997. *America's Communal Utopias*. University of North Carolina Press.

Platon, Sara, and Mark Deuze. 2003. "Indymedia Journalism: A Radical Way of Making, Selecting, and Sharing News?" *Journalism* 4 (3): 336–355.

Plunkett Research. 2008. Food Industry Overview. http://www.plunkettresearch.com.

Pollan, Michael. 2006a. My 2nd Letter to Whole Foods. http://www.michaelpollan.com.

Pollan, Michael. 2006b. *The Omnivore's Dilemma: A Natural History of Four Meals*. Penguin.

Poppendieck, Janet. 1998. *Sweet Charity? Emergency Food and the End of Entitlement*. Viking.

Porter, Michael, and Claas van der Linde. 1995. "Green and Competitive." *Harvard Business Review* 68 (3): 79–91.

Portes, Alejandro. 1994. "When More Can Be Less: Labor Standards, Development, and the Informal Economy." In *Contrapunto: The Informal Sector Debate in Latin America*, ed. C. Rakowski. State University of New York Press.

Portes, Alejandro, and Bryan Roberts. 2005. "The Free-Market City: Latin American Urbanization in the Years of the Neoliberal Experiment." *Studies in Comparative International Development* 40 (1): 43–82.

Postrel, Virginia. 2006. "In Praise of Chain Stores." *Atlantic Monthly*, December: 164–167.

Power, Thomas Michael. 1996. *Lost Landscapes and Failed Economies: The Search for a Value of Place*. Island.

Prakesh, Swati. 2007. "Beyond Dirty Diesels: Clean and Just Transportation in Northern Manhatten." In *Growing Smarter: Achieving Livable Communities, Environmental Justice, and Regional Equity*, ed. R. Bullard. MIT Press.

Princen, Thomas. 2002. "Distancing: Consumption and the Severing of Feedback." In *Confronting Consumption*, ed. T. Princen, M. Maniates, and K. Conca. MIT Press.

Province of Nova Scotia. 2008. Community Economic Development Investment Funds. http://www.gov.ns.ca.

Public Power. 2003. "The Energy Grows Greener. Public Power Utilities Are Leaders in the Move toward Greater Reliance on Renewable Technologies for Electricity Production." *Public Power* 61 (4): 12–17.

Public Power. 2006. "Ohio Wind: Municipal Utilities in Ohio Teamed Up to Build a 7.2-MW Wind Power Project." *Public Power* 64 (2): 36–40.

Putnam, Robert. 2000. *Bowling Alone: The Collapse and Revival of American Community*. Simon and Schuster.

Ratner, Lizzy. 2005. "Amy Goodman's 'Empire.'" *The Nation*, May 23: 27–31.

Redman, Charles, Carole Crumley, Fekri Hassan, Frank Hole, João Morais, Frank Riedel, Vernon Scarborough, Joseph Tainter, Peter Turchin, and Yoshinori Yasua. 2007. "Group Report: Millennial Perspectives on the Dynamic Interaction of Climate, People, and Resources." In *Sustainability or Collapse? An Integrated History and Future of People on Earth*, ed. R. Costanza, L. Graumlich, and W. Steffen. MIT Press.

Reece, Ray. 1979. *The Sun Betrayed: A Report on the Corporate Seizure of Solar Energy*. South End.

Reich, Robert. 1991. *The Work of Nations: Preparing Ourselves for Twenty-First Century Capitalism*. Knopf.

Reilly, Jasmine. 2007. "The Cornwall Sustainable Energy Partnership." *Local Economy* 22 (1): 85–91.

Relocalization Network. 2008. The Relocalization Network: Background and History. http://www.relocalize.net.

Renting, Henk, Terry Marsden, and Jo Banks. 2003. "Understanding Alternative Food Networks: Exploring the Role of Short Food Supply Chains in Rural Development." *Environment and Planning A* 35 (3): 393–411.

ReVision House. 2008. ReVision Urban Farm. http://www.vpi.org.

Reynolds, Paul, Nancy Carter, William Gartner, Patricia Green, and Larry Cox. 2002. *The Entrepreneur Next Door: Characteristics of Individual Starting Companies in America*. Kauffman Foundation.

Ricardo, David. 1929. *Principles of Political Economy and Taxation*. G. Bell.

Rifkin, Glenn. 2006. "Marking a Profit and a Difference." *New York Times*, October 5.

Roberts, Wallace. 1999. "Power Play." *American Prospect* 42 (January–February): 71–77.

Robertson, Roland. 1995. "Glocalization: Time-Space And Homogeneity-Heterogeneity." In *Global Modernities*, ed. M. Featherstone, S. Lash, and R. Robertson. Sage.

Rosen, Paul. 2001. "Toward Sustainable and Democratic Urban Transport: Constructivism, Planning, and Policy." *Technology Analysis and Strategic Management* 13 (1): 117–135.

Rotmans, Jan, René Kemp, and Marjolein van Asselt. 2001. "More Evolution Than Revolution: Transition Management in Public Policy." *Foresight* 3 (1): 15–31.

Rutland, Ted, and Sean O'Hagan. 2007. "The Growing Localness of the Canadian City, or, On the Continued (Ir)relevance of Economic Base Theory." *Local Economy* 22 (2): 163–184.

Sacks, Beth. 2004. "Vermont's Energy Efficiency Utility." Workshop at Sustainable Communities Conference, Burlington, Vermont.

Sakolsky, Ron. 2001. The LPFM Fiasco: Micropower Radio and the FCC's Low-Power Trojan Horse. www.lipmagazine.org.

Saldivar-Tanaka, Laura, and Marianne Krasny. 2004. "Culturing Community Development, Neighborhood Open Space, and Civic Agriculture: The Case of Latino Community Gardens in New York City." *Agriculture and Human Values* 21 (4): 399–412.

Sale, Kirkpatrick. 1980. *Human Scale*. Coward, McCann and Geoghegan.

Saleos. 2003. Railroaded: Part 4. Diesel Buses: What's Old Is New (Sorta). http://www.weeklydig.com.

Sandell, Clayton. 2006. "Reducing Your Carbon Footprint." ABC News, June 7. http://a.abcnews.com.

Sandro, Phillip. 1994. "Jobs and Buy Local Programs: Expected Employment Effects of Public-Sector Import Substitution in Chicago." *International Journal of Public Administration* 18 (1): 199–225.

Saporito, Bill. 2007. "Restoring Wal-Mart." *Time*, November 12: 46–52.

Sarver, Aaron. 2005. "Media for the People." *In These Times*, May 9: 10.

Sassen, Saskia. 2000. *Cities in a World Economy: Sociology for a New Century.* Pine Forge/Sage.

Saunders, Caroline, Andrew Barber, and Greg Taylor. 2006. Food Miles— Comparative Energy/Emissions Performance of New Zealand's Agriculture Industry. Research Report 285, Lincoln University. http://www.lincoln.ac.nz.

Scheinberg, Anne. 2003. "The Proof of the Pudding: Urban Recycling in North America as a Process of Ecological Modernization." *Environmental Politics* 12 (4): 49–75.

Schimmel, Bruce. 2005a. "The Blonde and the Blowhard." *Philadelphia City Paper*, May 26–June 1.

Schimmel, Bruce. 2005b. "The New Local." *Philadephia City Paper*, May 12–18.

Schimmel, Bruce. 2006. Bruce Andrew Schimmel. Biography. http://schimmel.com/bio.html.

Schlett, James. 2007. "Shoppers Asked to Buy from Local Businesses." *Schenectady Gazette*, August 22.

Schmelzkopf, Karen. 1996. "Urban Community Gardens as Contested Space." *Geographical Review* 85 (3): 364–381.

Schmelzkopf, Karen. 2002. "Incommensurability, Land Use, and the Right to Space: Community Gardens in New York City." *Urban Geography* 23 (4): 323–343.

Schmitt, John. 2000. "Inequality and Globalization: Some Evidence from the United States." In *The Ends of Globalization*, ed. D. Kalb et al. Rowman and Littlefield.

Schnaiberg, Allan. 1980. *The Environment: From Surplus to Scarcity.* Oxford.

Schnaiberg, Allan, and Kenneth Gould. 1994. *Environment and Society: The Enduring Conflict.* St. Martin's.

Schneiberg, Marc. 2007. "What's on the Path? Path Dependence, Organizational Diversity, and the Problem of Institutional Change in the US Economy, 1900–1950." *Socio-Economic Review* 5 (1): 47–80.

Schragger, Richard. 2005. "The Anti-Chain Store Movement, Localist Ideology, and the Remnants of the Progressive Constitution, 1920–1940." *Iowa Law Review* 90 (3): 1011–1094.

Schumacher, E. F. 1973. *Small Is Beautiful: Economics As If People Mattered.* Harper and Row.

Severson, Kim. 2006. "Why Roots Matter More." *New York Times*, November 15.

Shaffer, Amanda, Robert Gottlieb, Vanessa Zajfen, Mark Vallianatos, Benjamin Nyberg, and Peter Dreier. 2007. Shopping for a Market: Evaluating Tesco's Entry into Los Angeles and the United States. Urban and Environmental Policy Institute, Occidental College.

Sheban, Jeffrey. 2007. "Tested in Columbus, Wal-Mart Broadens 'Buy Local' Emphasis." *Columbus Dispatch*, April 17.

Shuman, Michael. 2000. *Going Local: Creating Self-Reliant Communities in a Global Age*. Routledge.

Shuman, Michael. 2006. *The Small-Mart Revolution: How Local Businesses Are Beating the Global Competition*. Berrett-Koehler.

Shuman, Michael. 2007. On the Lamb. http://www.ethicurean.com.

Silva, Eduardo. 2007. "The Import-Substitution Model: Chile in Comparative Perspective." *Latin American Perspectives* 34 (3): 67–90.

Silver, David. 2004. "The Coil of Cyberspace: Historical Archaeologies of the Blacksburg Electronic Village and the Seattle Community Network." In *Shaping the Network Society*, ed. D. Schuler and P. Day. MIT Press.

Singer, Hans. 1988. "The World Development Report 1987 on the Blessings of Outward Orientation: A Necessary Correction." *Journal of Development Studies* 24 (2): 232–236.

Sklair, Leslie. 2001. *The Transnational Capitalist Class*. Blackwell.

Slocum, Rachel. 2007. "Whiteness, Space, and Alternative Food Practice." *Geoforum* 38 (3): 520–533.

Smith, Alisa, and J. B. MacKinnon. 2007. *Plenty: One Man, One Woman, and a Raucous Year of Eating Locally*. Harmony.

Smith, Christopher, and Hilda Kurtz. 2003. "Community Gardens and Politics of Scale in New York City." *Geographical Review* 93 (2): 193–212.

Smith, Julia. 2007. "Beyond Fair Trade: Rethinking Producer-Consumer Relations." Presented at annual meeting of American Anthropological Association.

Smith, Terrence. 2003. Power to the People. http://www.pbs.org/newshour.

Soil Born Urban Agricultural Project. 2008. Soil Born Farms Urban Agricultural Project. http://www.soilborn.org.

Solar Region Freiburg. 2008. Freiburg Solar City. http://www.solarregion.freiburg.de.

Solomon, Deborah, and Greg Hitt. 2007. "A Globalization Winner Joins in Trade Backlash." *Wall Street Journal*, November 21.

Sonnino, Roberta, and Terry Marsden. 2006. "Alternative Food Networks in the South West of England: Towards a New Agrarian Eco-Economy?" *Research in Rural Sociology and Development*, vol. 12, 299–322.

South Central Farms. 2008. What We Are About? http://www.southcentralfarmers.com.

South Coast Air Quality Management District. 2000. Multiple Air-Toxics Exposure Study (MATES-II). http://www.aqmd.gov.

Sovacool, Benjamin, Hans Lindboe, and Ole Odgaard. 2008. "Is the Danish Wind Energy Model Replicable for Other Countries?" *Electricity Journal* 21 (2): 27–38.

Speth, James Gustave. 2008. *The Bridge at the End of the World: Capitalism, the Environment, and Crossing from Crisis to Sustainability.* Yale University Press.

Spiers, Elizabeth. 2008. "Neighborhoodlums: Exploding the Myths, Presumptions, and Pretension of the 'Buy Local' Bullies." *Fast Company*, June: 128.

Staeheli, Lynn, Don Mitchell, and Kristina Gibson. 2002. "Conflicting Rights to the City in New York's Community Gardens." *GeoJournal* 58 (2–3): 197–205.

Starr, Jerold. 2003. Community Radio at the Crossroads. http://www.cipbonline.org.

Stevenson, Steve, Daniel Lass, John Hendrickson, and Kathy Ruhf. 2004. "CSA across the Nation: Findings from 1999 and 2001 National Surveys." Presented at annual meeting of Agricultural, Food, and Human Values Society. http://www.cias.wisc.edu.

Stoker, Gerry. 2004. "New Localism, Progressive Politics, and Democracy." *Political Quarterly* 75 (S1): 117–129.

Stone, Kenneth. 1995. "Impact of Wal-Mart Stores and Other Mass Merchandisers in Iowa, 1983–1993." *Economic Development Review* 13 (2): 60–69.

Sustainable Business Network of Greater Philadelphia. 2003. White Paper on Regional Economic Development, Competitiveness, and Prosperity through Local Business Ownership. http://www.sbnphiladelphia.org.

Sustainable Connections. 2008. What We Do, Values and History. http://sustainableconnections.org.

Swann, Robert, and Karen Witt. 1995. Local Currencies: Catalysts for Sustainable Regional Economies. http://www.humanscale.org.

Swenson, Dave. 2004. Buying Local in Union County and Creston, Iowa: An Economic Impact Analysis. Department of Economics, Iowa State University.

Swenson, Dave. 2006. Buying Local in Marshall County and Marshallton, Iowa: An Economic Impact Analysis. Department of Economics, Iowa State University.

Szasz, Andrew. 2007. *Shopping Our Way to Safety: How We Changed from Protecting the Environment to Protecting Ourselves.* University of Minnesota Press.

Tainter, Joseph. 1988. *The Collapse of Complex Societies.* Cambridge University Press.

Tarasuk, Valerie, and Joan Eakin. 2003. "Charitable Food Assistance as Symbolic Gesture: An Ethnographic Study of Food Banks in Ontario." *Social Science and Medicine* 56 (7): 1505–1515.

Thompson, Janice. 2006. Clean Money Comparisons: Summaries of Full Public Financing Programs. http://library.publiccampaign.org.

Tierney, John. 2008. "10 Things to Scratch from Your Worry List." *New York Times*, July 29.

Toke, David, Sylvia Breukers, and Maarten Wolsink. 2008. "Wind Power Deployment Outcomes: How Can We Account for the Differences?" *Renewable and Sustainable Energy Reviews* 12 (4): 1129–1147.

Tolbert, Charles. 2005. "Minding Our Own Business: Local Retail Establishments and the Future of Southern Civic Community." *Social Forces* 83 (4): 1309–1328.

Tolbert, Charles, Michael Irwin, Thomas Lyson, and Alfred Nucci. 2002. "Civic Community in Small-Town America: How Civic Welfare Is Influenced by Local Capitalism and Civic Engagement." *Rural Sociology* 67 (1): 90–113.

Trauger, Amy. 2007. "Connecting Social Justice to Sustainability: Discourse and Practice in Sustainable Agriculture in Pennsylvania." In *Alternative Food Geographies: Representation and Practice*, ed. D. Maye, L. Holloway, and M. Kneafsey. Elsevier.

Troske, Kenneth. 1999. "Evidence on the Employer Size-Wage Premium from Worker-Establishment Matched Data." *Review of Economics and Statistics* 81 (1): 15–26.

Unity: Journalists of Color. 2004. Joint statement by UNITY, AAJA, NABJ, NAHJ and NAJA on the annual American Society of Newspaper Editors Newsroom Census. http://unityjournalists.org.

Unity: Journalists of Color. 2008. New FCC Rules Ignore Crisis in Minority Media Ownership. http://unityjournalists.org.

Upstream 21. 2008. What Makes Us Different. http://www.upstream21.com.

US Department of Agriculture. 2000. 2000 USDA Farmers Market Study Statistics. http://www.ams.usda.gov.

US Department of Agriculture. 2007. Farmers Market Growth: 1994–2006. http://www.ams.usda.gov.

Utne Reader. 1997. Age of the Mega-Alternatives. http://cafe.utne.com.

Valderrama, Andrés, and Beltran, Isaac. 2007. "Diesel Versus Compressed Natural Gas in *Transmilenio*-Bogotá: Innovation, Precaution, and the Distribution of Risk." *Sustainability: Science, Practice, and Policy* 3 (1): 59–67.

Van de Brugge, Rutger, Jan Tormans, Derk Loorbach. 2005. "The Transition in Dutch Water Management." *Regional Environmental Change* 5: 164–176.

Von Hassell, Malve. 2002. *The Struggle for Eden: Community Gardens in New York City*. Bergin and Garvey.

Walker, Gordon, Sue Hunter, Patrick Devine-Wright, Bob Evans, and Helen Fay. 2007. "Harnessing Community Energies: Explaining and Evaluating Community-Based Localism in Renewable Energy Policy in the U.K." *Global Environmental Politics* 7 (2): 64–82.

Walker, Jesse. 2002. "The Battle for Indie Radio." *Salon*, June 20. http://www
.salon.com.

Wallgren, Christine. 2006. "Local or Global Food Markets: A Comparison of
Energy Use for Transport." *Local Environment* 11 (2): 233–251.

Washington State University Energy Program. 2004. New Engine Technologies.
http://www.energy.wsu.edu.

Watkiss, Paul. 2005. The Validity of Food Miles as an Indicator of Sustainable
Development: Final Report. Department for Environment, Food, and Rural
Affairs, United Kingdom. http://statistics.defra.gov.uk.

Watt, Glen. 2000. NGV Transit Bus Fleets: The Current International Experience. International Association of Natural Gas Vehicles. http://www.iangv.org.

Watts, D., B. Ilbery, and D. Maye. 2005. "Making Connections in Agro-Food
Geography: Alternative Systems of Food Production." *Progress in Human Geography* 29 (1): 22–40.

Weinberg, Adam. 1998. "Distinguishing among Green Businesses: Growth,
Green, and Anomie." *Society and Natural Resources* 11 (3): 241–250.

Weinhold, Bob. 2002. "Fuel for the Long Haul: Diesel in America." *Environmental Health Perspectives* 110 (8): A458–A464.

Wicks, Judy. 2004. *Good Morning, Beautiful Business.* E. F. Schumacher
Society.

Wiener, Jon. 2007. "End of an Era at the *LA Weekly*." *The Nation*, July 16–23:
31–34.

Williamson, Thad, David Imbroscio, and Gar Alperovitz. 2002. *Making a Place
for Community: Local Democracy in a Global Era.* Routledge.

Wilson, Dominic, and Roopa Purushothaman. 2003. Dreaming with BRICs:
The Path to 2050. Global Economics Paper 99, Goldman-Sachs. http://www2
.goldmansachs.com.

Wilson, G. Thomas II. 2001. "FCC Policy and the Underdevelopment of Black
Entrepreneurship." In *The Information Society and the Black Community*, ed.
J. Barber and A. Tait. Praeger.

Wilterdink, Nico. 2000. "The Internationalization of Capital and Trends in
Income Inequality in Western Societies." In *The Ends of Globalization*, ed.
D. Kalb et al. Rowman and Littlefield.

Winner, Langdon. 1986. *The Whale and the Reactor: The Search for Limits in
an Age of High Technology.* University of Chicago Press.

Winter, Michael. 2003. "Embeddedness, the New Food Economy, and Defensive
Localism." *Journal of Rural Studies* 19 (1): 23–32.

Winter, Michael. 2004. "Geographies of Food: Agro-Food Geographies—
Farming, Food, and Politics." *Progress in Human Geography* 28 (5): 664–670.

Wisconsin State Journal. 2006. "Editorial: 'Buy Local' Pitch a Feel-Good Flop."
October 16.

Witt, Susan. 2008. Berkshares and Community Currencies. Lecture in Social Entrepreneurship Series, March 28, Rensselaer Polytechnic Institute.

Wolsink, Maarten. 2006. "Wind Power Implementation: The Nature of Public Attitudes: Equity and Fairness instead of 'Backyard Motives.'" *Renewable and Sustainable Energy Reviews* 11 (6): 1188–1207.

Wood, Barbara. 1984. *E. F. Schumacher: His Life and Thought*. Harper and Row.

Woodin, Michael, and Caroline Lucas. 2004. *Green Alternatives to Globalization: A Manifesto*. Pluto.

Woods, Michael. 2003. "Conflicting Visions of the Rural: Windfarm Development in Mid Wales." *Sociologia Ruralis* 43 (3): 271–288.

World Commission on Environment and Development. 1987. *Our Common Future*. Oxford University Press.

York, Richard, and Eugene Rosa. 2003. "Key Challenges to Ecological Modernization Theory." *Organization and Environment* 16 (3): 273–288.

Zenger Urban Agricultural Park. 2008. A Century-Old Working Farm. http://www.zengerfarm.org.

Index

Urban and Industrial Environments

Maureen Smith, *The U.S. Paper Industry and Sustainable Production: An Argument for Restructuring*

Keith Pezzoli, *Human Settlements and Planning for Ecological Sustainability: The Case of Mexico City*

Sarah Hammond Creighton, *Greening the Ivory Tower: Improving the Environmental Track Record of Universities, Colleges, and Other Institutions*

Jan Mazurek, *Making Microchips: Policy, Globalization, and Economic Restructuring in the Semiconductor Industry*

William A. Shutkin, *The Land That Could Be: Environmentalism and Democracy in the Twenty-First Century*

Richard Hofrichter, ed., *Reclaiming the Environmental Debate: The Politics of Health in a Toxic Culture*

Robert Gottlieb, *Environmentalism Unbound: Exploring New Pathways for Change*

Kenneth Geiser, *Materials Matter: Toward a Sustainable Materials Policy*

Thomas D. Beamish, *Silent Spill: The Organization of an Industrial Crisis*

Matthew Gandy, *Concrete and Clay: Reworking Nature in New York City*

David Naguib Pellow, *Garbage Wars: The Struggle for Environmental Justice in Chicago*

Julian Agyeman, Robert D. Bullard, and Bob Evans, eds., *Just Sustainabilities: Development in an Unequal World*

Barbara L. Allen, *Uneasy Alchemy: Citizens and Experts in Louisiana's Chemical Corridor Disputes*

Dara O'Rourke, *Community-Driven Regulation: Balancing Development and the Environment in Vietnam*

Brian K. Obach, *Labor and the Environmental Movement: The Quest for Common Ground*

Peggy F. Barlett and Geoffrey W. Chase, eds., *Sustainability on Campus: Stories and Strategies for Change*

Steve Lerner, *Diamond: A Struggle for Environmental Justice in Louisiana's Chemical Corridor*

Jason Corburn, *Street Science: Community Knowledge and Environmental Health Justice*

Peggy F. Barlett, ed., *Urban Place: Reconnecting with the Natural World*

David Naguib Pellow and Robert J. Brulle, eds., *Power, Justice, and the Environment: A Critical Appraisal of the Environmental Justice Movement*

Eran Ben-Joseph, *The Code of the City: Standards and the Hidden Language of Place Making*

Nancy J. Myers and Carolyn Raffensperger, eds., *Precautionary Tools for Reshaping Environmental Policy*

Kelly Sims Gallagher, *China Shifts Gears: Automakers, Oil, Pollution, and Development*

Kerry H. Whiteside, *Precautionary Politics: Principle and Practice in Confronting Environmental Risk*

Ronald Sandler and Phaedra C. Pezzullo, eds., *Environmental Justice and Environmentalism: The Social Justice Challenge to the Environmental Movement*

Julie Sze, *Noxious New York: The Racial Politics of Urban Health and Environmental Justice*

Robert D. Bullard, ed., *Growing Smarter: Achieving Livable Communities, Environmental Justice, and Regional Equity*

Ann Rappaport and Sarah Hammond Creighton, *Degrees That Matter: Climate Change and the University*

Michael Egan, *Barry Commoner and the Science of Survival: The Remaking of American Environmentalism*

David J. Hess, *Alternative Pathways in Science and Industry: Activism, Innovation, and the Environment in an Era of Globalization*

Peter F. Cannavò, *The Working Landscape: Founding, Preservation, and the Politics of Place*

Paul Stanton Kibel, ed., *Rivertown: Rethinking Urban Rivers*

Kevin P. Gallagher and Lyuba Zarsky, *The Enclave Economy: Foreign Investment and Sustainable Development in Mexico's Silicon Valley*

David N. Pellow, *Resisting Global Toxics: Transnational Movements for Environmental Justice*

Robert Gottlieb, *Reinventing Los Angeles: Nature and Community in the Global City*

David V. Carruthers, ed., *Environmental Justice in Latin America: Problems, Promise, and Practice*

Tom Angotti, *New York for Sale: Community Planning Confronts Global Real Estate*

Anastasia Loukaitou-Sideris and Renia Ehrenfeucht, *Sidewalks: Conflict and Negotiation over Public Space*

David J. Hess, *Localist Movements in a Global Economy: Sustainability, Justice, and Urban Development in the United States*